SEPTEMBER 2021

THE SIGNS AND APPOINTED FEASTS OF MESSIAH FROM SEPTEMBER 2015 TO SEPTEMBER 2021

PHIL RICHARDSON

Lunar Matrix

SEPTEMBER 2021 by Phil Richardson

Published by Lunar Matrix Publishers

LunarMatrixPublishers.com

Unless noted otherwise, all "Scripture quotations are taken from The Scriptures, Copyright by Institute for Scripture Research. Used by permission."

Scripture quotations marked NKJV are from the New King James Version of the Bible," Copyright © 1982 by Thomas Nelson. Used by permission. All rights reserved.

Italics in Scripture represent the author's added emphasis.

Cover design by Phil Richardson

Visit the author's website www.September2021.com

All the images in this book may be viewed in HD and downloaded off the website.

Available on Kindle from Amazon.com and other online stores.

International Standards Book Number 978-0-99677-551-9

Published: September 2, 2015

Table of Contents

An Important Introduction   **1**

to this 1st Version: **1**

   Allow Me To Take You On A Deep Spiritual Journey   *1*

   The Feast Days are the Key to Understanding these Latter Days!   *3*

   Understanding on How this Book was Written –
   Cleaning Up The Language!   *5*

   Truth or Tradition? Your Fork in the Road to Greater Spiritual
   Understanding!   *9*

   Good Friday or Passover?   *9*

   Easter or the First Fruits of Resurrection?   *11*

   Was the Messiah Really Born on December 25th?   *13*

   The Most Accurate Translation of the Bible   *14*

   My Journey into the Hebrew Roots of Christianity   *15*

Chapter 1   **17**

The Latter Days are all about the Ancient Jewish Wedding   **17**

   The Appointed Feasts of YHVH   *18*

   The Season of Repentance   *19*

   Shadow Pictures of Yom Teruah   *20*

   The Idiomatic Expressions of Yahshua   *21*

   The Signs and "Appointed Feasts"   *23*

   The Thief in the Night — an Idiom for Apathy   *26*

   Parallels of the Ancient Jewish Wedding   *30*

   The Bridal Price   *32*

   The Betrothal   *34*

   The Bride's Acceptance and Consent   *35*

   Sealing the Ketubah   *36*

   The Bridegroom   *38*

I Go To Prepare A Place For You   41

The Bride has her Baptism   42

Approval from His Father   43

Hosanna and the Coronation of the King   45

The Creator was Married Once Before!   49

The Messiah Died in Order to Marry His Bride!   51

Chapter 2   54

Daniel! Seal the Book Until the   54

Time of the End!   54

These Latter Days!   56

Are We Truly in the Latter Days?   57

The Time of Jacob's Distress   60

A Closer look at Daniel Chapter 12   62

June 7th, 1967 and Jerusalem   66

An Introduction to the Shmitah   67

The Shmitah and the Jewish Civil Calendar   70

Knowledge Would Increase   72

The Feast Days of Daniel Chapter 12   74

This Generation Shall By No Means Pass Away!   75

Observable Patterns and Signs in the Heavens   76

Determining the Jubilee   78

A Jubilee Year Cycle: 49 or 50 Years?   80

I Shall Make You a Burdensome Stone   81

Chapter 3   85

The 6,000 Years of Man's Rule   85

Identifying the Most Accurate Lunar Calendar System   85

The Jewish Calendar System   86

The Creator's Calendar System   87

The Abib Barley Calendar System   87

The Contrast Between the Spiritual and Civil Years   *90*

The 7,000 Year Plan of the Creator   *92*

Hebraic & Gregorian Days   *94*

An Intro to "Torah Calendar"   *97*

6,000 years and 120 Jubilees   *99*

A Messiah for all Religions   *101*

120 Jubilees?   *102*

Chapter 4   **105**

September 2015 and the Feast of   **105**

Yom Teruah   **105**

A Deeper look into Yom Teruah   *106*

The Mystery of the Shmitah   *108*

The "Shmitah Release Day"   *115*

The Breach   *117*

The "Shmitah Release Day" and the Connection to Yom Teruah 2015   *120*

Why the Connection with America?   *123*

America in Bible Prophecy?   *124*

The Israeli and Palestinian Peace Process and the Shmitah   *127*

Jade Helm 2015   *132*

Chapter 5   **135**

September 2015 and the Feast of   **135**

Yom Kippur   **135**

The Foundation of the 70 weeks   *138*

Cracking the Mystery of Daniel's 70th week!   *141*

The Creator's Jubilee and the Connection to Yom Kippur 2015   *147*

The Double Prophetic Fulfillment of Daniel's 7 weeks   *153*

The Pope, the U.S. and the UN   *158*

Chapter 6   **160**

September 2015 and the 160

Feast of Tabernacles 160

A Deeper look into Tabernacles 160

The Significance of Tabernacles in Our Time 162

The Blood Moons 164

The "Tetrad Blood Moons" 167

The "Blood Moon Tetrads" Announce the 70th week 174

The Final Super Blood Moon and the Connection to Tabernacles 2015 ... 176

The Three Pillar Foundation 177

Chapter 7 179

September 2017 and the 179

Mid-Tribulation Sign 179

Look, the Virgin Conceives and Gives Birth to a Son 180

The Roaming King Planet 185

Revelation Chapter 12 and Yom Teruah 186

Crowned with 12 Stars 188

A Sign Last Seen 3,865 Years Ago 189

Birthed at 41 weeks 191

Does this Sign Point to the Rapture? 193

Rabbi Judah Ben Samuel's 800 Year Old Prophecy Points to
September 2017 194

Saint Malechy's 870 Year Old Prophecy and Pope Francis,
the Final Pope! 198

Chapter 8 202

September 2014 and the Final 2,550 Days 202

My Aha Moment 202

A Closer Look into the Final 2,550 Days 204

The Metonic Lunar Cycle and the 86 Moons versus 87 Moons 207

A Closer Look at the 1,335 Days   *214*

President Obama and the Connection to Yom Teruah 2014   *216*

The "President" of the United Nations   *222*

A Covenant with the Many   *224*

Russia to Chair the UNSC in September 2015 and
Will Approve a Palestinian State!   *229*

Chapter 9   **234**

Putting It All Together: **234**

The Connection to September 2021   **234**

The Confirmation and Double Confirmation of June 7, 1967 and
September 24, 2014   *236*

Six Years of Tribulation   *242*

The Richardson Theory   *243*

The End of the 2,550 Days and the Connection to September 2021   *245*

The 7 Witnesses and the Divine Order of Seven   *246*

It's Too Perfect!   *248*

What we can Expect   *248*

The Beginning of the 7th Millennium   *257*

The "Destroyer of the Eye!"   *261*

Tearing Down the Veil Between Jew and Gentile   *263*

Shout, O Daughter of Jerusalem!   *265*

Some Additional Facts and Observations: *268*

Blessed are Those Who Shall be Found Watching!   *270*

Index   **272**

Scripture that supports calling upon the true name of
the Creator Yahweh: *272*

Mystery Babylon: *272*

A Summary of the Nine Harbingers   *276*

NOTES   **280**

AWAKENING BLAST   YOM TERUAH

MONEYJOBS
CRISIS

ECONOMIC SIGNS

TABERNACLES
POLICY
TETRADS 2015

MONITORING

An Important Introduction

to this 1st Version:

"It is the esteem of God to hide a matter, And the esteem of Kings to search out a matter" (Proverbs 25:2, NKJV)

Allow Me To Take You On A Deep Spiritual Journey

This journey I want to take you on started over 2,500 years ago. For Millennia, the greatest of the prophets of old; Jeremiah, Ezekiel, Daniel, Isaiah, Zechariah, along with John the Revealer, spoke about a time when the accumulation of man's desire would once again be reunited under a Babylonian World System. The Bible refers to this time when the world's systems would be identified as "Mystery Babylon." It is a time much like Nimrod's Babylon, when the world would unite together in thought, language, economy, government and religion. Today, the world's educational, media and political systems have embraced the values and ideas behind empty humanistic philosophies or the idea that mankind can solve today's problems apart from the Divine Creator, thus pushing him aside. In much of the same way, the churches of the West have embraced deceitful philoso-

1

phies intertwined with Scripture that have watered down the true understanding and meaning of the Good News.

This book was written in order to bring the reader into deeper insight and revelation as to the Signs and Appointed Times *(Appointed Feasts)* of these *Latter Days* as is so well documented by the Prophets of Old. For generation to generation, mankind have reflected on the prophecies from such writings from the Old Covenant (Old Testament) and New Covenant (New Testament) and have pondered on how, and when these events would play out at the End of the Age of Man and his rule on Earth.

It was Sir Isaac Newton, one of the greatest mathematicians and scientist of all time, who struggled with the very question of the timing of these Latter Days. He struggled to understand the timing of the prophecies of the ancient writings of the Book of Revelation up to his death in 1727 CE. Accounts of the life of Sir Isaac Newton recount how he spent the better part of his life writing his own commentary of over 1 million words [1] with regard to the enigmatic eschatological study of the Bible. The reason for this struggle is evident from the writings of the Prophet Daniel, as he was instructed to "hide the words, and seal the book until the time of the end and that many shall diligently search and knowledge shall increase" (Daniel 12:4).

Those prophecies from the 9th and 12th chapter of the Book of Daniel, along with the vast *knowledge* of the World Wide Web, are being fulfilled today. Over the centuries, the world's educational; media, religious and political systems have conspired, manipulated and twisted the truth for their gain. Thanks to the advent of computers, the average truth-seeker can harness the information from the internet and begin to destroy the walls of deception that have been built around him/her and society in general. As a result, the Theory of Evolution is being blown to pieces today, the dispersion of the northern 10 tribes of Israel are being revealed, and the false teachings and celebrations within the Christian faith are being challenged.

The Feast Days are the Key to Understanding these Latter Days!

With regard to the subject of this book, I look into the earth shaking events that are about to unfold on planet earth and how they correlate to the Messiah's return. **SEPTEMBER 2021** lays out the unstoppable correlation of major world events that highlight the Creator's incredible, divine connection of the coming Jewish Fall Feasts of Yom Teruah 2015, Yom Kippur 2015, Tabernacles 2015, Yom Teruah 2017 with the Fall Feast Days of 2021.

The Creator has chosen the Jewish people, who have been faithful in observing His Feasts for thousands of years. Unfortunately, it has been the plan of the enemy to blind us from the understanding of these feasts. This blindness has been caused partly by the use of the Gregorian calendar, and the mindset within Christianity that these feasts have been done away with, preventing us from making the deep spiritual connections to the end times. Contrary to popular belief, these feast, followed by observant Jews, are meant to be celebrated by followers of Jesus as well. As you will learn, these feasts that have been hidden by a veil, in these latter days, are being lifted and their shadow pictures of good things to come are being revealed. **SEPTEMBER 2021** *UNLOCKS* the mysteries behind the shadow pictures of these feasts and brings clarity to the start of the 7 years of Tribulation, the 2550 days, the Antichrist, the Bridegroom coming for his Bride (Rapture), the Great Economic Collapse, Judgment and the return of the Messiah.

The hidden mystery behind the feast days is one of the primary revelations that are starting to be unveiled to both Jew and Gentile. As this veil is

lifted, it is my prayer that Jew and Gentile will become united and will begin to realize the significance of the Torah, the Feasts and to the One by
Whose stripes we are healed.

> "But he was wounded for our transgressions, he was bruised for our
> iniquities: the chastisement of our peace was upon him; *and with his*
> *stripes we are healed*" (Isaiah 53:5)

> "Who his own self bare our sins in his own body on the tree, that we,
> being dead to sins, should live unto righteousness: *by whose stripes*
> *we were healed*" (1 Peter 2:24)

Discover the two key dates that will offer a confirmation and double confirmation to the count down date to **SEPTEMBER 2021**. Those two key
dates are June 7th, 1967 and September 24th, 2014. June 7th, 1967, the
day after the Six Day War, was an absolute key date of Jerusalem being
returned to the control and dominion of the Jewish people for the first
time in over 2,000 years after their dispersion abroad. This, along with Israel becoming a Nation in one day on the eve of Shavuot on May 14th,
1948, was the start of the countdown of the *Latter Days* as documented in
the Bible. The other key date is September 24th, 2014, which was the eve
of Yom Teruah, otherwise known as the Feast of Trumpets. Bible prophecy
was fulfilled on that day whereby *"he made a covenant with the many"* via
the Book of Daniel 9:27. Discover who "he" is as I go into detail about this
event in the 8th chapter of the book and show how this kicked off the final
2,550 days of man's rule.

Will you join me in this incredible Journey as we break through the veil of
deception and hidden knowledge, into the beginning of the seventh millennium, the end of man's rule and the finale of the Messiah's return?

Understanding on How this Book was Written – Cleaning Up The Language!

This book was not written using the typical Christian lingo. Instead, for a greater spiritual understanding of the things of God, it is prudent to "clean up the language" and to embrace truth over tradition. I am reminded of the warning associated with James 3:1, *"Not many of you should become teachers, my brothers, knowing that we shall receive greater judgment."* It is for this reason that I am compelled to bring you the truth. My prayer is that I will be able to do so conclusively throughout this book.

The Scriptures tell us that the original Hebrew is a pure language and that it is the language of the Creator. Greek, Latin, English, German, Spanish and the other languages are a mixture of each other that have adopted pagan meanings and terminology throughout the centuries. As a matter of fact, you would not be able to carry on a conversation in English with someone just 400 years ago. The language has changed that much.

The following prophecy states that the Creator will restore a once lost pure language: *"For then I will restore to the peoples a pure language,* That they all may call on the name of יהוה, To serve Him with one accord" (Zephaniah 3:9). Notice that it says He will restore to the peoples, not just the Jewish people. To restore means it was lost at one time. We have seen a restoration of this lost language, but not in its entirety. This may be seen clearly since Modern Hebrew is clearly different even from Palio Hebrew. Thus, this verse has not been fulfilled in its finality.

We find that the hand of the Almighty has set the Hebrew language in motion from the creation and has preserved its structure and meaning for the most part of well over 4,000 years. This can be validated partly through the discovery of the Dead Sea Scrolls throughout the Qumran region near the Dead Sea in Israel from the year 1946 to 1956. [2]

Within Christianity today, many believers do not fully recognize that God has a name. Ask any believer and more than likely the majority will say *The Great I Am, God* or *The Lord* as the most common response. However, these are simply titles and not His name. Fortunately, He does have a name and it is prevalent throughout the Scriptures. However, you have probably never noticed it simply because *The Lord* is a cover title of His true name.

The Creator's name, יהוה, being read from right to left, is made up of the Hebrew letters of Yod Hey Vav Hey. His name is commonly translated in English as Yahweh, Yahovah, Yahuwah or Yehovah. The reason for the different pronunciations stems from the facts that there are no vowels in the Hebrew language unlike the English language.

Going to *BlueLetterBible.org* and searching for *The Lord* will reveal his true name. The result will be Strong's #H3068 [3] that matches His true name יהוה which occurs 6,519 times in the Tanakh or Old Testament. Again, this is the Creator's name that was deliberately removed from the Scriptures. This is clearly a violation of His own word where He mentions multiple times within the Scriptures (see index I). One of the strongest examples of this comes from the 3rd Commandment,

> "You do not bring the Name of יהוה your Elohim to naught, for יהוה does not leave the one unpunished who brings His Name to naught."
> (Exodus 20:7)

The translation that I use states that we should not bring the name of יהוה your Elohim (the plural form of God) to naught, meaning, His name, Yahweh (YHVH), should not be brought to nothingness. Most current translations state that, "You do not take the name of the Lord in vain," meaning not to swear using His name. Keep in mind that the 10 Commandments were written by the finger of the Creator and it is His Com-

6

mandments that are of high importance to Him, and should be to us as well.

In regard to the name, Jesus, I will be using His Hebrew name within this book and not the name transliterated from the Greek. We can easily verify His true Hebrew name by going to BlueLetterBible.org and doing a search for Jesus. The result will be Strong's Number G2424 and the Greek spelling will be Iesous pronounced Yay-SOOS. Much like the title *The Lord*, Iesous, has been transliterated to the name by which we know Him today - Jesus. A further search for the Hebrew origin of His Hebrew name results in Strong's H3091. What we find is His Hebrew name of יהושע pronounced Yeh-o-shua, which occurs 218 times within the Old Testament. I bet you never realized that Jesus' name is mentioned 218 times in the Old Testament!

Jesus' Hebrew name is made up of Yod Hey Vav Shin and Ayin, correctly translated as Yehoshua, Yahshua, Yahushua or Yeshua. The name Jesus Christ in Hebrew would be Yahshua HaMashiach or simply translated, Joshua the Messiah in English. Yeshua in Hebrew means *Salvation*. Yahshua or Yahushua in Hebrew means *YHVH is Salvation* or *God is Salvation*. For the purpose of this book, I will refer to Him as Yahshua or the Messiah. Conversely, I will be using the Hebrew name יהוה (YHVH), the Almighty, or the Creator, to identify the Father or God throughout this book.

There are lots of opinions on how Jesus' Hebrew name should be spelled and pronounced. My preference is to place the name of the Father in His name. Here is a verse that supports this, "Set-apart Father, guard them in *Your Name which You have given Me,* so that they might be one, as We are" (John 17:11).

Hence, I will use Yahshua that means Yah is my salvation, over the more popular Jesus and, Yeshua, that simply means salvation. We also see the

Father's name in the names of the prophets such as the Prophets Zechariah (ZekarYah), Zephaniah (TsephanYah), Isaiah (YeshaYahu), and Nehemiah (NehemYah) as placing Yah, [4] the short form of the name of Yahweh, was common in those times and created esteem from the eyes of other people. We even see this in modern times as in the name of the current Prime Minister of Israel, Benjamin NetanYahu. The name of the Father is within his name. I simply believe that the name above all names would be identified as having the name of the Father in His name much like the names of the prophets versus Yeshua that simply means salvation. Clearly, Yahushua or Yahshua [5] would satisfy this.

While we are on the subject of the meaning behind the name, I would like to look a little deeper in the meaning behind the name of Yahwey (YHVH). His name, which can be verified on multiple fragments of the Dead Sea Scrolls is יהוה. His name being read from right to left, is made up of the Hebrew letters of Yod Hey Vav Hey. Each Hebrew letter has a meaning or symbol attached to it. As an example, the Hebrew letter Vav is the symbol of a Nail. The letter Hey is the symbol of Revelation as in "Behold, I bring you Revelation." The symbol attached to the letter Yod has a meaning of "Hand or Hand attached to an Arm."

Putting it all together, we find that The Creator's name literally means...

- **BEHOLD! THE NAIL IN THE HAND THAT BRINGS REVELATION!**

It's amazing to me that God's name identifies his Son as it was the Son who was nailed to the cross and has had such a profound influence on mankind. With regard to the name of Yahshua (יהושע), I will reveal the symbolic meaning behind His name in the final chapter of this book as you will realize that no other name is more fitting.

As it relates to the title *God*, I will mostly be using the Creator, the Almighty or His true name when describing God the Father. The reason for this is two-fold. God is a common *title* that represents all pagan deities, idols and other mighty ones within other cultures of the world. This is shown in the Bible as either God or god depending on the noun that the word represents. Secondly, the title *God* will be used by the False Prophet to unite the world under a New World Order Religious System so that the nations, peoples and tongues will embrace this Mystery Babylon Religion that will usher in the Anti-Messiah.

Truth or Tradition? Your Fork in the Road to Greater Spiritual Understanding!

What is your typical reaction when you discover something contrary to your belief system? As an example, what is your response when I say that Yahshua could not be the Messiah if he died on a Friday night and resurrected on a Sunday morning? Would you shrug this off without seeking more information? Would you do this because of the vast array of biblical scholars and pastors who could not be possibly wrong over the course of hundreds of years?

Is my question to you truth or tradition? In other words, when confronted with a truth that contradicts your belief system, will you chose truth over tradition? Unfortunately, most people will choose tradition because of peer pressure and a psychological condition known as cognitive dissidence.

Your choice of embracing the truth or rejecting it either takes you more into the light or away from it, and you will either become more spiritually blind or more spiritually enlightened depending on what path you take. Ultimately, what is offered in this book will definitely challenge your belief system.

Good Friday or Passover?

Yahshua did not die on a Friday evening known within Christianity as Good Friday. This is a false belief system that has helped to divide Jew and

9

Gentile for hundreds of years. Does not the Scripture state that Yahshua would be in the grave for 3 days and 3 nights?

"For as Jonah was three days and three nights in the stomach of the great fish, so shall the Son of Adam be three days and three nights in the heart of the earth." (Matthew 12:40)

Doesn't the Scriptures state that He was put in the grave just before the High Sabbath? Meaning that that particular High Sabbath could have been Wednesday, not just Saturday as a majority of Christians believe. The Sanhedrin and High Priest of that time recognized the High Sabbath as the Feast of Unleavened Bread that would have begun just a few hours from the death of Yahshua after sunset on Nisan 15.

"Therefore, because it was the Preparation Day, that the bodies should not remain on the cross on the Sabbath (for that Sabbath was a high day)…" (John 19:31, NKJV)

Let's see if we can't shed some light on this false belief system! Yahshua made it clear that there are 12 hours in a day and 12 hours in a night (John 11:9). Friday at sunset to Saturday at sunrise is one night. Saturday at sunrise to Saturday at sunset is one day. Saturday at sunset to Sunday at sunrise is the 2nd night. Scripture clearly says that the stone to the tomb had been removed on the first day of the week while it was still dark (John 20:1). The first day of the week is Sunday or more precisely Saturday after sunset to Sunday morning before sunrise. Thus, Yahshua must have arisen between sunset to sunrise on the first day of the week and within a 12-hour period of time.

Ultimately, what we have is one day and two nights. This does not line up with Scripture and must be rejected! It should have been rejected hundreds of years ago and leads me to ask the question, "Why have we tolerated this false belief system for hundreds of years?" The answer is more complicated than summed up here but is attributed to embracing false belief systems over truth, which always leads to spiritual blindness. Part of the confusion lies in understanding what a *High Sabbath* is as recorded in John 19:31.

The common understanding is that the High Sabbath follows Passover. This was the view held by the first century Jewish community and is why John 19:31 states that it (Passover) was a *Preparation Day* and that the bodies should not remain on the cross. Clearly, the Feast of Unleavened Bread was only a few hours away, which identifies it as the High Sabbath according to Leviticus 23:6-7. It would have been after sunset on Nisan 15 that the Jews would have celebrated the Passover Seder Meal. Interestingly enough, we see Yahshua celebrating His Passover Seder Meal, known as the *Last Supper*, just after sunset at the beginning of Passover on Nisan 14. There is a very good reason for this as Scripture indicates that Passover is the first day of Unleavened Bread, "In the first month, on the fourteenth day of the month, you have the Passover, a festival of seven days, unleavened bread is eaten" (Ezekiel 45:21). It was Yahshua and His Disciples who were observing the correct day as it was Passover Day that was a High Sabbath. [6]

Easter or the First Fruits of Resurrection?

So, you may be asking, what is the correct answer to when He died? The Scripture is clear that Yahshua died on Passover near the end of the day on Nisan 14 according to John 18:28. He died on Passover as the sacrificial Lamb, placed in the grave at sunset just prior to the Feast of Unleavened Bread and 72 hours later arose on the Feast of First-fruits being *Messiah the first-fruits* (1 Corinthians 15:23). Fifty days later, the Holy Spirit in-dwelt the 120 disciples (Acts 2:1-4), thus fulfilling Shavuot or Pentecost as it is known today. The Spring Feasts of YHVH have been fulfilled in totality with the sacrificial death and resurrection of Yahshua. With the Spring Feasts fulfilled in totality, we are now anticipating the Fall Feast being fulfilled in the very near future.

Here is another question I have: Why do we call the day that Yahshua resurrected from the grave as "Easter Sunrise?" Should it not be known as first-fruits of resurrection as indicated in Scripture? "But now Messiah has been raised from the dead, and has become the *first-fruit* of those having fallen asleep" (1 Corinthians 15:20). The truth of the matter is that we have inherited lies from our forefathers and have embraced falsehoods. The following Scripture and within context speaks of our current generation.

> "O יהוה, my strength and my stronghold and my refuge, in the day of distress *the gentiles* shall come to You from the ends of the earth and say, *"Our fathers have inherited only falsehood, futility, and there is no value in them." Would a man make mighty ones for himself, which are not mighty ones?* "Therefore see, I am causing them to know, this time I cause them to know My hand and My might. And they shall know that My Name is יהוה!" (Jeremiah 16:19-21)

Easter (the goddess Ishtar or Ashtaroth) was the pagan "mighty one" known as the "queen of heaven" that was married to Nimrod and later on to her son, Tammuz, after Nimrod's death. She reigned as queen of the Babylonian Empire and was worshipped as a pagan deity or mighty one.

Her "deity" has been attributed to fertility in the form of rabbits, dyed eggs and sun worship. As documented, Ishtar (Easter) was associated with Baal worship or sun worship and was always tied to the spring time when the vernal equinox (equal day and night) occurred. This is why Easter is always celebrated closest to the vernal equinox and not necessarily near Passover. This event of changing *times and laws* was decided at the Council of Nicaea in 325 CE, when the churches at that time, headed by the Roman

Catholic Church, "agreed that Easter, 'the Christian Passover', should be celebrated on the Sunday following the first full moon after the vernal equinox." [7]

There is a popular video out on the web by the name of *Zeitgeist* [8] and does a good job at discrediting Jesus based upon these false belief systems. Of course, those watching this video do not realize that the truth has been watered down by paganism and lies. How many millions of people are making eternal decisions based upon this false information and our unwillingness on standing for the truth?

"And have no fellowship with the fruitless works of darkness, but rather reprove them." (Ephesians 5:11)

Was the Messiah Really Born on December 25th?

Christmas is no different and is often times worst with regard to the pagan belief systems. December 25th is attributed to the birthdays of many pagan deities including Tammuz and Zeus to name a few. It is also known that this date is attributed to the "annual feast celebrated in the honor of the sun." [9] This makes sense because it is attributed to the sun beginning its return toward the northern tropic known as the Winter Solstice, slowly lengthening the days until spring. There is much that can be stated about this pagan belief system especially as it pertains to the original Santa and his evil elves, but I will stop here to make my point. The point here is, again regarding spiritual blindness. If one embraces lies, then that person will be spiritually deceived.

So, when did Yahshua enter the world? It was during the Fall Feasts when Mary and Joseph could not find room in the Inn before giving birth to Yahshua. There was no room because Jerusalem and the surrounding towns were filled with over 2 million pilgrims that came from other locations around Judah to celebrate the Fall Feast Days. This would have been the same time that the shepherds would have been shepherding their sheep out in the open fields at night. December would have been much too cold. Many within the Hebrew Roots Movement believe that Yahshua was born either on Yom Teruah or during the Feast Day of Tabernacles because the Bible states, "And the Word became flesh and pitched His tent among us" (John 1:14). This makes sense because during Tabernacles at that time, the Jews made temporary dwelling places known as sukkahs (tents) and lived in them for 7 days as they still do to this day. Likewise, Yahshua was born in a manger that could have been identified as a sukkah.

There are some who attribute His birth to Rosh Hashanah/Yom Teruah of that feast falling on the 1st of Tishri. The Hebrew words for *In the beginning* is Aleph b' Tishrei and is translated as *On the first of Tishri*. We know from Scripture that Joseph was required to take part in the census in His hometown. The Romans would not have required that census to have taken place during Tabernacles as it was required that all males were to present themselves to YHVH on that feast day in the town of Jerusalem. Neither do I want to leave out the possibility of Him being born on Yom Kippur known as the Day of Atonement as He will fulfill this feast day in the near future with His physical appearance. One thing is for sure, He was not born on the pagan solar day of December 25th.

The Most Accurate Translation of the Bible

The translation of the Bible should be of deep concern for the Christian. Using poor translations results in error and false conclusions that were never meant to be. One example of error and false conclusion is *Replacement Theology*. Because an accurate translation is key to understanding the Scriptures, I have chosen to use the most accurate translation to date that even exceeds the accuracy of the King James Version.

14

This translation I am referring to is the Institute for Scripture Research [10] Translation (ISR98). It may be viewed and/or downloaded for free on your computer, ipad or phone. Simply go to Bible.com and select ISR98. All of the quotes within this book, unless noted otherwise, are of this translation. On a side note, I also recommend HalleluYah Scriptures found at halleluyahScriptures.com.

My Journey into the Hebrew Roots of Christianity

My Journey started in 2011 when my wife and I began hitting a plateau of understanding within the Bible and what was being preached from the pulpits. I was simply becoming burned out and had an insatiable desire for the depth of meaning in the Scriptures that was not being satisfied. Some of you reading this can relate as if something is missing and you don't understand the yearning for more truth. It almost reminds me of the movie, *the Matrix*, where we find Neo searching for the truth on the internet. I now understand that this tugging on the heart is as a result of the Holy Spirit tugging on the heart of millions of believers worldwide as the Almighty is equipping us for these latter days and of the great harvest of souls.

It was about this time when the Almighty began to bring us divine connections with other believers who had incredible amount of insight, knowledge and wisdom as to our Hebraic Roots. Being a Christian, for the majority of my life, I embraced this newly discovered truth with a fresh new look at Jesus from a Hebraic Roots perspective.

Throughout this process, we were introduced to unique people who were instrumental in helping us connect with our Hebrew Messiah who had a deep understanding of the Hebrew Roots, the Feasts, the true Sabbath day of rest. There are, of course, other teachers and Pastors who have helped to connect us with the Hebraic Roots of our Christian faith such as Mark

Biltz, Michael Rood, Kenny Russell with BulldozerFaith.com and especially my friend and mentor Eliyahu Chiles and his wife Abiyah. The information presented within this book is a result of embracing truth over the prevalent traditions of today's Laodicean Churches.

I do not associate myself with any Christian denomination yet I grew up and called Calvary Chapel my home church for many years. Since embracing the Hebrew Roots of my Christian faith, I need to state that I do not embrace Judaism nor am I pretending to be Jewish or proclaiming to be from the tribe of Judah. I am, however, an American who is simply embracing the truth and a follower of Yahshua as I have been grafted into the olive tree of Israel through the Branch of Ephraim.[11]

For a majority of my adult life, the biblical eschatological study of the end time's events has always fascinated me. It is one area that absolutely proves the existence of the Almighty. I noticed that once I embraced the truth behind the Scriptures and turned away from the pagan Greek belief systems within Christianity, then the Creator began to lift the veil of spiritual darkness from my eyes and I started to make deep spiritual connections with certain patterns I was observing with regard to the Fall Feast days. What is presented to you today is a result of my deep search as it relates to the *End Times* and the return of the *Lion of the tribe of Judah* back to Earth.

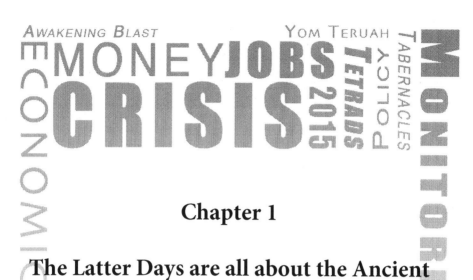

Chapter 1

The Latter Days are all about the Ancient

Jewish Wedding

There is little debate that when Yahshua spoke, He often used parables to help explain what He was trying to communicate because of the deep spiritual connections behind their meaning. Even today, we are still learning and discovering new meaning to what was spoken almost 2,000 years ago.

When Yahshua made the statement to the disciples that, "No man would know the day or the hour, not even the angels in heaven, but only my Father in heaven," was that statement to be taken literally? Did He literally mean in every sense of the word that we wouldn't know the timing of His return or that we just wouldn't know the day or hour? I believe it is true that we will not know the day or the hour, just like He said. That is a true statement! However, I do believe it is possible that we could know the month and year and even the *Appointed Feasts* that point to His return, which is precisely what I will lay out in this book by identifying the feasts and their patterns.

The Appointed Feasts of YHVH

The *Appointed Feasts* of YHVH (the LORD) are made up of a total of seven feasts. They're more popularly known today as the Jewish Feasts. You will notice that the Spring Feasts are made up of four feasts namely Passover, Unleavened Bread, First fruits and finally Shavuot. The Spring Feasts take place every year around April.

THE APPOINTED FEASTS OF YHVH

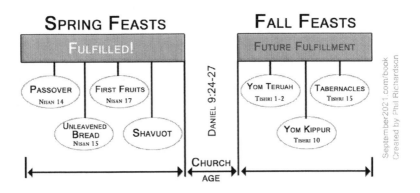

The Fall Feasts take place right around September. They are made up of three feasts, namely Yom Teruah (Feast of Trumpets), Yom Kippur (Day of Atonement) and Tabernacles (Sukkoth). It was Yahshua who fulfilled the Spring Feast through His death, burial and resurrection. Shavuot was fulfilled through the indwelling of the Holy Spirit on the 120 believers as recorded in the Book of Acts. It is my belief, among many others, that Yahshua will fulfill the Fall Feast this second time with Kingship, Power and Authority.

Notice that the Church Age as it is known is uniquely situated between the fulfillment of the Spring Feast and the Fall Feast. Based upon my observations, the Church Age began at the end of the 69 *weeks* [1] and will finalize at the beginning of the 70th *week* of *Daniel's Seventy week Prophecy.* The end of the 69 *weeks* finalized when Yahshua was *cut off* or died as the Passover Lamb.

The Season of Repentance

The season that leads up to the Fall Feast Days of Yom Teruah, Yom Kippur and Tabernacles is known in Hebrew as Teshuvah, translated as Repentance. This return to repentance begins on the first day of the 6th month of Elul and concludes 40 days later on Yom Kippur. Ten days prior to Yom Kippur begins the civil New Year known today as Rosh Hashanah. It is also known as Yom Teruah or the Day of Trumpets as translated in English. The Day of Trumpets officially begins on the Fall Feast days with the sighting of the crescent new moon on either Tishri 1 or Tishri 2. Because it can take up to two days for the visible sighting of the crescent new moon, within Jewish culture, it is known as *one long day.*

The period of time from Yom Teruah to Yom Kippur highlights the final 10 days of Teshuvah and is considered among the Jewish community as the High Holy Days. These final 10 days is also known as the 10 days of Awe that ends on the Day of Atonement or Yom Kippur, the most sacred Day of the Fall Feasts. Five days later come Tabernacles or the Feast of Sukkoth which ends eight days later on Shemini Atzeret known as the eight days of assembly.

The Feast Days are shadow pictures of good things to come intertwined with shadow pictures of judgments to an unbelieving world. Leviticus 23:24 states: "Speak to the children of Israel saying, in the seventh month on the first day of the month, you shall have a Sabbath-rest, a memorial of blowing of trumpets, a holy convocation." This passage clearly identifies Yom Teruah as that day of the blowing of the shofar.

Shadow Pictures of Yom Teruah

The Feast of Yom Teruah is the prime example of rehearsals and shadow pictures of good things to come, and not so good depending on whether or not you are covered by the Almighty's wings of protection. This feast ushers in the governmental civil calendar, and is associated by different idioms that identify these shadow pictures and what they represent. [2] The most common idioms associated with Yom Teruah are as follows:

- KIDDUSHIN NESU'IN MEANING "THE WEDDING OF THE MESSIAH"
- THE TIME OF JACOB'S TROUBLE OR THE "TRIBULATION"
- THE DAY OF THE AWAKENING BLAST OR "TERUAH"
- "YOM HADIN" MEANING THE "DAY OF JUDGMENT" OR "OPENING OF THE BOOKS"
- "YOM HAKESH" MEANING "THE HIDDEN DAY"
- "HA MELECH" MEANING THE "CORONATION OF THE MESSIAH"
- "YOM HAZIKKARON" MEANING THE "DAY OF REMEMBRANCE"
- "HA YOM HARAT OLAM" MEANING THE "BIRTHDAY OF THE WORLD"

The Feast of Yom Teruah starts the series of the High Holy Days every year and was vitally important 2,000 years ago as it is today. Recently, there has been a feverish build up to these Fall Feast days anticipated by millions of Jews and Hebrew Roots Christians around the world. This is a big event in Israel today especially the sighting of the new moon in the 7th month of Tishri. It is still a popular saying among those in Israel that, *No Man Knows the Day or Hour*" during this time. This phrase is attributed to the sighting of the crescent new moon and was said by the Temple High Priest back 2,000 years ago as was said by our High Priest, Yahshua the Messiah.

The Idiomatic Expressions of Yahshua

Yahshua taught in parables in order to reveal greater truth to those who had the spiritual blinders removed from their eyes, while concealing truth from the spiritually blind that did not nor would not embrace the truth.

The statement, "No man knows the day or the hour....but only my Father in heaven," was an idiom with a much deeper meaning than its interpretation today in our western mindset. Is it possible that Yahshua was using idiomatic language that the current Jewish culture would have understood, but that other cultures inclusive of our western culture, would not fully understand? I believe that not only is this feasible, but that this is in fact the case. Certainty, only that culture that understood the idioms of the day would be able to make the deep spiritual connections to what was being said.

An idiom is an expression or statement that has a deeper meaning attributed to it. As an example, when I say, *Don't burn your bridges!, what* am I saying? Most today would attribute that to keeping your relationships and opportunities in a healthy state and they would be correct. When I say, *I'm just killing time*, does that imply that I am trying to murder time if that were even possible? Of course not! What about, *It's raining cats and dogs!* We understand that it is really raining hard. But, how would other cultures interpret these words if they didn't understand our culture especially over the course of hundreds of years? We laugh at such interpretations today, because we understand the deeper meaning of what are behind these statements.

Regarding the Jewish culture at that time, the disciples and those listening to the words of Yahshua, "No man knows the day or hour...but only my father in heaven" instantly made the connection to the Feast of Yom Teruah and the Jewish Wedding. Today, we refer to it simply as the *Ancient Jewish Wedding*, but as you will discover, there is a deeper connection

21

to this ancient wedding and to the times we are living. Once you understand the details behind the Feast of Yom Teruah and the details behind the Ancient Jewish Wedding, then you will also make the connections.

There is a particular set of verses in Thessalonians that have been have been a stumbling block for many for some time.

"Now, brothers, as to the times and the seasons, you do not need to be written to. For you yourselves know very well that the day of יהוה comes as a thief in the night. For when they say, 'Peace and safety!' then suddenly destruction comes upon them, as labour pains upon a pregnant woman, and they shall not escape. But you, brothers, are not in darkness, so that this Day should overtake you as a thief. For you are all sons of light and sons of the day. We are not of the night, nor of darkness." (1 Thessalonians 5:1-5)

When I read this, I am now able to make certain connections and tie it into our current generation. In my mind, when I read this I can't help but to read it as such.

"Brothers, regarding the 'Signs' in the heavens and the 'Appointed Feasts Days of YHVH,' there is no need to be written to, because you understand the cultural idioms. You know very well that YHVH come as 'a thief in the night' to a sleeping church, and as a Bridegroom for His Bride on the Appointed Feast Days of Yom Teruah, at the Last Trump of the blowing of the shofar in some future year. For when they say 'Peace and safety,' then sudden destruction falls on that 'Great Day' of Atonement. But, we should not be in darkness, for we are the children of light who hear His voice and understand the times." (Phil's version)

That is the spiritual connection I am able to make with these verses because I understand the idioms behind the meaning. Now, let me break these verses down in detail, so you will be able to make these connections as well.

The Signs and *"Appointed Feasts"*

The phrase "Signs (Times) and Seasons" is first found in Genesis 1:14:

> "And Elohim said, "Let lights come to be in the expanse of the heavens to separate the day from the night, and let them be for signs and appointed times, and for days and years,"

This verse comes from the ISR98 *Institute for Scripture Research* version of the Bible. Most versions state, "and let them be for signs and seasons." The word *seasons* will be the focus here.

The Hebrew word for seasons is Mow'ed [3] that means appointed times, appointed feasts and seasons. In the Strong's Concordance, Mow'ed is identified as Strong's number H4150. Unless noted otherwise, all references for this book come from the online concordance of *blueletterBible.com*. What we find is that this Hebrew word is used 223 times within the Old Testament. Within the 223 times, it is translated 150 times as congregation, 23 times as feasts, 13 times as seasons and 12 times as times. Within the context of the congregation, it is used to describe either the *Tabernacle of the Congregation* or the *Tent of the Congregation,* which represents the tent or structure that housed the Holy of Holies. In every case, when Mow'ed is used 23 times in context as *Feasts,* it is used to describe the actual Feast Days of Passover, Unleavened Bread and Tabernacles. The 13 times Mow'ed is used in context to describe *seasons,* it is used 10 times to highlight the Feast Days. The following are some of the verses that confirm this:

"These are the feasts [H4150] of the LORD, even holy convocations, which ye shall proclaim in their seasons." [H4150] (Leviticus 23:4, NKJV)

"Let the children of Israel also keep the Passover at his appointed season." [H4150] (Number 9:2, NKJV)

"In the fourteenth day of this month, at even, ye shall keep it in his appointed season: [H4150] according to all the rites of it, and according to all the ceremonies thereof, shall ye keep it." (Numbers 9:3, NKJV)

"But at the place which the LORD thy God shall choose to place his name in, there thou shalt sacrifice the Passover at even, at the going down of the sun, at the season [H4150] that thou camest forth out of Egypt." (Deuteronomy 16:6, NKJV)

"He appointed the moon for seasons: [H4150] the sun knoweth his going down." (Psalms 104:19, NKJV)

This last verse clearly shows the context of seasons as referring to the *Feast Days of the Lord*. It is clear that the moon does not dictate the seasons as in winter, spring, summer and fall. Only the sun, the spring and fall equinox dictate the actual seasons because the actual seasons are based on the sun and the tilt of the earth as indicated in Genesis 1:14. The moon is used to highlight the Feast days, which are entirely Lunar Feasts. Psalms 104:19 is clearly using *seasons* in reference to the Feast days.

It is critical that I make these connections with seasons because it is critical that you make the spiritual connection to *Signs and Seasons as* literally meaning *Signs and Appointed Feast Days*. This is the true translation of this text and is highly important in making connections to the times in which we live, because the time is short.

24

With regard to *Signs,* the Hebrew word is Owth [4] and means a sign, signal, a distinguished mark, banner, remembrance, miraculous sign, omen and warning in that particular order. When I think of the 1949 to 1950, 1967 to 1968 and the 2014 to 2015 Lunar (Blood) Tetrad Moon cycles, that we are currently in the midst of, I can't help but identify these *Blood Moons* as an exact interpretation of the meaning of the Hebrew word Owth. These *Blood Moon Tetrads* are four uninterrupted total lunar eclipses that happen in the spring and fall in back to back years. It's during a total lunar eclipse that the moon appears as blood.

In order to make a point regarding the word *Owth,* these *Blood Moon Tetrads* act as a heavenly sign or signal with flashing red lights. These four flashing red lights are a miraculous sign or *distinguished mark.* The distinguished mark is a good definition of these Lunar Moon Tetrads as you will discover in chapter six. It is possible that this is a bad omen of things to come to the world and especially in regard to the Jewish Nation of Israel. The Lunar Tetrads act as a warning, but aren't always accurate in that definition because these Tetrads sometimes occur after the event like the case after Israel was declared a nation in 1948. This implies that these Tetrads are more of a *distinguished mark* that identify or highlight key events that has to do with the Jewish People and the land of Canaan (Israel) and also identifies a time of liberation or judgment. I go in depth on these *Blood Moon Tetrads* in chapter six.

It is known among the Jewish culture that lunar eclipses are a bad omen to Israel, while solar eclipses are bad omen to the nations. It was on Nisan 1, the first month of the Spiritual Year, of 2015 that there was a solar eclipse. The same phenomena will happen this year in the month of Tishri being the first month of the Jewish civil calendar year.

The remaining of verse 1 of Thessalonians 5 states that, *"you do not need to be written to."* What a stumbling phrase! If you read this phrase in its proper context with regard to the Jewish culture, then it makes perfect sense. The Apostle Paul is clearly identifying *Signs and Appointed Feast Days* to Season (H4150) as the *Appointed Feast* Days. This is why he made the statement that you do not need to written to, because it was obvious within the Jewish culture that this in reference to these Fall Feast Days especially Yom Teruah (the Day of Trumpets) to Yom Kippur (Day of Atonement) or more specifically *The Last Trump* and *The Great Trump* in that order. The 2nd verse of Thessalonians 5 states, *"For you yourselves know very well that the day of* יהוה *comes as a thief in the night."*

Why would he state that you yourselves know very well? It was because they understood the meaning behind the idiomatic language pointing to the Fall Feast Days. There are two expressions in this verse that needs to be viewed deeper. They are, *The Day of* יהוה or *The Day of The Lord* and *Comes as a Thief in the Night.* These statements are idioms and as such have a much deeper meaning behind them. Let us start with a *Thief in The Night.*

The *Thief in the Night* — an Idiom for Apathy

There are both positive and negative attributes associated with this idiom. Within the Jewish culture at that time, just before a Jewish wedding, the bridegroom would come for his bride in the middle of the night often to her unexpected surprise because she did not know the day or hour he would come, but knew the general timing of his arrival. This event was often attributed to him coming as a *thief in the night.* This was a joyous occasion and the bride needed to have oil in her lamp because the groom would come at a time when *No man would know the day or the hour.* Therefore, she needed to be prepared along with her bridesmaids. Of course, she would not wait around for her bridesmaids as the groom would *snatch* her up off the ground to be carried back to her new home prepared for her by her groom. This is the positive aspect of this idiom. Another name for this

26

day is Yom HaKeseh meaning *the Hidden Day* as in the groom coming for his bride as *a thief in the night*. This day is also associated by the name of Kiddushin Nesu'in meaning *the Wedding Ceremony* or *the Wedding of the Messiah*.

Someone who is caught unaware would be the negative aspect of the idiom, *a thief in the night*. The prime example of this would be the example of the five wise and foolish virgins or bridesmaids. The wise bridesmaids were eagerly awaiting the sounds of the shofar and the coming of the bridegroom, while the foolish bridesmaids were not and thus would miss his coming.

> "Remember therefore how thou hast received and heard, and hold fast, and repent. If therefore thou shalt not watch, *I will come on thee as a thief,* and thou shalt not know what hour I will come upon thee." (Revelation 3:3, NKJV)

There is another idiom in regard to coming as a thief and that has to do with keeping his garments. Here is the verse spoken by the word of Yahshua:

> "Behold, *I come as a thief.* Blessed is he that watcheth, and keepeth his garments, lest he walk naked, and they see his shame." (Revelation 16:15, NKJV)

To fully appreciate this statement, we must travel back in time to when Herod's Temple was standing and still in operation 2,000 years ago. This idiom has to do with the temple guards that would guard the temple gates and courts especially at the night watch. There were 24 stations that needed to be manned by a total of 240 guards and 30 priests.[5] Because these guards would need to be awake and on guard, those guards that had fallen asleep would not be treated lightly.

As was the custom, the Captain of the Temple would make his rounds every night, approaching the guards where they would arise and salute the Captain. If the Captain found any guards who had fallen asleep, he would set their clothes on fire with his torch. While the guards' clothes were on fire, he would begin to shed his clothes running naked and ashamed. Thus, the Captain of the Guard would be known to come as *a thief in the night.* Yahshua was obviously using this idiom to describe what was spoken in Revelation 16:15 and can be attributed to other Scriptures with the Bible. This is why the term *a thief in the night* can be applied to the sleeping church. In regard to *the Day of the Lord,* this in reference to Yom Kippur or the Day of Atonement as it is also called. This day is a terrible and dreadful day and implies great judgment. This day is also known as *the Great Day.* This is especially meaningful in that it is quoted from the 16th chapter of the Book of Revelation and as such applies to our time.

Likewise, Yom Teruah is attributed to judgment as it is known as Yom HaDin or *the Day of Judgment* or the opening of the books in order to judge. Many Jews believe this will mark the time of Jacob's trouble. Another name for Jacob is Israel. Today we would read this as *Israel's trouble* or the start of the *7 years of tribulation* that is known in the Christian community. You can see why the ten days that follow Yom Teruah is a critical period of time until Yom Kippur as this *Great Day* will begin Great Judgment.

Many Jews believe that Israel will be saved on the Day of Atonement in some future year. This thought or belief is key! Let me state that again! Many Jews believe that Israel will be saved on Yom Kippur, known as the Day of Atonement. This future Yom Kippur will be discussed in the final chapter of this book.

28

"Come, my people, enter thou into the chambers, and shut thy doors about thee: hide thyself as it were for a little moment, until the indignation be overpast. For, behold, the LORD cometh out of his place to punish the inhabitants of the earth for their indignity: the earth also shall disclose her blood, and shall no more cover her slain." (Isaiah 26:20-21, NKJV)

"No one is able to come to Me unless the Father who sent Me draws him. And I shall raise him up in the last day." (John 6:44)

The Scripture in Isaiah is yet another example of the shadow pictures of good things to come along side with great judgment. This Scripture hints that the Groom will come for his Bride whereby they will both enter the wedding chamber. This lines right up with the Ancient Jewish Wedding where they enter the wedding chamber first, and then emerge from their chambers to be presented to the entire wedding party and guests.

Continuing with Thessalonians 5: 3-4, "For when they say, 'Peace and Safety!' then suddenly destruction comes upon them, as labour pains upon a pregnant woman, and they shall not escape. *But you, brothers, are not in darkness, so that this Day should overtake you as a thief.*"

You may have picked up on this. When Paul says, *this Day*, he is making a reference to Yom Kippur because it is Yom Kippur that is known as *the Great Day* or *just the Day*. It is also a day of the blowing of the shofar much like Yom Teruah, but is known as one long blast or *the great shofar* as it is often referred within the Jewish communities. Some believe this final blowing of the shofar on the Day of Atonement will usher in the return of the Messiah on this day in some future year. I speak about this in the final chapter. The implication here is that we are not to be ignorant of the times in which we live. We do not want to be found sleeping in the

29

case of the Temple Guard or unprepared in the case of the bride or the 5 foolish bridesmaids.

For when they say *"Peace and Safety, then sudden destruction."* Let's not forget the words of Yahshua, for today we hear and read about wars and rumors of wars. We can pick up the paper or read on news sites regarding peace and safety. *"For we are all sons of light and sons of the day. We are not of the night nor of darkness."* Let's not be in darkness as to the times!

Parallels of the Ancient Jewish Wedding

When Elohim (The plural form of God) created marriage between one man and one woman, he attributed this same pattern of marriage to His Son and His future bride. The Hebrew wedding is much different from our western weddings, so in order to paint an accurate picture of how Yahshua will one day come for His earthly bride, I need identify and explain the 12 Jewish events and customs that make up this wedding.

There are 12 events that make up the typical Ancient Jewish Wedding. They are in order as follows:

1. THE SELECTION OF THE BRIDE BY THE SON'S FATHER.

2. THE ESTABLISHMENT OF THE BRIDAL PRICE AND ACCEPTANCE.

3. THE BRIDE AND GROOM ARE BETROTHED TO ONE ANOTHER ONCE THE BRIDAL PRICE IS ACCEPTED.

4. A WRITTEN DOCUMENT DRAWN UP CONTAINING THE PROMISES OF THE GROOM AND THE RIGHTS OF THE BRIDE.

5. THE BRIDE'S ACCEPTANCE AND CONSENT.

6. GIFTS WERE GIVEN TO THE BRIDE AND THE COVENANT WAS SEALED ONCE THE BRIDE DRANK FROM THE CUP OF WINE.

7. THE BRIDE HAS HER MIKVAH (BAPTISM), WHICH IS A RITUAL CLEANSING.

8. THE BRIDEGROOM DEPARTS FROM HER, GOING BACK TO HIS FA-
    THER'S HOUSE FAR AWAY TO PREPARE THE BRIDAL CHAMBER.

9. THE BRIDE WAS "SET APART" UNTIL HIS RETURN TYPICALLY ONE TO
    TWO YEARS.

10. THE BRIDEGROOM WOULD RETURN FOR HER, UPON THE APPROVAL
    FROM HIS FATHER. HE WOULD RETURN WITH A COMPANY OF WED-
    DING GUESTS, WITH THE BLOWING OF THE SHOFAR AND WITH A
    SHOUT, "BEHOLD THE BRIDEGROOM COMES."

11. THE BRIDEGROOM WOULD ABDUCT OR RAPTURE HIS BRIDE, USU-
    ALLY IN THE MIDDLE OF THE NIGHT. THE EXPRESSION USED WAS AS
    "A THIEF IN THE NIGHT."

12. LASTLY, THERE WOULD BE "THE MARRIAGE SUPPER" WITH A HOST
    OF WEDDING GUESTS WHO HAD BEEN INVITED BY THE GROOM'S FA-
    THER. IT WOULD LAST FOR SEVEN DAYS OR LESS.

If this is your first time reading this, then you have already made some connections to the Messiah (Yahshua) and are more than likely scanning well known verses in your head that have remained a mystery to you until now. It should have become clear to you that Yahshua was using cultural wedding idioms with regard to his second return back to earth.

Now, let's dive deeper into these 12 steps and apply familiar Scriptures that will begin to paint a picture in your mind of how Yahshua will one day return for his bride.

> "For I am jealous for you with a jealousy according to Elohim. For I gave you in marriage to one husband, to present you as an innocent maiden to Messiah." (II Corinthians 11:2)

Paul is clearly making the connection of a wife to her husband as a maiden or virgin to the Messiah. Ephesians 5:25 is a similar reference, "Husbands,

31

love your wives, as Messiah also did love the assembly and gave Himself for it." Here we see the assembly would be the assembly of believers attributed to a wife as Messiah as a loving husband.

In step one, we see that the father of the groom searches for a potential bride for his son. Likewise, the Father has searched and found a Bride for His Son and it is the body of believers known today as the Church. The Father is looking for a perfect and pure Bride for His Son. Keep in mind that the entire body of believers does not make up His Bride as is so commonly understood. There seems to be two separate groups for the wedding. Scripture suggests that the bride and groom are made up of one group, while the wedding party and guests make up the second. As you can see, there are believers in Yahshua who will be a part of the wedding party group and the more prized group being the Bride.

What group we eventually become a part of is more difficult to explain. What comes to my mind are the words from Yahshua himself in John 14:15, *"If you love me, you will keep my commandments."* I believe observing his commandments are a healthy first step.

The Bridal Price

"Ask of me a bride price and gift ever so high, and I give according to what you say to me, but give me the girl for a wife." (Genesis 34:12)

"Knowing that you were redeemed from your futile way of life inherited from your fathers, not with what is corruptible, silver or gold, but with the precious blood of Messiah, as of a lamb unblemished and spotless," (I Peter 1:18,19)

"Or do you not know that your body is the temple of the Holy Spirit who is in you, whom you have from God, and you are not your own? For you were bought at a price; therefore glorify God in your body and in your spirit, which are God's" (I Corinthians 6:19-20, NKJV)

As was the custom, once the father has selected a potential bridal candidate for his son, he would then approach the father of the potential bride and offer a bridal price for her on behalf of his son, this along with the ketubah or the contract. We see throughout the Scripture that brides in ancient times were purchased with a price. We clearly see this demonstrated when Rebekah accepted the initial bridal price of the nose ring and bracelets made of gold for her pledge of marriage to Isaac as recorded in the entire chapter of Genesis 24. The reason for the bridal price was to show the father of the bride what worth his daughter was to the potential groom and his love for her. We also see this in the Scriptures of Jacob when he married Leah instead of Rachel. In the 29th chapter of Genesis we see Jacob serving Laban for seven years as a bridal price for his beloved Rachel who he was betrothed to marry. So, the bridal price can be finances or the greater price of servitude, as in the case of Jacob, seven years.

One of the greatest expressions of love is to lay down your life for others such as your bride. This expression of love far exceeds gold and silver or any kind of wealth. Likewise, as the Bride of Messiah, we were paid by a very high bridal price, that being the death of Yahshua and the shedding of his blood for the redemption of sin. This bridal price is beyond even servitude, for there is no greater love than to lay one's life for their friends (John 15:3). It was the first-fruits of the Messiah's death that resulted in His Bride receiving many gifts in the form of forgiveness, eternal life, the fruit of the Spirit and the gifts of the Spirit.

There are of course many more gifts to speak of, but to summarize my point, all of these gifts are of great value and cannot be bought with worldly riches such as gold and silver. The gift of eternal life that has been freely given had a great cost to both the Father and the Son and is the greatest gift that we as believers can receive.

The Betrothal

The bride and groom are betrothed to one another once the bridal price is accepted and a written document is drawn up containing the promises of the groom and the rights of the bride. This step is known as the betrothal and is similar to an engagement today whereby a fiancé has accepted a proposal and has received a ring as a bridal price. Back then, there was a much greater sense of commitment as they were entering a legal binding contract or covenant. This covenant was in the form of a marriage contract known as a ketubah, which was presented to the father of the bride. This covenant would consist of the groom's promises to his bride. The bride, in return, would cherish her ketubah. Once a couple entered a covenant of betrothal, they were legally married in the eyes of the law. The final step to seal this covenant and to make it binding was for both parties, especially the bride, to drink the cup of wine. The drinking of the cup was what *Sealed* the marriage. Although legally married, physical contact was refrained and consummation was forbidden.

Much like the ketubah, we have a marriage covenant known as the Bible. The transliteration of *New Testament* and *Old Testament* are Catholic/Latin in origin and originate from *New Covenant* and *Old Covenant* as in a marriage covenant or contract. Much like the ketubah, the Bible contains the promises that await those who embrace the Messiah. Likewise, we are to cherish what is written and to place His word and His Torah on our hearts.

"See, the days are coming," declares יהוה, "when *I shall make a new covenant with the house of Yisra'ĕl and with the house of Yehudah,* not like the covenant I made with their fathers in the day when I took them by the hand to bring them out of the land of Egypt, My covenant which they broke, though I was a husband to them," declares יהוה "For this is the covenant I shall make with the *house of Yisra'ĕl* after those days, *declares יהוה: I shall put My Torah in their inward parts, and write it on their hearts.* And I shall be their Elohim, and they shall be My people" (Jeremiah 31: 31-33)

This prophecy is directed to the northern House of Israel. The southern House of Judah, the Jewish people, have always had the Torah written on their hearts, even in their rebellion. This Scripture applies more for the northern kingdom that assimilated themselves within the Gentile Nations. *The new covenant, ketubah, is for both houses of Israel,* the Jews and for the aspersion of Israel that have lost their identity. I would like to note that it was on Shavuot that YHVH presented His ketubah in the form of the *Ten Commandments* to his Bride— the 12 tribes of Israel.

The Bride's Acceptance and Consent

If she did not accept his offer then the espousal would be broken and the father of the groom would begin searching for another candidate for his son. Because YHVH is a gentleman who does not force anyone into a relationship with Him, we see that those who chose him must be pure. We see this in Scripture regarding Isaac and Rebekah in Genesis 24:57- 58, where Rebekah was asked concerning Isaac: "Will you go with this man?" She said, "I will go."

We have a choice! Either we accept Yahshua and obey His commands that make up the ketubah (the Bible), or we reject His free offer. Unfortunately, the majority of the world rejects Him and His free offer.

"Enter in through the narrow gate! Because the gate is wide – and the way is broad – that leads to destruction, and there are many who enter in through it. *"Because the gate is narrow and the way is hard pressed which leads to life, and there are few who find it."* (Matthew 7: 13-14)

Sealing the Ketubah

The ketubah, once presented, would need to be sealed by the partaking of the cup filled with wine and would represent the final act of acceptance. In doing so, the marriage covenant would become a legal and binding agreement and they would be betrothed as bride and groom.

I can't help but make the connection of what Yahshua did for us on the cross. The new covenant that would save us from the sting of death, was not sealed until the shedding of his blood. This is why drinking the cup sealed the deal and made it a legal binding contract. If she refused the cup, then the betrothal would be annulled. The partaking of the cup was the deal maker or the deal breaker. Likewise, we are entering into a binding contract when we partake in the communion. According to 1 Corinthians 11:27-30, "We are not to take communion lightly as those who eat and drink in an unworthy manner bring on disease, sickness and even death." It is for this reason that communion is to be taken serious in much the same way you would want your spouse to take his or her vows seriously prior to the wedding.

We see another example of this during the Passover Seder regarding the 4 cups of the Seder. These 4 cups represent sanctification, deliverance, redemption, and restoration.[6] This is what YHVH did for the children of Israel when He took them out of Egypt. Exodus 6 identifies these 4 works of YHVH…

1	"I will bring you out" — sanctification
2	"I will save you" — deliverance
3	"I will redeem you" — redemption
4	"I will take you as My people" — restoration

Likewise, the Messiah has given us all of these aside from the final cup of restoration. He has *sanctified* us by calling us to be set apart by living the life different from the world much like the children of Israel were separated and sanctified from the Egyptians who were being punished for following false gods and all that was an abomination to God.

As YHVH delivered Israel from slavery and heavy bondage, Yahshua has delivered us from the bondage of sin through the shedding of his blood on that Roman cross. We are no longer slaves to sin or the fruits of bondage that lead to death, but rather delivered with the hope of eternal life.

He has *redeemed* all of mankind by His death and resurrection. However, He has not *restored* the world. Not Yet! This is the final cup of the Passover Seder that Yahshua refused to drink on that Passover night nearly 2,000 years ago.

"And taking the cup, and giving thanks, He gave it to them, saying, "Drink from it, all of you. "For this is My blood, that of the renewed covenant, which is shed for many for the forgiveness of sins. *"But I say to you, I shall certainly not drink of this fruit of the vine from now on till that day when I drink it anew with you in the reign of My Father."* (Matthew 26:27-28)

"This cup is the renewed covenant in My blood. As often as you drink it, do this in remembrance of Me. 'For as often as you eat this bread and drink this cup, you proclaim the death of the Master until He comes.' " (1 Corinthians 11:25-26)

We see that Yahshua clearly identified this 4th cup as the cup of the *renewed covenant* of restoration or the b'rit chadashah applied as the "renewed covenant in my blood."

The Bridegroom

Yahshua understood His mission at His first coming! He understood that He would be returning to his Father's house where he would eventually be drinking this final cup in His Father's kingdom with His Bride at the *appointed time* of his Father. Yahshua and His disciples were actually entering into a marriage covenant by drinking from the cup of restoration whether they realized or not, much in the same way that we are doing so today. I bet you will never partake of communion the same!

> "And before the Festival of the Passover, יהושע knowing that His hour had come that He should move out of this world unto the Father, having loved His own who were in the world, He loved them to the end." (John 13:1)

He was making an idiomatic statement with this final cup that restoration would not take place until that day "when I drink it anew with you in the reign of My Father." This verse implies that the wedding day will either be in heaven and/or during the millennial reign on earth.

The 4th cup of the Seder represents the coming Messianic Era, the Kingdom of Heaven and the final and full *Restoration* of this world. The beginning of the 7th Millennium will usher in the Kingdom of God where one righteous king will reign.

Yahshua has already been declared the Messiah, much like a newly elected President of the United States is considered President on or after November 2nd of an election year depending on when Tuesday falls on the calendar. The President-elect will officially become President at the swearing in ceremony on January 20th or 21st for a four-year term. At the swearing in ceremony, he inherits all the power and authority that comes with his seat and position. Yahshua, being Messiah Elect, is awaiting His swearing in ceremony that will happen sometime at the beginning of the 7th Millennium at the Mow'ed or *appointed time* of Yom Kippur in the very, very, near future.

Another verse that comes to my mind is the scroll of Isaiah that Yahshua read from as is recorded in Luke 4:16-21:

> "And He came to Natsareth, where He had been brought up. And according to His practice, He went into the congregation on the Sabbath day, and stood up to read. And the scroll of the prophet Yeshayahu was handed to Him. And having unrolled the scroll, He found the place where it was written: 'The Spirit of יהוה is upon Me, because He has anointed Me to bring the Good News to the poor. He has sent Me to heal the broken-hearted, to proclaim release to the captives and recovery of sight to the blind, to send away crushed ones with a release, to proclaim the acceptable year of יהוה And having rolled up the scroll, He gave it back to the attendant and sat down. And the eyes of all in the congregation were fixed upon Him. And He began to say to them, "Today this Scripture has been filled in your hearing.' "

You may or may not have noticed, but He stopped reading right in the middle of the sentence that ended on the, *acceptable year of יהוה.* Why did He not continue reading the remainder of the verse? The remainder of the verse states, "and the day of vengeance of our Elohim, to comfort all who mourn,..."

The day of vengeance of our God is meant to be fulfilled in the end of days during the Fall Feasts and was not meant to be fulfilled during his first coming. His first coming was as an innocent lamb, in humility, humbleness and without worldly appeal or the authority of the world. That dominion was, and still is, under the authority of the god of this world. The full Scripture of Isaiah 61:1-3 is as follows:

> "The Spirit of the Master יהוה is upon Me, because יהוה has anointed Me to bring good news to the meek. He has sent Me to bind up the broken-hearted, to proclaim release to the captives, and the opening of the prison to those who are bound, to proclaim the acceptable year of יהוה, and the day of vengeance of our Elohim, to comfort all who mourn, to appoint unto those who mourn in Tsiyon: to give them embellishment for ashes, the oil of joy for mourning, the garment of praise for the spirit of heaviness."

Isn't it interesting that that coma separating these two statements would make up a time frame of almost 2,000 years! This same principle will be applied to another remarkable prophecy within the 9th chapter of the book of Daniel. I discuss this in detail in chapter eight.

This Scripture alludes to restoration after the *Day of the Lord,* to comfort all that mourns. Regarding restoration, this is still going on today and will continue until the final restoration of all things. We have seen and are seeing a restoration of the Jewish people back to their land. We are seeing a restoration of the name of the Creator —Yahweh. We are seeing a restoration of the son's name — Yahshua. We are witnessing Christians coming out of their paganism and doctrine, embracing their Hebrew Roots,

40

embracing the Feasts, embracing the Torah and much more. There is indeed restoration taking place.

I Go To Prepare A Place For You

Once the cup was partaken, she was now legally his bride and betrothed to him. At that point and as was the custom, the groom would make the declaration that he would go to his father's house in order to prepare a room for both him and the bride. Which is known as the bridal room.

> "In My Father's house are many staying places. And if not, I would have told you. I go to prepare a place for you. 'And if I go and prepare a place for you, I shall come again and receive you to Myself, that where I am, you might be too.'" (John 14:2-3)

He would promise to come back for her once the bridal room was finished and once He had the approval from His Father for only the Father had the authority to send His son for His bride. The Father would send His Son for His Bride under His terms and according to His *appointed time.*

The Jewish custom was not to set a date for the wedding unlike our western culture. The date would remain a mystery and only the father of the groom would have an idea to when that time would be. Traditionally, the wedding would take place up to one to two years (spiritually 1,000 to 2,000 years).

During this time, the bride was to be set apart and was to honor her ketubah best identified by *the word of YHVH.* She was to be eagerly awaiting his return as she would not know how long he would be gone. As such, she would always need to be prepared as he would come at a day and hour that she might not expect. Her lamp was to be filled with oil and she would need to be ready to depart at the father of the grooms choosing. Likewise,

41

her bridesmaids, who were often made up of her family members such as her sisters and who lived under the same roof, would need to be ready with their lamps filled with oil.

As the weeks and months passed, worry and doubt would set in and she would begin to wonder if he would indeed come back for her. As believers, it is easy to fall under the same doubt. As the world becomes more lawless and wicked, will Yahshua truly come back for us as He promised? Will it be this year, next year or 30 years from now? I believe He is closer than we realize! Will your lamp be filled and burning?

The Bride has her Baptism

Another one of the cultural steps is the ritual cleansing of the bride being mikvah or immersed in water otherwise known today as being baptized. The reason for this is two-fold. One is for physical purification and the other is for spiritual purification. The word mikvah means being immersed into a stream of living water such was the time when Yahshua was mikvah'd in the Jordan River by the High Priest, Yochanan ben Zechariah,[7] known as John the Baptist. The mikvah is a representation from the old life and coming up out of the water to new life.

> Mark 16:15-16, "And He said to them, 'Go into all the world and proclaim the Good News to every creature. He who has believed and has been immersed, shall be saved, but he who has not believed shall be condemned.' "

When Esther was chosen to become queen, she went through a purification process of one year. We can see during her purification that she was to remain set apart and pure.

As the Bride of Messiah, we have been immerse into the living water as part of the purification process both physically and spiritually in order to shed our old life of sin into a new life of obeying his word. *"Old things pass away, all things become new."*

Approval from His Father

After a period of time, after the chamber room was built, and after the father had determined that his son was ready, for only the father had that authority, he would send his son back to where his bride and bridesmaids were located, where they would be eagerly awaiting his return.

Because the bridegroom is righteous and true, he would return to her as had promised accompanied by a *host* of those who made up of the wedding party, bridesmaids and guests. This was a happy, joyous occasion as there would be laughter, shouts of joy, the blowing of the shofar (Trumpet) and dancing. The groom's best men would go ahead of the wedding party and would proclaim, *"Behold! The bridegroom comes."*

He would come for her at a day and hour that she did not expect usually at the midnight hour. The bride would begin to hear the singing, shouts of laughter and the blowing of the shofar in the distance. This would give her just enough time to gather her things but not always enough time to warn her bridesmaids. When he arrived along with the wedding party, he would snatch her up as a "thief in the night" where they would begin the long journey back to his father's house. The Hebrew word that describes this event is nissuin and that word is derived from the root word of nasa - which means to *carry.*[8] Thus, the custom of the groom was to hoist his bride in the air, where she would be placed safely in a carriage being carried off to the groom's added chamber room at his father's house.

"Let us be glad and rejoice and give honor to Him, for the marriage of he Lamb is come and his wife has made herself ready. And to her was granted to be arrayed in fine linen, clean and white, for the fine linen is the righteousness of saints." (Revelation 9:7-8)

This final culminating event where the bride is hoisted in the air speaks of the rapture of the bride. During the entire trip, she would be covered and hidden by her wedding garments and by her veil. Her identity would be hidden from the wedding party and guests. This is the idiom used for Yom Teruah being a *day of hiding* known as Yom HaKesh.

We see this in the Scriptures when Jacob married Leah instead of Rachel. We see that Jacob served Laban for seven years as a bridal price for his beloved Rachel whom he was betrothed to marry. Laban, instead, switched his daughters and he married Leah to Jacob instead. How was this possible without Jacob knowing this? It was because of the wedding dress and the veil that covered her. The bride was hidden!

The ten maidens or virgins recorded in Matthew 25:1-13 are not the bride, but rather the bridesmaids as the groom would *snatch* his bride into the air as he would never leave his bride! The bridesmaids would join the weeding party back at the father's house where the wedding would take place. But then, who are the foolish maidens and whom do they prophetically represent?

"Then the reign of the heavens shall be compared to ten maidens who took their lamps and went out to meet the bridegroom. "And five of them were wise, and five foolish. "Those who were foolish, having taken their lamps, took no oil with them, but the wise took oil in their containers with their lamps. "Now while the bridegroom took time, they all slumbered and slept. "And at midnight a cry was heard, 'See, the bridegroom is coming, go out to meet him!' "Then all those maidens rose up and trimmed their lamps. "And the foolish said to the wise, 'Give us of your oil, because our lamps are going out.' "But the wise answered, saying, 'No, indeed, there would not be enough for us and you. Instead, go to those who sell, and buy for yourselves.' "And while they went to buy, the bridegroom came, and those who were ready went in with him to the wedding feast, and the door was shut. "And later the other maidens also came, saying, 'Master, Master, open up for us!' "But he answering, said, 'Truly, I say to you, I do not know you.' "Watch therefore, because you do not know the day nor the hour in which the Son of Adam is coming," (Matthew 25:1-13)

The 5 foolish maidens describe a sleeping church, much like the church from Laodicean mentioned in Revelation chapter three that have been caught up with the cares of this world. The oil may refer to the Holy Spirit or righteousness and those five foolish virgins that did not have enough oil may represent those believers not being filled by the Rauch and not being clothed with "the garments of salvation (Yeshua)" that is required in order to be the bride of Messiah.

Hosanna and the Coronation of the King

After their long journey from the Bride's hometown (Earth) to the Father's house (Heaven), they would arrive where they would be married and proclaimed husband and wife. Soon afterwards, they would be the honored couple at the Great Wedding Feast.

On the couples wedding day, the groom will be seen as the king and the bride as the queen. The groom would dress as much like a king as his finances would allow. If the groom came from a wealthy family, then he would wear a gold crown along with fine linen and royal garments. The bride, likewise, would be dressed in a way that reflects his queen. The Book of Esther reflects this. After 12 months of preparation with oil, myrrh and perfumes, she (Esther) would prepare for her role as queen.

> "I greatly rejoice in יהוה, my being exults in my Elohim. For He has put *garments of deliverance on me*, He has covered me with the robe of righteousness, as a bridegroom decks himself with ornaments, and as a bride adorns herself with her jewels" (Isaiah 61:10).

The Hebrew word for deliverance is yesha' (Strong's H3468) that literally means salvation and is the root word for the name of Yeshua.

As the groom, bride and the accompanied wedding party approached the father's house, they would hear the words, "Blessed is He who comes in the name of יהוה!" Psalm 118:26. Likewise, when Yahshua was approaching Jerusalem during his Triumphal Entry, the people were quoting this prophetic phrase verbatim. It was Yahshua who was announcing himself as the Bridegroom to Israel on that prophetic day.

> "And the crowds who went before and those who followed cried out, saying, *"Hoshia-na to the Son of Dawid! Blessed is He who is coming in the Name of יהוה! Hoshia-na in the highest!"* (John 12:13).

The Hebrew word of Hoshia-na would be Hosanna in English. This saying is the joyful wedding cry of the bride to the groom. It was Yahshua, as he was entering Jerusalem riding on the colt or donkey, where he mentioned that even *the stones would cry out* an obvious reference to Scripture being fulfilled through him as the Messiah on that day thus fulfilling prophecy,

> "Rejoice greatly, O daughter of Tsiyon! Shout, O daughter of Yerushalayim! See, your Sovereign is coming to you, He is righteous

46

and endowed with deliverance, humble and riding on a donkey, a colt, the foal of a donkey" (Zechariah 9:9).

"Hoshia-na to the Son of Dawid! Blessed is He who is coming in the Name of יהוה*! Hoshia-na in the highest!,"* was referenced to not only as a husband, but also as King, a King who will radically save them at their greatest hour of need, still being a future event.

As He made his triumphant entry past the crowds and towards Jerusalem, He would make the following statement,

"Yerushalayim, Yerushalayim, killing the prophets and stoning those who are sent to her! How often I wished to gather your children together, the way a hen gathers her chickens under her wings, but you would not! "See, your House is left to you laid waste. *And truly I say to you, you shall by no means see Me until the time comes when you say, 'Blessed is He who is coming in the Name of* יהוה*!'* " (Matthew 23:37-39)

Remember that the new covenant was for both houses of Israel, the southern kingdom making up the Jews and the tribe of Benjamin, and the northern kingdom identified as the 10 tribes. In this passage he is clearly identifying the southern kingdom. The prophecy of the houses being laid waste was in reference to the destruction of Jerusalem in 70 CE.

"Let Your dead live, together with my dead body, let them arise. Awake and sing, you who dwell in dust; for Your dew is a dew of light, and let the earth give birth to the departed spirits. *Go, my people, enter your rooms, and shut your doors behind you; hide yourself, as it were, for a little while, until the displeasure is past. For look,* יהוה *is coming out of His place to punish the inhabitants of the earth for their crookedness.* And the earth shall disclose her blood, and no longer cover her slain." (Isaiah 26:19-21)

Interestingly enough the passage in Isaiah 26 states at the time that the dead would arise, that His people would enter their rooms in order to hide themselves, for a little while until the displeasure is past as YHVH will punish the inhabitants of the earth. This passage seems to line up with John 14:2-3, *"In My Father's house are many rooms. I go to prepare a place for you."*

It seems that this passage speaks of these main events happening in one moment of time: The dead in Messiah shall arise first; then the bride shall be taken and will enter into her wedding chamber (room); she will be hidden from tribulation as YHVH punishes the inhabitants of the earth. In other words, what this passage is alluding to is the so-called rapture, the wedding and tribulation starting at one instance in time. If you have read this far, then you can see how all of these events can happen on the feast days of Yom Teruah.

It will be this future *Appointed Feast* that Yahshua and his Bride will be known as King and Queen to all who attend the wedding party. When they arrived from their long trip, the bride and groom would enter the bridal chamber as the wedding party would wait outside. Once inside the chamber, they would consummate the marriage for the first time. The friend of the bridegroom would wait outside the room until the groom would announce the news to his friend. The stained linen would offer proof of the bride's virginity and with that, the identity of the bride would be unveiled and there would be a great and joyous wedding celebration. The bride and groom would spend the next 7 days in the bridal chamber together, coming out to join in the celebrations with the wedding party and guests from time to time where there would be food, dancing and a

48

great celebration. As was the custom, the wedding party/feast would last for seven days.

Playing of music and dancing was a regular part of the celebration. This feast is identified in the 19th chapter of the Book of Revelation as *the Marriage Supper of the Lamb!* There seems to be an equal split of opinions with regard to when this event takes place and where. In reference to the location, there seems to be two choices, that being heaven or earth. If this prophecy is a reflection of the Ancient Wedding Feast, which I believe it is, then I believe this Great Feast not only takes place in heaven, but also back on earth. I discuss this in the final chapter of the book as well as my theory on the approximate time as there is a great deal of reasoning on this and can only be explained once you understand the logic behind my reasoning, so keep reading!

"And I heard, as it were, the voice of a great multitude, as the sound of many waters and as the sound of mighty thunderings, saying, 'Alleluia! For the Lord God Omnipotent reigns! Let us be glad and rejoice and give Him glory, for the marriage of the Lamb has come, and His wife has made herself ready. And to her it was granted to be arrayed in fine linen, clean and bright, for the fine linen is the righteous acts of the saints.' Then he said to me, Write: 'Blessed are those who are called to the Marriage Supper of the Lamb!' And he said to me 'These are the true sayings of God.' " (Revelation 19:6-9)

The Creator was Married Once Before!

Would it surprise you to hear that YHVH (God) was married once before? The Scriptures record that YHVH was married to all 12 tribes that made up Israel. We see mention of this in the Book of Jeremiah.

"And after she had done all these, I said 'Return to Me.' But she did not return. And her treacherous sister *Yehudah* saw it. 'And I saw that for all the causes for which backsliding *Yisra'ĕl* had committed adultery, *I had put her away and given her a certificate of divorce;* yet her treacherous sister *Yehudah* did not fear, but went and committed whoring too.' " (Jeremiah 3:7-8)

At the time of this prophecy, Israel had been broken into two kingdoms, [9] the northern kingdom made up of 10 tribes known as "Israel/Ephraim" [10] and the southern kingdom known as "Judah/Jews" made up of the tribe of Judah, the tribe of Benjamin along with a remnant of the tribe of Levi. The northern kingdom is also referred to as the House of Ephraim, the House of Israel or just Israel. This event of the tribes being divided happened in 931 BCE. [11] Here is the scriptural basis for this...

"Then Ahijah took hold of the new garment that was on him, and tore it into twelve pieces. And he said to Jeroboam, "*Take for yourself ten pieces,* for thus says the Lord, the God of Israel: '*Behold, I will tear the kingdom out of the hand of Solomon and will give ten tribes to you* ....And to his son I will give one tribe, that My servant David may always have a lamp before Me in Jerusalem, the city which I have chosen for Myself, to put My name there... And I will afflict the *descendants of David* because of this, but not forever.' " (1 Kings 11:30-31, 36, 39, NKJV)

This Scripture shows that YHVH gave a certificate of divorce to the northern kingdom known also as the *aspersion* or *the Lost sheep of the House of Israel* as referred to by Yahshua. [12]

It was her *sister* Judah (the Jewish people) that were spared for a period of time, but nonetheless her offspring would and did suffer judgment as is well documented historically. *"And I will afflict the descendants of David because of this, but not forever"* (1 Kings 11:39). The descendants of David are clearly a reference to the Jewish people (the tribe of Judah) and yet another fulfillment of Bible prophecy.

The prophet Jeremiah goes on to say that YHVH will make a new (marriage) covenant with both Houses of Israel.

"I will make a new covenant with the House of Israel and the House of Judah" (Jeremiah 31:31).

The Messiah Died in Order to Marry His Bride!

How is it that the Scriptures speak of how YHVH would make a new marriage covenant with a wife that he issued a divorce decree. Does not the Torah forbid such a thing?

"They say, 'If a man divorces his wife, And she goes from him, And becomes another man's, May he return to her again?' Would not that land be greatly polluted? But you have played the harlot with many lovers; Yet return to Me," says the Lord." (Jeremiah 3:1, NKJV)

How can the Creator break his own law, his own Torah? The short answer is that He can't. He is unable to break his own word as this is contrary to what the Scriptures indicate because that would go against His character. So how can YHVH remarry his bride?

This is an incredible mystery and not an easy question to answer. There are some clues that Scripture leaves us.

"Hear, O Yisra'ĕl: יהוה our Elohim, יהוה is one!" (Deuteronomy 6:4)

51

"Hear, O Israel: The Lord our God, the Lord is one! (Deuteronomy 6:4, NKJV)

The title *God* comes from the Hebrew word Elohim. Elohim is a word that is plural, not singular. Yet, this passage refers to *YHVH (The Lord) our Elohim being* one is a mystery in itself. This verse implies that the Almighty is greater than one even though Scripture confirms that He is one. What a mystery!

The mystery revealed is found in none other than Yahshua! John 1:1 states, *"In the beginning was the Word, and the Word was with Elohim, and the Word was Elohim."* What I have discovered is that the *Word of YHVH* is Yahshua. Because He is *echad* [13] with Elohim, when He died, He not only paid the penalty of sin, but we discover that He is able to remarry his bride. The implication is that Yahshua, known as the *Word of YHVH* was married to both houses of Israel.

This topic is so deep that I would highly recommend you watch a video titled, *Identity Crises* by Pastor Jim Staley. It's free on Youtube or you can order a copy!

The Scripture identifies His name as the *Word of YHVH* among His other names that can be found throughout the Scriptures especially in the Old Covenant (Old Testament). The following set of verses from the Book of Revelation identifies just a few of his many names,

"And I saw the heaven opened, and there was a white horse. And He who sat on him was called *Trustworthy and True*, and in righteousness He judges and fights. And His eyes were as a flame of fire, and on His head were many crowns, having a Name that had been written, which no one had perceived except Himself - and having been dressed in a robe dipped in blood – and His Name is called: *The*

Word of יהוה And the armies in the heaven, dressed in fine linen, white and clean, followed Him on white horses. And out of His mouth goes a sharp sword, that with it He should smite the nations. And He shall shepherd them with a rod of iron. And He treads the winepress of the fierceness and *wrath of Ĕl Shaddai.* And on His robe and on His thigh He has a name written: *SOVEREIGN OF SOVER-EIGNS AND MASTER OF MASTERS.* And I saw one messenger standing in the sun, and he cried with a loud voice, saying to all the birds that fly in mid-heaven, "Come and gather together for the sup-per of the great Elohim, to eat the flesh of sovereigns, and the flesh of commanders, and the flesh of strong ones, and the flesh of horses and of those who sit on them, and the flesh of all people, free and slave, both small and great." And I saw the beast, and the sovereigns of the earth, and their armies, gathered together to fight Him who sat on the horse and His army." (Revelation 19:11-19)

Chapter 2

Daniel! Seal the Book Until the

Time of the End!

"But you, Daniel, hide the words, and seal the book until the time of the end. Many shall diligently search and knowledge shall increase." (Daniel 12:4)

The Jews are a unique people. Never before have a tribe of people who lost their homeland, assimilated into other nations and cultures, have successfully gone back to re-inhabit their homeland. This is an amazing feat considering the fact that over 1,800 years have transpired from being driven out in 70 CE to re-inhabiting their land once again in the 20th century. Most biblical scholars prior to the 20th century must have thought that the Scripture dedicated to Israel re-inhabiting their land must have been allegory and not a literal future fulfillment due to the enormous feat that would have needed to take place in order for this to come to pass. But, as we know, nothing is impossible for the Almighty as Bible prophecy will be fulfilled to even the smallest detail.

We know from history that a growing number of Russian and Eastern European Jews began to make their way back to the land of Canaan known today as Israel that began back in 1905 during the Zionist movement. This act would provide the momentum for other Jews to make their way back to their land along with persecution and anti-Semitism as the motivating force. This initial push would eventually become reality initiated by the Balfour Declaration of 1917 and the eventual backing of the *Jewish State* by the U. N. and the United States after the horrors of the holocaust during WWII. This fact of the Jews re-inhabiting their land makes me ponder the majesty of the Almighty in that He can't go against His word. Genesis 17:8-9 declares such a promise:

" 'Also I give to you and your descendants after you the land in which you are a stranger, *all the land of Canaan, as an everlasting possession; and I will be their God.*' And God said to Abraham: *'As for you, you shall keep My covenant, you and your descendants after you throughout their generations.*' " (NKJV)

" 'Therefore see, the days are coming,' declares יהוה, 'when it is no longer said, 'יהוה lives who brought up the children of Yisra'ĕl from the land of Mitsrayim,' but, 'יהוה lives who brought up the children of Yisra'ĕl from the land of the north and from all the lands where He had driven them.' *For I shall bring them back into their land I gave to their fathers.*' " (Jeremiah 16:14-15)

" 'For behold, the days are coming,' says the Lord, 'that I will bring back from captivity My people Israel and Judah,' says the Lord. 'And I will cause them to return to the land that I gave to their fathers, and they shall possess it.' " (Jeremiah 30:3, NKJV)

Scripture declares that both houses will inhabit Israel in the latter days. Most are only aware of the Jews coming back to Israel, but Scripture indicates that the *northern kingdom of the House of Israel* will come back as well with her sister Judah known as the *southern kingdom of Judah*. We are beginning to see this as there is a huge interest in identifying the lost 10 tribes of *Israel*. This is actually a hot topic right now especially when you realize that one of the promises of YHVH was that He would make Abraham's seed more numerous than the stars and that his great grandchildren Ephraim and Manasseh would become great and powerful nations (Genesis 48:20).

These Latter Days!

In this chapter, I will attempt to make my case that we are indeed in these final days known as the *latter days*. The term *latter days* is backed by numerous Scriptures that point to a period of time from the Messiah's first coming to His second coming back to earth otherwise known as the final Age of man. My focus, within this book, will be to highlight the period of time from the re-birth of Israel until the Messiah's return, a period of roughly 70 to 90 years. Within this book, I will use this term *latter days* as having its beginning with the re-gathering of the Jewish people back to the land of Israel at the turn of the 20th century and with the emphasis on the year 1948 when the Jewish nation, once again became a nation.

> "Who has heard such a thing? Who has seen such things? Shall the earth be made to give birth in one day? Or shall a nation be born at once? For as soon as Zion was in labor, She gave birth to her children." (Isaiah 66:8)

This amazing prophetic day of the nation of Israel being born in one day fell on May 14th, 1948 that coincided with the eve of Shavuot. The fact that it fell on the eve of Shavuot tells me that the Creator divinely orchestrated this as this was the *Appointed Feast* when Israel was first recognized as a nation when they were presented with the Ten Commandments on Mount Sinai after their exodus out of Egypt. I make a good case within this book that major events that have fallen and will fall on the feast days are divinely inspired and directed by the Almighty especially on the eve (the moment or up to 24 hours before) of these major feast days.

Much like the Spring Feasts of Passover, Unleavened Bread and First-Fruits being fulfilled through Yahshua, the actual prophetic fulfillment of the middle feast, the Feast of Shavuot (Pentecost), was fulfilled 50 days later when according to the Book of Acts, the Ruach Ha Codesh or Holy Spirit fell on the 120 disciples while they were awaiting this gift as promised by Yahshua as recorded in John 14:16. The gift of the Holy Spirit is again an idiom associated with the ancient Jewish wedding whereby the groom would shower his bride with gifts. Instead of worldly possessions, the Messiah's gifts would be worth far greater.

Are We Truly in the Latter Days?

The term latter days, latter years and time of the end is mentioned throughout the Bible and mostly signify a period of time just prior to the return of Yahshua/Jesus coming to rule with great authority. My focus with these latter days will be to focus on the prophetic period of time of roughly 100 years from when the Jews began to migrate back to their homeland up to the present day with a laser focus into the future as most of the latter day prophecies are still to take place such as the Psalm 83 war, the Gog and Magog war, the prophecies concerning Jerusalem being a burdensome stone, Damascus being destroyed by fire and others.

There are numerous prophetic Scriptures that speak of Judah re-inhabiting their homeland in the latter years rebuilding the waste cities. Here is a handful among many.

"After many days you shall be called up. *In the latter years you shall come into the land of those brought back from the sword and gathered from many people on the mountains of Yisra'ĕl, which had been a continual waste. But they were brought out of the gentiles, and all of them shall dwell safely.*" (Ezekiel 38:8)

"And I shall turn back the captivity of My people Yisra'ĕl. And they shall build the waste cities and inhabit them. And they shall plant vineyards and drink wine from them, and shall make gardens and eat their fruit. *"And I shall plant them on their own soil, and not up-root them any more from their own soil I have given them," said* יהוה *your Elohim!"* (Amos 9:14-15)

"And speak to them, 'Thus said the Master יהוה, *"See, I am taking the children of Yisra'ĕl from among the gentiles, wherever they have gone, and shall gather them from all around, and I shall bring them into their land. "And I shall make them one nation in the land, on the* mountains of Yisra'ĕl. And one sovereign shall be sovereign over them all, *and let them no longer be two nations,* and let them no longer be divided into two reigns."* (Ezekiel 37: 21-22)

"And they shall have borne their shame, and all their trespass they committed against Me, when they dwell safely in their own land, with none to make them afraid, *when I have brought them back from the peoples and gathered them out of the lands of their enemies. And I shall be set apart in them before the eyes of many gentiles. 'And they* shall know that I am יהוה their Elohim, who sent them into exile among the gentiles, and then gathered them back to their own land, and left none of them behind. 'And no longer do I hide My face from them, for I shall have poured out My Spirit on the house of Yisra'ĕl,' declares the Master יהוה." (Ezekiel 39: 26-29)

"Look, the days are coming," declares יהוה, "that the ploughman shall overtake the reaper, and the treader of grapes him who sows seed. And the mountains shall drip new wine, and all the hills melt. *"And I shall turn back the captivity of My people Yisra'ĕl. And they shall build the waste cities and inhabit them. And they shall plant vineyards and drink wine from them, and shall make gardens and eat their fruit. "And I shall plant them on their own soil, and not uproot them any more from their own soil I have given them," said יהוה your Elohim!"* (Amos 9:13-15)

"Thus said the Master יהוה, *"On the day that I cleanse you from all your crookednesses, I shall cause the cities to be inhabited, and the ruined places shall be rebuilt, and the land that was laid waste tilled instead of being a ruin before the eyes of all who pass by. "And they shall say, 'This land that was laid waste has become like the garden of Ĕden. And the wasted, the deserted, and the destroyed cities are now walled and inhabited.' "Then the gentiles which are left all around you shall know that I, יהוה, have rebuilt the destroyed places and planted what was laid waste. I, יהוה, have spoken it, and I shall do it."* 'Thus said the Master יהוה, "Once again I shall let the house of Yisra'ĕl inquire of Me to do for them: I shall increase their men like a flock. "As a set-apart flock, as the flock at Yerushalayim at her appointed times, so shall the wasted cities be filled with flocks of men. And they shall know that I am יהוה." (Ezekiel 36: 33-38)

These prophetic verses clearly speak of the *latter years* when the Jewish people would re-inhabit the land of Canaan that had been a continual waste for over 1800 years while being brought back from the sword out of the gentile nations to never be uprooted again. It is amazing to see what was written down over two millennium ago coming to fulfillment within our generation. This is an accurate prophetic description of the events that happened after World War II representing the period of time just prior to 1948 to the present day as they continue to come out of the gentile nations such as the European countries as a result and in part to the rise of Islamic fundamentalism and a steady rise of anti-Semitism.

Indeed we have seen Israel flourish greatly to where they now supply Europe with a large supply of their produce. They are one of the world's biggest producers of fresh citrus fruit as well as exporter [1] with a wide variety of fruits and vegetables grown. They also continue to win international awards for their wine and their cows produce the highest amount of milk per cow in the world. Truly astonishing!

Who is the source of the Jews going back to their land? Most would attribute it to a correlation of events that transpired from the Balfour declaration, to the recognition by the United Nations, to the Zionist movement, and to even to Jerusalem being captured by the British Empire. However, according to this passage, it is the Creator YHVH that did this. He is the one who is in control and His divine influence is evident to those who are watching. Even the gentiles will know that it is because of Yahweh that these events are taking place.

The Time of Jacob's Distress

Another term that describes these last days is the time of Jacob's trouble or Jacob's distress. These expressions speak of the tribulation. Here we see a verse in Jeremiah that identifies this future event.

"Oh! For great is that day, there is none like it. And it is the *time of Ya'aqob's distress, but he shall be saved out of it.* 'And it shall be in that day,' declares יהוה of hosts, 'that I break his yoke from your neck, and tear off your bonds, and foreigners no more enslave them." (Jeremiah 30:7-8)

This is the only verse in the Bible concerning the words Jacob's distress. The Jewish people mostly understood it as the Day of the Lord. Much like Christianity, Judaism teaches of a period of time of great distress for a period of seven years or less with their future Messiah saving them as identified by the prophets. But, it is not all doom and gloom especially for those who place their trust in the Creator as the reference of being saved out of it *in that day.*

We see hints of salvation through Yeshua on that day as being saved out of it and being no more enslaved as can be found in Daniel 12:1 and other similar Scriptures. It is the Fall Feasts that are often attributed to great judgment and equally of salvation from Yom Teruah to Yom Kippur. For it is on a Yom Kippur that announcements the beginning of a 50th year of Jubilee according to Leviticus 25:8 and other Scripture, whereby the captives and slaves are set free and where foreigners no longer enslave them. The phrase, For *great is that day* is often an expression to the *Day of the Lord* as a great and terrible day. Yom Kippur is often associated with the day of judgment from the Almighty and is considered by the Jewish people as the highest holy day of the year, a day of fasting and repentance in order to be found worthy to escape judgment. *He shall be saved out of it* also speaks of Yom Teruah whereby the Bridegroom comes for his bride at a period of time where, *"no man knows the day or hour."*

There are passages from the Book of Zephaniah that speak of a time of trouble or day of distress on the day when the ram's horn (shofar) is blown as a warning. There are two *Appointed Feast* Days that use the shofar as a warning - Yom Teruah and Yom Kippur known as the *Last Trump* and *Great Trump,* in that order. The blowing of the shofar on Shavuot, on the other hand, is known as the *First Trump* as it was the first recorded blowing of the shofar as shown in Exodus 19:16-19. Here is a verse that either speaks of Yom Teruah or Yom Kippur,

> "That day is a day of wrath, a day of distress and trouble, a day of waste and ruin, a day of darkness and gloominess, a day of clouds and thick darkness, a day *of ram's horn and alarm* – against the walled cities and against the corner towers." (Zephaniah 1: 15-16)

This day of distress and time of trouble may be different from *Jacob's trouble* otherwise known as the seven years of tribulation. It could be that there is more than one day of distress or for that matter more than one *Day of the Lord,* but more than likely the *Day of the Lord* (The Day of YHVH) will be the final culmination Day of when the Messiah returns to fight for Israel.

A Closer look at Daniel Chapter 12

With regard to the latter days, there seems to be no greater chapter within the Bible that speaks of the time we live in than the 9th and 12th chapter of the Book on Daniel. The 12th chapter is especially important and once deciphered, you will see how it applies today. Due in part to this entire chapter being so KEY in understanding these latter days, the entire chapter has been included for reference. I have highlighted key phrases and words that I will be referencing throughout this book. This entire prophetic chapter describes future events with some small exceptions that I will discuss.

(Daniel 12:1-13, emphasis added in bold.)

1"Now at that time Mika'ĕl shall stand up, the great head who is standing over the sons of your people. *And there shall be a time of distress, such as never was since there was a nation, until that time. And at that time your people shall be delivered, every one who is found written in the book,*

2*and many of those who sleep in the dust of the earth wake up, some to everlasting life,* and some to reproaches, everlasting abhorrence.

3"And those who have insight shall shine like the brightness of the expanse, and those who lead many to righteousness like the stars forever and ever.

4"But you, Dani'ĕl, hide the words, and seal the book until the time of the end. *Many shall diligently search and knowledge shall increase.*"

5Then I, Dani'ĕl, looked and saw two others standing, one on this bank of the river and the other on that bank.

6And one said to the man dressed in linen, who was above the waters of the river, "How long until the end of these wonders?"

7And I heard the man dressed in linen, who was above the waters of the river, and he held up his right hand and his left hand to the heavens, and swore by Him who lives forever, that it would be *for a time, times, and half a time. And when they have ended scattering the power of the set-apart people, then all these shall be completed.*

8And I heard, but I did not understand, so I said, "My master, what is the latter end of these matters?"

9And he said, "Go, Dani'ĕl, for the words are hidden and sealed till the time of the end.

10"Many shall be cleansed and made white, and refined. But the wrong shall do wrong – and none of the wrong shall understand, but those who have insight shall understand.

11"And from the time that which is continual is taken away, and the abomination that lays waste is set up, *is **one thousand two hundred and ninety days.***

12"Blessed is he who is waiting earnestly, and comes to **the *one thousand three hundred and thirty-five days.***

13"But you, go your way till the end. And rest, and arise to your lot at the end of the days."

First off, the entire Book of Daniel is estimated to be between 2,200 to 2,500 years old and the 12th chapter concerns the time we are living in right now. Verse one starts out as the time of distress such as never was seen in a nation. To me, this could be the start of Daniel's 70th week as described in the 9th chapter of Daniel. The events in this verse are very similar to *Jacob's distress* mentioned in Jeremiah 30:7-8. Both Jacob's trouble and the time of distress are directly referenced to the tribulation. Again, we see a reference of "your people being delivered" as an idiom for the groom coming for his bride. Those who wake up out of the dust of the earth has a direct reference to 1 Corinthians 15:51-52:

"See, I speak a secret to you: We shall not all sleep, but we shall all be changed, in a moment, in the twinkling of an eye, *at the last trumpet*. For the trumpet shall sound, and the dead shall be raised incorruptible, and we shall be changed."

The event described in 1 Corinthians speak of the *rapture* or more precisely the Groom coming for his Bride wherein those who are living will be changed in such a way that our mortal bodies will be changed to immortals. The term last *trumpet* is an expression used on the Feast of Yom Teruah as previously discussed, so these two passages clearly identify the beginning of the Fall Feast Days and it will more than likely be on Yom Teruah and even this ten day window of time from Yom Teruah to Yom Kippur that we, "shall all be changed, in a moment, in the twinkling of an eye, at the last trumpet." In the third verse, we see an amazing reference to our generation and the *time of the end…*

"But you, Dani'ĕl, hide the words, and seal the book until the time of the end. Many shall diligently search and knowledge shall increase."

Daniel was instructed to hide the words and seal the book until such a time when knowledge would increase and many would diligently search. Today we live in the era when information travels at light speed. The whole world is connected instantaneously through technological advances in the form of satellites, wireless transmission, computers, software and the World Wide Web. The vast array of information and knowledge is overwhelming. Any individual can now harness the power of the internet and become an expert in any topic they chose and many have done just that. Never before in the history of mankind, has the floodgates of revelation and knowledge been so readily available to the average seeker of truth. One such example of this knowledge that was sealed and now has been unsealed has to do with the past and future signs in the heavens. By using an open source software known as *Stellarium*, one can now harness the power of computers to peer into the heavens in order to discover *Signs*. I discuss these *Signs* in the 6th and 7th chapter of this book.

The reference to the *time of the end* is inferred to mean the final 7 weeks (7 years) that begins the final *week*, or the 70th *week*, as indicated in the ninth chapter of the book of Daniel. Briefly stated, Daniel 9:24 indicates that there would be a total of 70 *weeks* decreed for the Jewish people, "*Seventy weeks* are decreed for your people and for your set-apart city (Jerusalem)..." The next two verses indicate a period of time of 7 weeks (49 years) and 62 weeks (434 years) that would need to pass before the final 70th *week* (7 years) could begin. It is this 70th *week* that is accredited to the *tribulation* timeline of the final seven years of man's rule.

As you will discover, this *time of the end* is also attributed to the jubilee for it is the jubilee that is directly linked to *the Sabbath of years* or Shmitahs as they are known as well as the start of *the 50th Year of Jubilee*.

June 7th, 1967 and Jerusalem

As briefly mentioned in the Introduction, the date of June 7th, 1967 is **ABSOLUTELY KEY** in deciphering the *time of the end* and it is this date that is directly connected to the set apart city of Jerusalem. I will be making the case on how the prophetic time clock began to start ticking when Jerusalem was taken back under the governmental control of the Jewish people on that divine day.

It would have been the seventh day following the 6 Day War that would have fallen on June 7th, 1967 and it was on this day that the dominion of this city, for the first time in over 2,000 years, switched back into the hands of the Jewish people, out of the hands and dominion of the Gentiles.

We know that the decree to rebuild Jerusalem was the prophetic key time to the beginning of the weeks countdown over 2,400 years ago and so it was the case back on June 7, 1967. This date, as you will discover, was divinely orchestrated and is intimately tied into the Shmitah and the final *50th Year of Jubilee.*

An Introduction to the Shmitah

The Shmitah is a Hebrew word that means *to release* or *to let go.* The Shmitah, otherwise known in the Scriptures as *Sabbath of years,* is one completely unique year, out of seven years. These Shmitahs have been observed and now identified thanks to the U.S. Stock Market and the reunification of Jerusalem. The Shmitahs and jubilees go hand in hand and are intimately linked to each other. Here is the scriptural support for these Shmitahs:

> "And you shall count *seven Sabbaths of years* for yourself, seven times seven years. And the time of the seven Sabbaths of years shall be to you forty-nine years. 'You shall then sound a ram's horn to pass through on the tenth day of the seventh month, on the Day of Atonement cause a ram's horn to pass through all your land.' And you shall set the fiftieth year apart, and proclaim release throughout all the land to all its inhabitants, it is a Jubilee for you." (Lev 25: 8-9)

The following is a visual representation of the Shmitah.

7 Year Shmitah Cycle

1	2	3	4	5	6	Shmitah 7

<small>September 2021 com book
Created by Phil Richardson</small>

So, we see that the Shmitah (*the seventh Sabbath of years*) is identified as one special seventh year. This cycle repeats until a full 49 years have been completed. Thus, the full 49 years are made up of seven times seven Sabbaths of years (7x7). The jubilee is a set apart year that follows this fully completed 49 years, meaning that the 50th Year of Jubilee begins the day after the completion of a full 49 years on the day deemed to be the holiest day of the year — Yom Kippur. It is Yom Kippur that falls on the 10th day of the seventh month and it is on this day that the ram's horn or shofar is blown that announces the 50th Year of Jubilee that would ends exactly 359 days later on the eve of Yom Kippur the following year.

The Jubilee, without exception, always falls on the Day of Atonement (Yom Kippur) with the blowing of the ram's horn, on the 10th day of the 7th month. This Jubilee year is attributed to blessings by the Almighty such as slaves being set free, property (houses and land) being returned to their original owners, family members reuniting, justice, liberty, the yield of their crops being supernaturally supplied to last up to 2 year and more. The Jubilee was a time of rejoicing and celebration and most importantly rest. It was commanded that the children of Israel (all 12 tribes) were to honor not only the weekly Sabbath, and not only the Shmitah year Sabbath, but also the Jubilee Sabbath that would occur right after the 49th year Shmitah.

This is what we saw in June of 1967, a return of not only Jerusalem, but also, the Gaza Strip, the Sinai Peninsula, the West Bank and the Golan Heights. And out of this return to the original land owners, united families and a return of the captives from out of the four corners of the world back to Israel. In addition, a time of rest, rejoicing and celebration.

The following graph shows seven sets of Shmitahs or sevens. You will notice that the smaller square boxes represent the Shmitah years and the 49th Shmitah ends where it appears that the 50th Year of Jubilee begins. In reality, the Shmitah ends on Elul 29 or the eve of Yom Teruah. It is Yom Teruah that begins the Civil year while Elul 29 would end the Civil Year. Counting down 10 would bring us to Yom Kippur when the Jubilee is announced. Thus, there is a 10-day window between the Shmitah ending and the Jubilee beginning. Within Judiasm, this time period is known as the *Ten days of Awe.* More on this later! Notice that the *50th Years of Jubilee* graph shows the Shmitah years landing on years 7, 14, 21, 28, 35, 42 and 49.

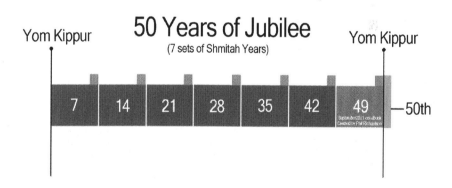

Here is the verse right after the description of the 49th Shmitah,

"And ye shall hallow the fiftieth year, and proclaim liberty throughout all the land unto all the inhabitants thereof: it shall be a jubilee unto you; and ye shall return every man unto his possession, and ye shall return every man unto his family." (Leviticus 25:10, NKJV)

In addition, the blowing of the ram's horn or shofar is different from the blowing of the shofar on Yom Teruah. This can be confusing when reading this in the Scriptures. On Yom Kippur, the blowing of the shofar is known as *the Great Trump* and is only blown once as apposed to being blown multiple times on Yom Teruah where the blowing of the last shofar is known as *the Last Trump*.

The Shmitah and the Jewish Civil Calendar

As briefly mentioned, the Shmitah officially begins on Tishri 1 (around September) of the Jewish calendar, that being the beginning of the first day of the civil calendar. It is the same day known as Rosh Hashanah, the head of the year or New Years to the Jewish People. With the Shmitah beginning on Tishri 1, it will end 359 days later on the last day of the civil calendar on Elul 29, that being the eve of Yom Teruah. If I were to make a comparison with regard to the Gregorian civil calendar, then the beginning of the civil calendar would begin January 1st and would end December 31st. Just remember that on the Jewish calendar, their civil year begins in the seventh month of Tishri whereas their spiritual year begins in the first month of Nisan, right around April. See the following image for a visual perspective on this.

The Spiritual and Civil Years
The First 7 Lunar Months of a 12 Month Cycle

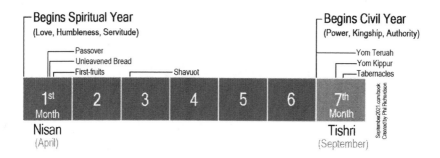

Notice that the Spiritual Year that begins on Nisan 1, incorporates the Spring Feats of Passover, Unleavened Bread, First fruits and Shavuot (otherwise known as the Feast of Weeks) and follows the Shmitah pattern of 6 and then the 7th. In this case, it would be 6 months and then the 7th month would be the beginning of the civil year, that being the Fall Feast Days of Yom Teruah, Yom Kippur and Tabernacles. If you have been paying attention, then you will have noticed this pattern of the Shmitahs in the 7 day week, 7 months, 7 lunar cycles, 7 years, 50th Year of Jubilees, the 7 millenniums and more.

The following graph, *the Fall Feast Days & the Civil Year,* is a visual representation of the Fall Feast Days:

The Fall Feast Days & the Civil Year!

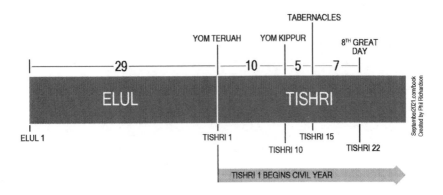

Within Judaism, the Fall Feast Days actually begin 29 days prior on Elul 1, which is the beginning of the 6th month on the Jewish Calendar. From Elul 1, the countdown will begin until Yom Teruah with the sighting of the crescent new moon that would announce the beginning of the Fall Feast celebrations. Notice, the ten-day period between the two Feasts of Yom Teruah and Yom Kippur that represent the *Ten days of Awe*. It is this 39 day window of time that is represented by the Hebrew word, teshuvah that means repentance. Yom Teruah would begin day #1 one of the ten day countdown of repentance until Yom Kippur, the Day of Judgment when *the Books are Opened*. Thus, the beginning of the 50th Year of Jubilee would represent judgment on a future Yom Kippur.

Knowledge Would Increase

With regard to knowledge increasing, we know that knowledge is power and the amount of knowledge and revelation has just exploded in these past 10 years alone. As an example, one of the websites that has helped me enormously in my understanding of the times is *TorahCalendar.com*. This site was created back in 2008 and I consider it a very accurate Hebraic lunar/solar calendar system that incorporates the solar/lunar Gregorian dates as well. The lunar/solar calendar known today as the Jewish calendar, is what I consider to be the Creator's calendar less the Talmudic Hellel II interpretations as well as the year 5775 as it currently stands today.

You will be surprised to learn what year it actually is. Torah Calendar uses the calculated astronomical sighting of the moon and is the same system NASA uses and is extremely accurate. With the Torah Calendar website, one can search back and forward thousands of years to see how the feast days line up with the blood moons with incredible accuracy. This is knowledge we never had even just 10 years ago. With programs such as *Stellarium*, we can know search the heavens back and forward thousands of years that have enabled us to identify *Signs* such the star of Bethlehem and even the *Mid-Tribulation Sign* in the future.

Thanks to the discovery by Pastor Mark Biltz back in 2008, we now have knowledge and understanding of the lunar moon Tetrads known as the *Blood Moon Tetrads* today. This revelation has helped me to identify this period of time and this revelation has opened up other doors of understanding with regard to Daniel's 49 years and final 7 years and their unique relationship to the Shmitah and Jubilee as you will discover.

The remainder of verse one of the 12th chapter of Daniel describes a period when, "they have ended scattering the power of the set-apart people, then all these shall be completed." The set apart people are the Jewish people. This passage seems to indicate that when the Jewish people are dwelling in their own land, then all will be complete. I would like to say that they will be dwelling safely, however, Scripture indicates that there will be great trouble yet for the Jewish people. YHVH will use this pain so that they will eventually cry out, *"Hoshia-na to the Son of Dawid! Blessed is He who is coming in the Name of יהוה! Hoshia-na in the highest!"* (John 12:13). It will be Yahshua who will save them at their greatest hour of need and is generally how the Creator works. This is why he is known as *the Eleventh Hour God.*

The Feast Days of Daniel Chapter 12

I bet you never realized that Daniel speaks of the *Jewish* Feast Days in Daniel Chapter 12! Not directly at least! There are three time periods mentioned in Daniel chapter 12. They are 1260, 1290 and 1335 days. It is amazing to me that when you add the sum of 1260 plus 1290 days, one comes to 2,550 days. That is not the amazing part! The amazing part is when calculated from Yom Teruah, it falls on Yom Kippur, seven 360-day cycles plus 30 days later, or 2,520 days plus 30 days. See the simplified graph labeled as *Daniel Chapter 12.*

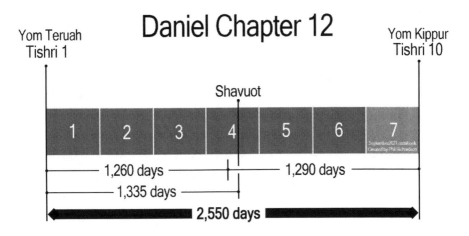

This graph is a simplified version and as such, not all seven-year cycles have the same results of falling on Yom Kippur. In other words, when starting on Yom Teruah of any given year and counting forward 2,550 days, the result would be the final day falling on Yom Kippur or not falling on Yom Kippur. That reason for this has to do with intercalation. Intercalation is the term used to describe balancing the moon cycle with the solar year. For example, a 13th lunar month is added to the Jewish calendar about every 2 to 3 years to balance the seasons of the harvest. Because of the process of intercalation, the moon cycles either balance out to be 86 moons or 87 moons over a 2,520 day period of time. It is this difference that is known as the Metonic Lunar Moon Cycle and plays a major role in determining if the final day of the 2,550 days will fall on Yom Kippur or not. I cover this topic more in depth in chapter eight.

This Generation Shall By No Means Pass Away!

"Truly, I say to you, this generation shall by no means pass away until all this takes place." (Matthew 24:34)

When Yahshua made this statement, He had just given a laundry list of events that would take place on earth prior to His return inclusive of false prophets, false messiahs that would betray many, famines, earthquakes in varies places, rumors of wars, the abomination of desolation, the sun and moon not giving their light after the distress of those days, etc. The majority of the events mentioned in the 24th chapter of Matthew still point to future fulfillment.

Almost 2,000 years have passed since Yahshua spoke those words. Who was *this generation* that He was speaking of? Could He have been referring to that current generation? I believe, like most, that He was speaking of a future generation that would see these things take place. More specifically, since this prophecy was spoken in Jerusalem, I believe that this prophecy speaks of Israel and more specifically Jerusalem. The re-birth of Israel that fell on the eve of Shavuot is what began the latter days. There is a passage in Psalms that speaks to me with regard to a full generation.

"The days of our lives are seventy years; Or if due to strength, eighty years." (Psalm 90:10)

This passage indicates that the days of our lives are from 70 to 80 years. This is very accurate as most people live this long well into their golden years. What is interesting is that those who were born in May 1948 will turn 70 years old in May 2018. What is also interesting is that there will be ten sets of Shmitah years from this same period of time or 70 years (10 x 7). There will be seven Shmitahs from June 7th, 1967 (7 x 7 =49) and ten Shmitahs from May 15, 1948, the re-birth of Israel (10 x 7 =70).

If we incorporate the Feast Day of Shavuot, we notice something very interesting. Again, May 14th, 1948 fell on the eve of Shavuot. Seventy solar years from this date comes to within one week of Shavuot 2018. Do you remember the 1,335 days on the graph? It falls on the eve of Shavuot. If we were to subtract 1,335 days from the eve of Shavout 2018, we would come to the eve of Yom Teruah 2014 (September 24, 2014). This was also a highly important day as I go deeper into this in the eighth chapter of this book.

Observable Patterns and Signs in the Heavens

Some of the connections I have been able to make concerning our generation being the final generation until the return of the Messiah is by observing patterns. These patterns seem to fall on the eve of major feast days. When I use the term eve, I am referring to the moment before, or up to 24 hours before, much like we might understand Christmas eve as being the night before Christmas. I will now briefly mention these patterns and signs and will expand on them in forthcoming chapters.

The patterns that can be observed have to do with the signs in the heaven of mostly solar and lunar eclipses. It is clear that part of the purpose of the

Creator creating the sun and moon was for this purpose as indicated in Genesis 1:14. With regard to lunar eclipses, we are within the tail end of four total lunar eclipses known as the *Tetrad Blood Moons*. I have double-checked and have confirmed these tetrads on the NASA lunar eclipse webpage. Their webpage will show them under their eclipse type heading as *total* and there will be a series of 4 total eclipses without interruption. The unique thing about these tetrads has to do with them lining up with the Spring and Fall Feast Days of Passover and Tabernacles. I discuss these lunar and solar patterns in chapter six.

These *Blood Moons* leads me to discuss the *Revelation Chapter 12 Sign* of the woman clothed with the sun, with the moon at her feet with a garland of 12 stars above her head, giving birth. The scriptural reference for this is Revelation 12:1-2. This is indeed a *Great Sign* seen in the heavens as witnessed by John who wrote the Book of Revelation. I have been able to observe this sign by using the open source software, *Stellarium* and have been able to document this sign only twice, once 3,865 years ago in 1850 BCE and the other time in the very, very near future.

Would it surprise you to hear that this sign of the woman being clothed with the sun and with the moon at her feet, happens at the end of the 6th moon and beginning of the 7th new moon every year on the lunar calendar system? Are you starting to pick up on the Shmitah patterns, this time with the 7th new moon? This event undoubtedly speaks of the Constellation Virgo (The Virgin as in Mary) and always falls on Yom Teruah. It is always on Yom Teruah when she is clothed with the sun while the moon is at her feet. I have documented this and have made a YouTube video of these astronomical events, but as you will discover, there is only one other future event where she has a garland of 12 stars above her head while giving birth and it is this *Great Sign* that John spoke about and what I have coined as the *Mid-Tribulation Sign*. I go into this in detail in chapter seven of this book.

Determining the Jubilee

As discussed, the Shmitah is one unique year out of seven lunar years that can be observed. It becomes obvious when we account for the *Shmitah Release Day,* that is one set apart day out of 2,520 day that falls on the last day of the civil calendar that being the last day of the Shmitah cycle. This *Shmitah Release Day* always falls on the final day of the seventh year, that being Elul 29. These dates have been observed in the past and they are divinely orchestrated as documented by Messianic Rabbi Jonathan Cahn in his teachings on the *Harbinger* and *The Mystery of the Shemitaha* books. I go into detail regarding these fascinating events in chapter four.

The question remains,"How do we determine the beginning of the Jubilee year?" Are there patterns that we can observe within the past 100 years that point to divine order? Furthermore, are the jubilees still relevant today and what might be the requirements in order to observe these jubilees? There are many opinions associated with this topic. There are many who suggest that the jubilee can't be observed because it can only be observed when all 12 tribes are represented in Israel [2] and some even suggest that the jubilee cycles had to have stopped when Israel ceased being a nation after 70 CE. Still many claim that the Shmitah can't clearly be identified. With that said, there are those who suggest that we are within a Shmitah cycle right now, as is my strong-held position.

I would like to state that these jubilees and Shmitahs can be observed by looking at the patterns. The Creator has revealed these patterns to us and it is just a matter of tuning into his frequency and understanding what He is trying to say.

With regard to the jubilee, we can look back throughout history at some very interesting events that have happened in the past and that have significantly impacted the Jewish people and the land of Israel. One of these significant events was the Balfour Declaration that established a Jewish

State in a letter dated November 2, 1917. This was a simple letter from then Secretary of State of the British Empire, Arthur James Balfour to Lord Rothschild for the "establishment in Palestine of a national home for the Jewish people." [3] This was a result of Zionism or the political aspirations of the Jewish people to establish their own land of Palestine, known today as the land of Israel. Remarkably, just one month after this mandate, a British General by the name of Allenby walked into Jerusalem by foot with the British Military and took the 400-year reign away from the Ottoman Empire. [4] This event happened on Hanukkah December 17, 1917 and brought the land of Israel one step closer to the vision of the Zionist.

So, we see there is something very significant with the year 1917 as being a jubilee year. Not only does it reflect the British Mandate of 1917, but also Jerusalem being taken from the Ottoman Empire by General Allenby. The other event that was very significant to the Jewish people happened on the eve of Shavuot, May 14th, 1948 with their nation being born in one day, a fulfillment of Bible prophecy. If the Balfour Declaration were the seeds, then May 14th, 1948 was the harvest day! How appropriate considering that it is on Shavuot (Feast of Weeks) that we are to bring our harvest to the Creator.

> "Count seven weeks for yourself. Begin to count seven weeks from the time you begin to put the sickle to the grain. "And you shall perform the *Festival of Weeks* to יהוה your Elohim, according to the voluntary offering from your hand, which you give as יהוה your Elohim blesses you." (Deuteronomy 16:9-10)

Fifty years later from 1917 brings us to the year 1967 and it was on June 7th, 1967, known today as *Yom Yerushalayim*, that the Jewish people regained the dominion of Jerusalem back in their control for the first time in over 2,000 years. Are you beginning to pick up on the patterns? Are you beginning to see the divine order in these events? Will more land be delivered to Israel in this up and coming *50th Year of Jubilee* as they did in the past two? I discuss more on the jubilee in the next chapter.

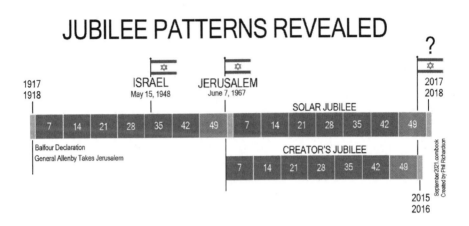

Notice the image above titled, *Jubilee Patterns Revealed*. The past two jubilees are clearly identified beginning in the year 1917 & 1967. The 50th Year of Jubilee is identified at the end of the 49th year and is a 359-day period of time beginning on Yom Kippur (YK) and ending on the eve of Yom Kippur the following year. The 50th Year of Jubilees has been identified from YK 1917 to YK 1918, YK 1967 to YK 1968 and YK 2017 to YK 2018.

You will notice that these jubilees are solar-based jubilees of 365.24 days per year. In addition, notice the second jubilee that I have coined as the *Creator's Jubilee*. I will discuss this special jubilee in chapter five.

A Jubilee Year Cycle: 49 or 50 Years?

While we are on the subject of the jubilee, I must account for those who believe that a full jubilee cycle is 49 completed civil years versus what has been presented to you thus far as a full jubilee cycle being 50 completed civil years. My position is to simply discuss the two prevailing view points and to not to justify the validity of one over the other because Scripture is simply not clear on this. The prevailing Scripture for the jubilee states,

> "And you shall count seven Sabbaths of years for yourself, seven times seven years. And the time of the seven Sabbaths of years shall be to you forty-nine years. 'You shall then sound a ram's horn to pass through on the tenth day of the seventh month, on the Day of Atonement cause a ram's horn to pass through all your land. 'And you shall set the fiftieth year apart,' " (Leviticus 25:8-10)

I follow the view point of Torah Calendar that believe, "the Jubilee Cycle consists of 50 Civil Years - seven Shemittah Cycles and a Jubilee Year." [5] This cycle makes a lot of sense from the stand point of the three Ages that point to 40 Jubilees each (2,000 years) making up 120 jubilees that would account to 6,000 years that scripturally seem to line up perfectly especially when Genesis 6:3 is taken into account and for various other reasons that I will discuss throughout this book.

After viewing a presentation given by Messianic Rabbi Jonathan Cahn, I realized that for those who hold to a 49 Year Jubilee, they believe that the 50th Year of Jubilee will begin on Yom Kippur 2015 and will end one year later in 2016. Those who hold to a 50 Year Jubilee believe that it will begin on Yom Kippur 2017 and will end in 2018. Amazingly, because of the *Creator's Jubilee, THEY ARE BOTH CORRECT!* The Creator has made it possible that both viewpoints are valid through the *Creator's Jubilee* and *Solar Jubilee.* Amazing! See the *Jubilee Patterns Revealed* graph for a confirmation of this.

I Shall Make You a Burdensome Stone

81

The Bible declares that whoever blesses Israel will be blessed and whoever curses Israel will be cursed. Since the United States came into existence, this nation has become a safe harbor for those who have been persecuted and exiled. We have welcomed all people into this land where each individual has had the same rights and liberties for hundreds of years with the exception of the slave trade early on. This nation has also harbored Jews from around the world who have suffered and who came to America for those same protections and opportunities. To date, there are well over 12 million Jews who call the United States home. The United States was also the first country, aside from Britain, to openly call for the existence of a home for the Jews in the land of Palestine and we have been Israel's closest allies since its inception.

It is evident that the United States has blessed Israel and we have been blessed because of it. But, what happens when we openly start to curse Israel as we are seeing now through the current Administration? What happens when we openly embrace Iran over Israel? Is there such a verse in the Bible that highlights this?

The Bible is clear that Jerusalem would be rejected by all nations in the latter days. We even see the United States, the closest ally to Israel, distancing itself from her. If the United States rejects Israel, then who is left to defend her? The answer can be clearly seen in the following verse.

"Behold, *I will make Jerusalem a cup of drunkenness to all the surrounding peoples,* when they lay siege against Judah and Jerusalem. And it shall happen in that day that I will make Jerusalem a very heavy stone for all peoples; all who would heave it away will surely be cut in pieces, *though all nations of the earth are gathered against it...It shall be in that day that I will seek to destroy all the nations that come against Jerusalem."* (Zechariah 12: 2-3, 9,)

This Scripture is clear that all nations, including the United States, will eventually be gathered against Jerusalem and the Jewish people. Taking such a stance against Israel is not wise and those nations who do so will face judgment from the God of Abraham, Isaac and Jacob. This Judgment Day will more than likely fall on some future year on Yom Kippur. When the nations no longer support Israel, then the nations will experience the strong arm of the Almighty as he defends Israel to the detriment to those who come against her.

We can expect to see Jerusalem making the top news stories in the years ahead as Jerusalem will become a stumbling block or heavy stone for all peoples and the nations. This will more than likely involve the Palestinian people and their desire for a State of their own. I would also imagine that the nations of the world, through the General Assembly of the United Nations will rule against Israel and for a State of Palestine. We see such legislation being introduced by France that will be introduced at this up and coming 70th General Assembly meeting of the United Nations starting on September 15 (Yom Teruah) this year.

Also, could another issue be the Non-Nuclear Proliferation agreement that states that no middle eastern countries posses' nuclear weapons? Because of recent revelations, the world is now aware that Israel possess' these weapons. This was a strong assumption for many years, but now that facts are out. We are starting to see this as just recently Iran's Foreign Minister Mohammad Javad Zarif has called for Israel to abandon her nuclear weapons. According to an article by Yahoo News, "Israel is widely believed to be the only owner of nuclear weapons in the Middle East, with about 80 warheads, according to the Federation of American Scientists. Israeli officials, however, have never publicly confirmed the existence of their nuclear arsenal." [6]

Will the U.N. force Israel to give up her weapons of mass destruction? I seriously doubt it! Doing so would spell certain death from the enemies that surround her and her enemies abroad. As the nations continue to abandon Israel, there is a warning in these last days to those Gentile Nations who come against Jerusalem...

"In that day יהוה shall shield the inhabitants of Yerushalayim. And the feeble among them in that day shall be like Dawid, and the house of Dawid like Elohim, like the Messenger of יהוה before them! *"And it shall be in that day that I seek to destroy all the gentiles that come against Yerushalayim."* (Zechariah 12:8)

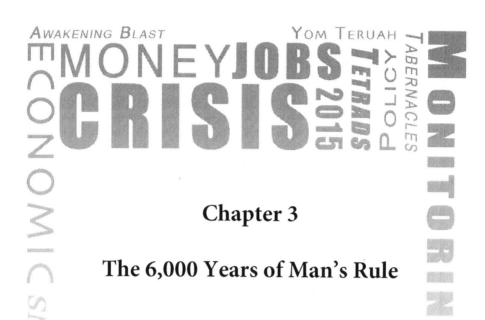

Chapter 3

The 6,000 Years of Man's Rule

In the last chapter, I briefly touched on the patterns, connections and unique relationship between the Shmitas, Jubilees and the Lunar Moon Tetrads. My goal in this chapter is to identify what year we are actually in from a Biblical perspective.

Identifying the Most Accurate Lunar Calendar System

Before I get into those topics of discussion, I need to explain in detail the Creator's calendar system. Other names attributed to this calendar system would be the Hebraic calendar, the lunar calendar and lastly, the Jewish calendar. Since both calendars are lunar and Hebraic, and for the purpose of simplicity, I will be comparing just two of them, that being the Creator's calendar and the Jewish calendar. These calendars are different from the Gregorian calendar in that they are lunar/solar-based, and are based upon twelve new moon cycles around the earth, whereas the Gregorian calendar is a solar/lunar and is based upon the earth making a complete cycle around the sun in 354.24 days. The primary difference is that YHVH's calendar is lunar-based while the Gregorian calendar is based on the sun. If we are trying to line up Bible prophecy with the Gregorian calendar, then we will miss the prophetic boat completely!

The ancient Egyptian, Assyrian, Babylonian, Indian, Mayan and Hebraic Civilizations all used a 360-day per year lunar moon calendar system. The Egyptians eventually switched to a solar calendar,[1] but for hundreds if not thousands of years, these cultures observed the lunar-based 360-day per year calendar system. There are some clues in Scripture that indicate this system. The earliest account of this is found in Genesis 7:11, 24 and Genesis 8:3-4, whereby, it was recorded that 150 days had elapsed over 5 lunar cycles from the 17th day of the 2nd moon to the 17th day of the 7th moon, or 30 days per month. Additionally, 1 Kings 4:7 mentions twelve months in one year, thus twelve times thirty giving us 360-days per year. It is this 360-days per year system that seems to coincide with Bible prophecy as well.

Regarding the names of the lunar months, there are only 4 lunar months attributed to Hebrew names within the Old Testament, those being Aviv (the first month), Ziv (second month), Ethanim (seventh month) and finally Bul (eighth month).[2] After the Babylon exile, the Bible gives a complete list of the Babylonian names for the Jewish months. However, the Bible refers to the lunar month cycles by their order such as the first month and seventh month. The Jewish calendar system uses these Babylonian names such as the first month of Nisan and the seventh month of Tishri. For simplicity's sake, I use these Babylonian names as they are common in the Jewish culture and Scripture backs these names.

The Jewish Calendar System

The Jewish calendar follows the Hillel II calculated system [3] that was established between 320 to 385 CE. It was Hillel II who held the office of Nasi of the Rabbinical Sanhedrin during that time. This calendar follows a nineteen-year cycle in order for the lunar calendar to realign with the solar cycle. An extra month, known as an Adar II, is added to each of the 3rd, 6th, 8th, 11th, 14th, 17th, and the 19th leap months. This extra Adar means that the typical 12th month becomes a 13th month in a one-year cycle roughly every two to three years. Before this calculated system was implemented, there had to be two witnesses that would confirm the sighting of the crescent moon on any given new moon. The most important sighting took place on the first month of Nisan just prior to the Spring Feasts of Passover. This determined the start of the year and not the seventh lunar month of Tishri. The second most important sighting was the crescent moon sighting on the 7th month of Tishri that would begin the Fall Feast Day Celebrations.

The Creator's Calendar System

The Creator's calendar system does not follow the Rabbinical Hillel II system. This astronomical calculated calendar determines the first month by the potential visible sighting of the crescent of the moon from Jerusalem based upon exact calculations of the moon in relation to the sun. The Creator's calendar does not account for clouds, rain or smog that would impair the physical sighting of the crescent, thus throwing off the start of the first month. The first of the year is determined by the spring equinox that places month 1 of day 15 (Unleavened Bread) either on or after the spring equinox. This way, the moon and sun determine the month and the year as stated in Genesis 1:14 and not necessarily the sighting of the crescent new moon that might be obscured by bad weather in Jerusalem at that time. This system eliminates man's error that might be caused by bad weather.

The Abib Barley Calendar System

There is one other calendar system rising in popularity that is being used by a particular sect of Jews known as the Karaites. The Karaites do not follow the Hillel II system but rather traditionally still follow the visible sighting of the crescent new moon according to what is laid out in the Torah. To these Jews, the sighting of the crescent new moon known as *Hodesh Ha-Aviv* or the *New Moon of the Aviv* is especially important as this first month is based upon the sighting of the Abib Barley or ripened barley. The Karaite Jews go one step further and may observe a leap month based upon the confirmation of the barley being ripened or Abib (Aviv). In other words, instead of placing the Feast of Unleavened Bread on or after the spring equinox, they may move the start of the first month in advance by one month because the barley is not Abib. There is a growing movement within the Hebrew Roots Christianity crowd that follows this same system for declaring the first month.

The Karaite Jews find their support in basically 5 Scriptures; Exodus 13:4, 23:15, 34:18 and Deuteronomy 16:1 are the only verses in the entire Bible that mention the word Abib or Aviv. By using *BlueletterBible.com* as a reference, the word abib (Strong's H24) means (I) fresh, young barley ears, barley and (II) Month of ear forming, of green crop, of growing green Abib, month of exodus and Passover. The definition of Abib in relation to these four verses is being used to describe the name of the month. The other Scripture that gives this idea credence is found in Leviticus 23:15, "And you shall count for yourselves from the day after the Sabbath, from the day that you brought the sheaf of the wave offering: seven Sabbaths shall be completed." The reasoning behind this is that in order to officially begin the counting of the fifty days that leads to Shavuot, the First fruits offering must be made available.

I do not necessarily prescribe to this way of thinking regarding the barley needing to be ripened within the land of Israel. In doing so, this system becomes purely speculative dictated by the weather, the barley being ripened, and the opinion of two or three witnesses. In my opinion, this system is flawed because it places Genesis 1:14 in the back seat as the sun and the moon were created for *signs* (*owth*) and *Appointed Feast* (*Mow'ed*). If we are off one month in our calendar system because of the barley not being ripened, then we are going to miss His *Divine Appointments*. Additionally, there is no way to properly determine if feast days line up with biblical events such as Yahshua's birth and death nor of future events.

According to the Karaite Jews, the sighting of the barley for 2015 was Abib. Thus, Passover was observed on the first month of Nisan 14 by all, inclusive of Hebrew Roots Christians, Jews and by Karaite Jews. This is particularly important for unification purposes as you will discover. I do agree with the viewpoint of Torah Calendar regarding the Abib Barley dictating the start of the first month...

They state, "If people want to believe that the barley determines the Hebrew Year, then the Creation Calendar will be of no benefit for them. For they are logically inferring that it is impossible to precisely know exactly when certain events occurred in history, as there are no records of how the barley has developed for every year in history. For those who persist in this belief that barley is required to determine the Hebrew Year, it would appear sheer folly trying to understand the dates in the historical past that are mentioned in the Scriptures. From this perspective it would be impossible to determine the Hebrew Year, Month and Day of the Messiah's birth, death and resurrection as an example, as there are no known existing records of how the barley had developed in those years.

In conclusion, a seeker of truth will spiritually deduce that an equitable method for determining the Hebrew Year for all time using both the sun and the moon must not only exist, but that such a method must be precise and uniform for every year of the 7000 Year Plan of Elohim if the elect – the chosen people – are to know where they are in time. Elohim teaches us that a Hebrew Year is not determined by a subjective "call" made by men, a call which is based solely on observance of the developmental stage of a plant seen at the end of Month 12 – a practice of which is nowhere to be found in Scripture. The Creator's calendar is mathematically determined by both the sun and the moon, and will always under normal conditions provide for the existence of Aviv or Carmel grain in Israel on or before Day 16 of Month 1. The Creation Calendar meets every historical, astronomical and prophetic requirement of Scripture, and for this reason, it may be considered the calendar of Elohim." [4]

The Contrast Between the Spiritual and Civil Years

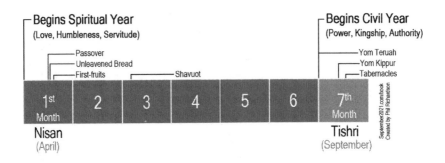

There is one other aspect of the Creator's Calendar that I would like to point out and that has to do with the Spiritual Year and the Civil Year. As mentioned, the spiritual year begins on Nisan 1 in the springtime and the civil year begins on Tishri 1 in the fall. There seems to be a dividing line between the two in that the spiritual year represents humbleness, meekness, sacrifice, servitude and love. We see a reflection of this when Israel left Egypt. They were humbled by the events that transpired with the fi-

90

nale of the first Passover sacrifice of the lamb's blood on their doorpost. It was because of this act of obedience and the actual blood that the angle of death passed over the Israelites but not the Egyptians.

This is also a reflection of Yahshua, the Sacrificial Lamb of Elohim. The Scripture is clear that He was born in a manger under the most humble of circumstances, acquiring no earthly possessions or power, while separating His power for love and dying under the most humiliating of circumstances. Here are a few verses from the prophets of old that speak of this humble Messiah, fulfilled through Yahshua...

"Rejoice greatly, O daughter of Tsiyon! Shout, O daughter of Yerushalayim! See, your Sovereign is coming to you, He is righteous and endowed with deliverance, humble and riding on a donkey, a colt, the foal of a donkey." (Zech 9:9)

"He was oppressed and He was afflicted, but He did not open His mouth. He was led as a lamb to the slaughter, and as a sheep before its shearers is silent, but He did not open His mouth." (Isaiah 53:7)

In direct contrast, the civil year of the Creator's calendar speaks of government, great power, authority, kingship and control by conquest. The civil calendar begins with the feast of Yom Teruah that is represented by the Coronation of the Messiah and judgment followed by Yom Kippur represented by either forgiveness or judgment and followed by the seven-day celebration of Tabernacles.

We know that His second coming will not be in humility such as riding on the colt of a donkey, but rather as a Conquering King with a sword of conquest as described in Revelation chapter nineteen.

Part of the reasons that Jews to this day reject their Jewish Messiah is because the Scriptures speak of a conquering Messiah along with a humble Messiah who would need to suffer rejection and agony. Rabbis debate among themselves as to whether or not the Scriptures speak of one Messiah who will fulfill all Scripture or of two separate Messiahs; one who will come humbly and rejected, and the other who will reign with great power. I have some news for them! Both prophecies speak of just one Messiah!

The 7,000 Year Plan of the Creator

The Jewish calendar reflects the year 5775. By Tishri 1, on Rosh Hashanah of this year, it will change to 5776. This means that the Jewish calendar documents 5775 years since the creation of Adam and Eve. This date of 5775, however, seems to conflict with the biblical records that are so well documented. The biblical accounts place the creation of Adam and Eve closer to the 6,000 year mark. This implies that the Jewish year may be off by as much as 225 years. Let's see if we can make sense of this.

There are some great sites that have painstakingly calculated the amount of years from Adam to Yahshua. There are certain websites [5] that document this and they have determined approximately 4,000 years using a number of Scriptures inclusive of Genesis, Exodus, Judges, I Kings, II Chronicles and the unbroken genealogical account recorded in the first chapter of Matthew. Thus we find that the Bible is a good source for determining the amount of years since creation. As an example, within the entire fifth chapter of Genesis, the period of time from Adam to Noah of being approximately 1,056 years is laid out.

Before I go much deeper into the actual biblical year, I would like to highlight the 7,000 year plan of the Creator in order to make some astounding connections to our time. II Peter 3:8 states, "... Let not this one matter be hidden from you: that with יהוה one day is as a thousand years, and a thousand years as one day."

My understanding is that the 1,000 years or the millenniums follow this Scripture as well as what has been documented in this book. In other words, the millennium cycles follows the creation plan set forth in the first chapter of Genesis. Whereby, in 6 days Elohim (God) created all that was to be created and in the 7th day He rested. We see this principle throughout Scripture from the Sabbath day of rest, to the Shmitah Principles to the number seven and the sequences of sevens such as 49 days and/or years as being divinely inspired and for that matter orchestrated by divine means. The 7,000 years can be easily understood by looking at it in a frame of reference to a one-week period of time of seven days. The beginning of the first day would be Sunday and would follow suit to Monday to Tuesday and so on until Saturday with Saturday being the Sabbath of Rest.

Seven Days as to Seven Millenniums

with יהוה one day is as a thousand years, and a thousand years as one day.

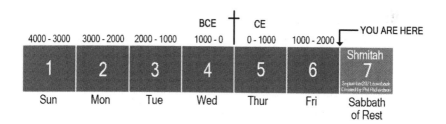

Likewise, the years follow the same pattern. We have 6 years and then the seventh year is the Shmitah year or Sabbath of years. And much like the days and years, we have the millenniums. The millenniums would follow

93

the same pattern. 4,000 years before the common era (BCE) and 2,000 years of the common era (CE) that would account for 6 millennia.

Hebraic & Gregorian Days

If I were to make an accurate description of this within a Hebraic mindset and in terms of the creation week recorded in the first chapter of Genesis, then the start of Friday night would begin sunset and would continue until sunrise Friday morning. This 12-hour period of time would be considered the night and the 12-hour day, in a Hebraic mindset, would begin sunrise to sunset making up 24 hours in totality. In other words, the night would precede the day and it would be 12 hours of night and then 12 hours of day that would make up the 24-hour day. See the figure below for a visual representation.

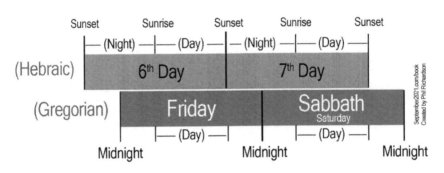

This is entirely different from our western mindset whereas we understand Friday to begin right at midnight and would continue until 11:59 pm the next day that would make up the 24-hour day. The 12 hour night and 12 hour day is more foreign to our way of thinking whereas the day proceeds the night. This is the opposite of the Hebraic mindset and is the reason that the weekly Sabbath begins on Friday night just after sunset and ends Saturday night just before sunset.

To view it another way, Shabbat would start around 6pm Friday night and would last until 6pm Saturday night and would account for 24 hours. If I were to state this in terms of where we are on the prophetic weekly timeline, then I would say we are in the 6th day of Friday night just a few seconds away from sunset, just about ready to enter the Sabbath of Rest or the start of Saturday, just moments before the beginning of the 7th Day Sabbath of Rest or the 7th Millennium of rest.

Additionally, Leviticus 23:3 is clear that we may *"work for 6 days, but on the seventh day, their must be a Sabbath of complete rest."* The seventh day was to be set apart and holy and observed by those who would obey him. This was in reference to 7 literal days, but this same Shabbat principle also applies to the year as well. Just a few more chapters in Leviticus 25:3-4 states,

> "Six years you sow your field, and six years you prune your vineyard, and gather in its fruit, but in the seventh year the land is to have a Sabbath of rest, a Sabbath to יהוה. Do not sow your field and do not prune your vineyard."

We see this same principle with the years as it applies to the days of the week. You may work 6 days then the Sabbath; you may work 6 years then the Sabbath. Throughout Scripture the seventh (7th) is set apart by the Creator. I hope you are grasping these principles as it is important in order to understand this book.

Using this reasoning, many Rabbis and Pastors believe that the 1,000 year reign of Messiah will occur in the 7th Millennium or from the beginning of the year 6,001 to the ending of the 7,000th year from creation known throughout Scripture as the *Millennial Reign*. If we apply one day is as a 1,000 years, then we can see that as there were 6 days of creation, there should also be 6,000 years for the rule of man. The implication is that at the end of the 6th day would begin the 7th day of the Sabbath rest. Likewise, at the end of the 6th Millennium or year 6,001 would usher in the 7th Millennium or the Millennial Sabbath of rest. I realize I am being redundant here, but this principle is important to grasp. I go deeper on this topic in the final chapter of this book.

The 6,000 year Countdown to the Shmitah of Liberty

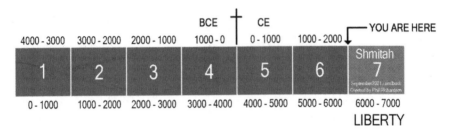

So, in taking another look at II Peter 3:8, we see that this mystery was not meant to be hidden as it was referencing the 7,000 year plan of the Almighty. Another clue is found in Exodus 21:2, "When you buy a Hebrew servant, he serves six years, and in the seventh he goes out free, for naught." It is at the beginning of this 7th year on Yom Teruah that all servants and slaves were to be set free. This is the principle behind the Shmitah year. It was required on the Shmitah year to *Let Go* and *to Release* the debt and bondage in order to set us free. The Shmitah year was to be a year of Liberty! Likewise, the beginning of the 50th Year of the Jubilee was to announce Liberty throughout the land where not only slaves and servants were to be set free, but land and possessions were to be returned to their original owners! This is the same concept of the Shmitah! In the case of the Jubilee, this would be announced on Yom Kippur whereas the Shmitah would be announced on Yom Teruah. In both cases, there would be a blowing of the shofar in order to set the captives free. These events speak of the Groom coming for his Bride, in order to set her free from the coming destruction.

An Intro to "Torah Calendar"

There is a website that I have mentioned a few times thus far that has been instrumental in my understanding of the times in which we live and that is *TorahCalendar.com*. I will refer to them from now on as *Torah Calendar*. This group has done a majestic job in laying out the 7,000 year plan of Elohim (God) and is where I have received my understanding on this topic.

This is no ordinary calendar system but rather an elaborate database that ties the Hebraic lunar months, years since creation, jubilee cycles, Sabbath of year or Shmitah cycle, lunar and solar eclipses, Gregorian and Julian dates and so much more. Take notice of the image below.

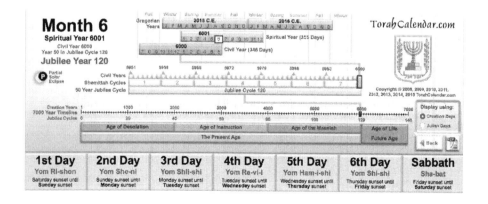

This snap shot from their site lays out a 7,000 year plan as previously mentioned breaking each millennium down into 20 jubilees and two millennium per age represented by the Age of Desolation, the Age of Instruction and finally the Age of Messiah, that we are currently in. These three ages would make 6,000 years or six millennium. As stated, the beginning of the seventh millennium would begin at year 6,001. This final millennium, the seventh, is known as the Age of Life and is believed by myself and many others to be the Age when the Messiah will reign from Jerusalem with great esteem and power.

According to *Torah Calendar*, we are in the year 6,000 right now as shown by the red mark (please note: high quality colored images can be viewed from September2021.com). You will notice that this snap shot highlights the 6th month known as the month of Elul (August 2015) and says spiritual year 6,001 and civil year 6,000. This is just one month prior to September 2015 and I chose this month to make a point.

I believe Torah Calendar is off exactly one year (360-days), whereas the spiritual year should read 6,000 and the civil year should read 5,999. The reason for this is that their Shmitah cycle is off by one year, shown by the small red square that is highlighting the jubilee year or 50th year of the Shmitah cycles. You will notice they have 7 sets of 7 years (49) years displayed with the 50th Year of Jubilee on display highlighted in red. The reason I believe they are off has to do with not being lined up with the *Creator's Jubilee* that began on June 7, 1967 and that will begin the 50th Year of Jubilee this September 2015 and thus civil year 6,000. I believe the reason for this is that they didn't have knowledge of this information back in 2008 as this knowledge had not yet been revealed. Other than that their calendar system is excellent! Again, I cover this topic in greater detail in the final chapter of this book.

6,000 years and 120 Jubilees

There is a direct relationship between 6,000 years and 120 jubilee cycles. A one thousand year period of time contains twenty jubilees. A jubilee cycle contains 50 years, so 50 years times 20 jubilees equals 1,000 years or one millennia. Thus, two millennia would account for 40 jubilees and so on.

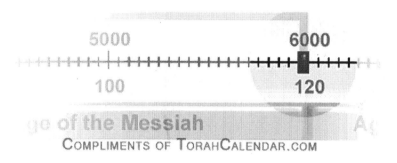

Torah Calendar has done a great job in breaking this down and reflects these three periods of times known as ages. The first age would be the Age of Desolation and covers a two thousand year period of time (40 Jubilees) roughly from 4,000 BCE to 2,000 BCE or from the period of time from Adam to Abraham. This period of time is also documented in the first chapter of Matthew in regard to the time period from Adam to Abraham being 13 generations. It was during this age that the earth experienced the worldwide flood, the confusion of the language in Babylon and the scattering of peoples and tongues to different regions of the world. See the image below that shows these three ages.

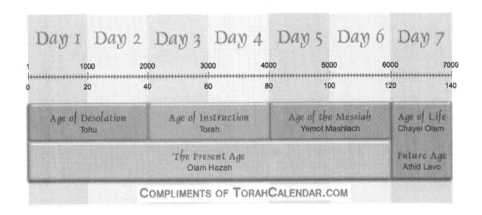

Day 1 Day 2 Day 3 Day 4 Day 5 Day 6 Day 7

| Age of Desolation | Age of Instruction | Age of the Messiah | Age of Life |
| Tohu | Torah | Yemot Mashiach | Chayei Olam |

| The Present Age | Future Age |
| Olam Hazeh | Athid Lavo |

COMPLIMENTS OF TORAHCALENDAR.COM

The second age would have been the Age of Instruction. This two thousand year period of time (40 Jubilees) would have covered roughly the dates from 2,000 BCE to 1 BCE or from the time of Abraham to Yahshua with Yahshua being born September 3 to 2 BCE. Matthew also documents that from the period of time from Abraham to Yahshua was 13 generations. It was during this period of time that the twelve sons of Jacob multiplied into a great number of people within Egypt where future generations became slaves under the Pharaoh's reign. They eventually escaped under the mighty hand of YHVH to Mount Sinai where they would have received the Torah of Instruction.

Lastly, the Age of Messiah is another two thousand year period of time (40 Jubilees) roughly from 1 BCE to 2,000 CE. It was during this Age when the Messiah was born into this world, died and then resurrected. This Age is almost complete until the beginning of the Age of Life, highlighted as the blue rectangle, which is a 20-jubilee period of time or a 1,000 year period of time known as the 1,000 Year reign of the Messiah. All in all, their have been a total of 120 jubilees in the past 6,000 years that are almost entirely complete. To be more precise, the 120th jubilee will finalize on Tishri 10, 2015 or on Yom Kippur 2015.

A Messiah for all Religions

Interestingly enough, it is not just Christians who are anticipating this final millennium, but also Jews, Muslims, Buddhism, Hinduism, Judaism and other religions that identify a future messiah who will bring order and set up a government of peace. The official website of Islam (*discoveringislam.org*) says that they anticipate that their messiah will appear in 2015 or 2016. According to an article from *WND*, titled, *Mahdi to Return By 2016, Followed By Jesus?*, the author documents very well that aside from Christians anticipating their Messiah, the Muslims are anticipating theirs as well known as the Mahdi. Both the Bible and Quran put forth end-times narratives that are very similar in many aspects but opposite in others.

As quoted from *discoveringislam.org,* they state, "Based on our numerical analysis of the Quran and Hadith, the official beginning of the End of Time and the coming of the Imam Mahdi will most likely be in 2015 (or 2016) and Jesus Christ will come down from Heaven to Earth in 2022, insha Allah (if Allah is willing)." [6] What I find intriguing, is that they believe in a seven years of tribulation much like within Christianity and Judaism.

If they believe Yahshua is to come back in 2022, then they also believe that tribulation must start in 2015. Remember that this is the official view of Islam who, according to Pew Research, has over 1.6 billion followers. Within Christianity, there are 2.2 billion followers. Just these two religious groups account for 53% of the world's population. In addition, the Buddhist recognize that their future messiah, known as Maitreya, will appear in order to bring complete order.[7] Likewise, within Hinduism, their messiah is known as the final Maha Avatara who will end the present age of darkness and destruction and who will offer salvation.

My point in all of this is to identify that all of the major religions, representing over 75% of the world's population, believe in a time of great conflict and tribulation; whereas, their particular messiah will save them and restore order. In other words, over three quarters of the world's 7.3 billion inhabitants have a worldview of a future 7 years of tribulation and a messiah who will save them. I don't know about you, but I can see a setup of a false *"Man of Peace"* who will lead the world astray claiming to be a messiah for all religions.

120 Jubilees?

I would like to highlight a verse that I find intriguing and could possibly points to these Jubilees. The verse is found in Genesis 6:3:

"And יהוה said, "My Spirit shall not strive with man forever in his going astray. He is flesh, and his days shall be one hundred and twenty years.""

The Hebrew word that is translated as year, is shaneh (Strong's H8141) and is often translated as year in the Scriptures. What I find interesting is that the word means: A. as division of time; B. as measure of time; C. as indication of age; D. a lifetime (of years of life).

Could it be that aside from year, that the word shaneh should be jubilee considering the significance of a jubilee to the Almighty's measure of time? If that were the case, then 120 jubilee cycles would amount to 6,000 years (120 x 50 years) with the 6,001st year marking the beginning of the 7th millennium. To be clear, I am not stating that this Scripture should read jubilees instead of years, but rather to read it in terms of its spiritual significance of where we are in the Biblical account of time. It is likely that it could mean 120 jubilees instead of years yet, I would rather view it in its spiritual significance of one year being one jubilee.

In one of their pdf's [8] provided on the *Torah Calendar* site, I discovered something that I thought was noteworthy to discuss. This would have to do with the six waterpots that were turned into wine as Yahshua's first public miracle. The following quote from the pdf mentioned above:

"In John 2:1-11, יהושע the Messiah alluded to the idea that the Marriage of the Lamb will occur after six millennial days are filled to the brim. It was at Cana that the Messiah turned water into wine at a marriage after six waterpots were filled to the brim. This first public miracle of יהושע the Messiah is deeply prophetic, as it convinced the disciples that יהושע was the Messiah who would rule in the Millennial Kingdom at the end of 6000 Civil Years of mankind's history. The first six millennial days of mankind's history are further grouped into three ages: the Age of Desolation, the Age of Instruction and the Age of the Messiah.

So, we see the prophetic message behind these six waterpots being turned into wine during a marriage ceremony. We know the that the beginning of the 6,000 year coinciding with the seventh millennium is alluded to within Scripture as being a time when the marriage of the Bridegroom to the Bride will take place coinciding to the 7th day of the Shabbat rest. The Book of Hosea alludes to this. This book is summarized in describing two kingdoms of Israel of first being chastised and then being redeemed in the latter days. Specifically, in Hosea 6:1-4, we read about a description of time that takes on enigmatic prophetic overtone of these latter days."

"Come, and let us turn back to יהוה. For He has torn but He does heal us, He has stricken but He binds us up. 'After two days He shall revive us, on the third day He shall raise us up, so that we live before Him. 'So let us know, let us pursue to know יהוה. His going forth is as certain as the morning. And He comes to us like the rain, like the latter rain watering the earth.' "Ephrayim, what would I do with you? Yehudah, what would I do with you?" (Hosea 6:1-4)

The latter rains are synonymous with the latter days as it correlates with the Fall Feast Days being a part of the fall harvest that rely on the latter rains. These latter rains tie into the Fall Feast Days. What I find particularly interesting is being revived after 2 days and being raised up on the third day so that we live with him. Using the understanding from II Peter 3:8 of "one day is as a thousand years," then we would read as: "After 2,000 years, He shall revive us, on the next day after the 2,000 years on the beginning of the third millennium, He shall raise us up as in the clouds or as a bride." Of course this speaks of Yahshua and all of this would take place at the end of the Age of Messiah and just prior to the Age of Life.

You will notice in the Book of Hosea that there is a division of two groups namely Ephrayim and Judah (Yehudah). The phrase, "He shall raise us up" speak of the Groom coming for his Bride!

Chapter 4

September 2015 and the Feast of

Yom Teruah

Back in chapter one, I attempted to make direct connections with the idioms associated with the Ancient Jewish Wedding to the Feast of Yom Teruah. In this chapter, I will cover more on the shadow pictures applies to the fall of this year (2015) with special attention to the start of Jacob's trouble or tribulation. As a review, the following are the common idioms associated with this feast.

- KIDDUSHIN NESU'IN MEANING "THE WEDDING CEREMONY" OR "THE WEDDING OF THE MESSIAH"
- THE TIME OF JACOB'S TROUBLE OR THE "TRIBULATION"
- THE DAY OF THE AWAKENING BLAST OR "TERUAH"
- YOM HADIN MEANING THE "DAY OF JUDGMENT" OR "OPENING OF THE BOOKS"
- YOM HAKESH MEANING "THE HIDDEN DAY"

- HA MELECH MEANING THE "CORONATION OF THE MESSIAH"
- YOM HAZIKKARON MEANING THE "DAY OF REMEMBRANCE"
- HA YOM HARAT OLAM MEANING THE "BIRTHDAY OF THE WORLD"

A Deeper look into Yom Teruah

It is on Yom Teruah in synagogues around the world that a series of trumpet sounds can be heard in observance of Leviticus 23: 23-25, with the blowing of the shofar as a holy convocation or as a *Day of Remembrance*. Traditionally, there are a series of trumpet sounds that are routinely blown on this feast that marks the beginning of the Fall Feast Days; a held blast known as Tekiah, followed by three broken blasts called Shevarim, followed by nine broken blasts called Teruah. These are blown a total of 99 times and the 100th blast, called the Tekiah Gedolah, being the final blast otherwise known as *the Last Trump*. Interestingly, all of the four different shofar blasts are all connected to Yom Kippur in that it represents the last sound or call to repentance and to search our hearts in a desire to change our ways before the Day of Atonement just 10 days later. It is on Yom Kippur that *the book is opened* and the sound of the shofar can be heard one last time. It is at this time that the Creator either forgives or allows judgment.

The sounding of the shofar on Yom Teruah of the sighting of the crescent moon, *where no man knows the day or the hour,* is a *wake-up* blast and a reminder that the Day of Atonement is fast approaching and thus a ten day count down of repentance and soul searching - a time to turn back to YHVH. It is important to realize that the blowing of the shofar is a command noted as *the blowing of trumpets*. Trumpets in this particular passage is the Hebrew word for Teruah. [1] The Strong's Concordance definition is an alarm of war, battle cry and shout of joy. Of the 36 times this word Teruah is used within the Tenakh, it is used 14 times to describe revival and exaltation.

106

There are a number of websites [2] that have documented the biblical Scriptures and Parashat readings associated with these idioms attributed with Yom Teruah. I will not be doing this, for the sake of time, but will now begin to highlight the discoveries and connections that Messianic Rabbi Johnathan Cahn has been able to make with regard to his two books, *The Harbinger* and *The Mystery of the Shemitah.* In this chapter, I will be paraphrasing the teachings of Mr. Cahn and the amazing connections that he has been able to make in regard to the Shmitah and a particular *Shmitah Release Day* once every 7 years (2,520 days).

We Christians, especially from a westernized background, have almost completely lost the importance of respecting and obeying the 4th Commandment of the Seventh Day of Rest. Keep in mind that it still is one of the Ten Commandments, the last I checked! This seventh day (Sabbath) is directly associated with the Shmitah and I believe its importance and relevance is being reignited in these latter days as Bible prophecy *CAN'T* be separated from the Shmitah. Part of the plan of the Creator is to use tribulation to strip paganism and false belief systems away from the church as well to enforce His Commandments,

> "O יהוה, my strength and my stronghold and my refuge, *in the day of distress the gentiles* shall come to You from the ends of the earth and say, "Our fathers have inherited only falsehood, futility, and there is no value in them." Would a man make mighty ones for himself, which are not mighty ones? *"Therefore see, I am causing them to know, this time I cause them to know My hand and My might. And they shall know that My Name is יהוה!"* (Jeremiah 16:19-21)

This Scripture from the Prophet Jeremiah is one for our time as this day of distress is not far off. This passage indicates that we will be going through tribulation to some degree, maybe to help purify us for the Groom that traditionally is reserved for one year. The Creator's plan is to have paganism and false doctrine completely stripped from the Church, much like he did to ancient Israel, by force if need be. What a great day it will be when we all call upon His true name as a united body of believers!

The Mystery of the Shmitah

Mr. Cahn makes a very good case of how the United States seem to follow clear pattern of warnings or harbingers in much the same way that ancient Israel experienced these harbingers. I will be paraphrasing Mr. Cahn's major points regarding the Shmitah and will be adding my own commentary as well. All material retrieved from his book will be identified by quotation marks and page number with regard to his second book.

As such, my goal in this chapter is to highlight commentary from Mr. Cahn in order to build a case for the Shmitah, first as a divine tool used by the Almighty for either blessings or curses and to help validate the Shmitah with regard to the jubilee. In doing so, I hope to portray the seriousness of this up and coming *Shmitah Release Day of* Elul 29, 2015 (September 13, 2015). Mr. Cahn refers to the day as simply the *Shemitah day*. Secondly, my goal is to also point out some overlooked analysis when it comes to the northern kingdom of Israel as mentioned only once by Mr. Cahn in his second book as stated, "The mystery begins in the last days of ancient Israel, the northern kingdom, as nine harbingers, prophetic signs, warnings of national judgment and destruction, appear in the land." [3] The identification of the northern kingdom of Israel is really critical to understanding how the United States fits into the warnings associated with the Shmitah as I will help identify the significance of the northern kingdom.

If you are not familiar with the *Harbinger*, then allow me to briefly cover it here. The author suggests that the Creator is bringing warnings and judgments against the United States much like he did against ancient Israel. These warnings are ultimately impending judgment that will not stop unless there is true repentance. According to Mr. Cahn, "The Bible reveals a clear pattern: before judgment, God warns. In the days of ancient Israel God sent warning of impending national judgment through varied means, through visions, through dreams, through audible voices, through prophetic utterances, through signs, through the written word, through prophetic acts, through supernatural occurrences, and through the outworking of natural events." [4] These nine harbingers are listed in order as the Breach, the Terrorist, the Fallen Bricks, the Tower, the Gazit Stone, the Sycamore, the Erez Tree, the Utterance and the Prophecy. For the sake of time, I will not be going into detail on these nine harbingers, but rather have listed each of the nine harbinger summaries in the Index section of this book.

History documents that the northern kingdom of Israel was attacked by their enemies in 732 BC. It was this attack that led to defiance and not repentance by the people or by their leaders. So, instead of a call of teshuvah (repentance) by the leadership, and a turning away from their sins of not obeying His Commandments and Statutes written down in the Torah, they instead became prideful and arrogant because of their strong national identity. He continues, "After the attack in 732 BC the people of Israel made a vow. The words of that vow were recorded by the prophet Isaiah: "The bricks have fallen, but we will rebuild with hewn stone; the sycamores have been cut down, but we will plant cedars in their place." [5]

In other words, the nation pridefully vowed to rebuild with stronger materials increasing the height and majesty of their "high towers" such as would be the result of using cut or hewn stone rather than the more inferior bricks. This statement was an act of defiance!

Ultimately, Mr. Cahn is able to make a convincing argument that the United States follow these same patterns of these nine harbingers as did the northern kingdom of Israel and it is these warnings that coincide with the Shmitahs. As stated by Mr. Cahn, "The first harbinger was manifested on American soil on September 11, 2001, as America's hedge of protection was lifted. An enemy was allowed to make an incursion, a strike on the land. America's national security was breached. The strike was contained, limited in time and scope. It was a shaking, a wake-up call, an alarm. But in the wake of 9/11 America did exactly as ancient Israel did in the wake of the ancient attack. America refused to turn back and, in fact, became even more defiant in its apostasy. And the ancient harbingers of judgment then began to manifest. But 9/11 didn't take place in just any year; 9/11 took place in the Year of the Shemitah." [6]

Of the 7 things YHVH hates, Pride would be number one on his list, "These six matters יהוה hates, And seven are an abomination to Him: A proud look, A lying tongue, And hands shedding innocent blood..." (Proverbs 6:16-17). One of the interesting observations from Scripture is the reference of the Creator wanting to bring down high towers that represent arrogance, pride and the idea that man can strive separate from him. Isaiah 2:12,15,17 states, "For יהוה of hosts has a day against all that is proud and lofty, against all that is lifted up, so that it is brought low;......and against every lofty tower, and against every strong wall, ...And the loftiness of man shall be bowed down, and the pride of men shall be brought low. And יהוה alone shall be exalted in that day."

The Creator is against the proud and in favor of the humble. This theme is prevalent throughout the Scriptures and what can be observed by the rise and fall of nations. The earliest example we have of this is ancient Babylon that said in their heart, "Come, let us build ourselves a city, and a tower whose top is in the heavens; let us make a name for ourselves . . ." (Genesis 11:4).

The Creator is in the business of building and restoring relationships. He can't have a relationship from those who are proud and arrogant. This in itself is a mystery. How can an all-powerful Creator, who created the trillions of stars, have a loving relationship with people whom He created with a free will especially to those who reject Him? The solution, from the Creator's perspective, seems to be the humbling of the proud and those who reject Him, so that they in return will embrace Him at their greatest hour of need.

It was the Tower of Babel that represented open defiance against the Creator and thus the need to humble the proud. Mr. Cahn goes on to identify those nations with the most economic and political influences. They are the ones with the highest towers (buildings) and thus the world's chief financial centers of influence, "Paralleling America's rise to world power was the rise of New York City. As America became the greatest power on earth, New York City would become the chief of cities." [7] It was simply a shift from the Old World system to the New World System, "The center of the world's financial realm had shifted from the Old World to the New, from the British Empire to the United States. The world's financial center was no longer London, but now New York City—the same city that now boasted the earth's highest towers." [8]

Prior to 9-11, America boasted the highest towers (World Trade Center 1 & 2), but now it has been overtaken by the Asian nations now overtaking America's role in the world. Notice how the rise and fall of a nation's highest buildings seems to represent the rise and fall of that particular nation. In the case of America, Mr. Cahn documents that all 9 harbingers have been identified and have come to pass. According to the pattern of the harbingers upon ancient Israel, these warnings lead to judgment as the northern kingdom of Israel became captive to Assyria in 721/722 BCE, just 11 years from their initial attack. Will the fate of the United States fall victim to the same pattern?

The premise of Mr. Cahn's second book, *The Mystery of the Shemitah*, builds upon his first book while going into great detail with regard to *the Sabbath of years* also referred to in the book as the Shemitah. The first mention of this Shmitah year within the Scriptures comes after the 12 tribes of Jacob (Israel) left Egypt as commanded by the Almighty, entering into Mount Sinai where Moses delivers unto Israel the Ten Commandments and the beginning of what is known as the Torah. The Torah in essence became the written instructions or laws whereby the children of Israel agreed to be bound by it and to follow the commandments of YHVH. I like to compare this event to the Ancient Jewish Wedding, whereby the bride would accept the Ketubah (Torah) that would state the promises of the bridegroom and the drinking from the Passover Seder cup that would seal the contract. Interestingly, Israel in totality went through her ritual cleaning by being mikveh'd or baptized in the Red Sea, more precisely identified in the Gulf of Aquaba between Saudi Arabia and Egypt.[9]

Once betrothed, Israel was to remain faithful to her ketubah (Torah) and especially the Ten Commandments. All the commandments were of equal importance, but there was a special commandment of obeying the Sabbath day of rest. By doing so, it set them apart from the world and identified their desire to follow His commandments. It is obeying His commandments that prove your love for Him. Even Yahshua made mention of this, "He who possesses My commands and guards them, it is he who loves Me. And he who loves Me shall be loved by My Father, and I shall love him and manifest Myself to him." The greatest commandment was to "love YHVH with all your heart, mind and soul." His words have not changed!

Aside from following and obeying the Ten Commandments, they were also required to obey *the Sabbath of years* as an act of obedience and to allow rest not only for Israel, but also for the land from being planted and harvested. By obeying, the Almighty would not only provide a double portion of manna on the sixth day of the week, but would also provide a double harvest in the sixth year to carry them through the Shmitah year. The crops that would grow during the Shmitah would be reserved for the poor among them (Exodus 23:10-12; Leviticus 25:1-7).

The laws and economy of ancient Israel were based upon an agrarian cycle directly related to farming and the agrarian laws within the Torah associated with land rights. One of the Creator's laws had to do with the release of debts on the Shmitah year, "At the end of every seven years you make a release of debts" (Deuteronomy 15:1). It was on this last day of the *Sabbath of years* that lenders were required to forgive or "release" borrowers from their debt. Over time, the last day of the Sabbath year began to be known as the day of release or in Hebrew, the Shmitah. It was this Shmitah that became a great blessing to the nation and it would become a time of reflection and celebration. When they were in obedience, YHVH would greatly bless the inhabitants of the land.

"...For יהוה does greatly bless you in the land which יהוה your Elohim is giving you to possess as an inheritance, only if you diligently obey the voice of יהוה your Elohim, to guard to do all these commands which I am commanding you today. "For יהוה your Elohim shall bless you as He promised you. And you shall lend to many nations, but you shall not borrow. And you shall rule over many nations, but they do not rule over you." (Deuteronomy 15:4-6)

Thus, "The Shemitah was a sign of the nation's covenant with God. Everything they had, the land and all its blessings, was dependent on that covenant and their relationship with God. It was all entrusted to them, but it belonged to God. If they turned away from God, then their blessings would be removed, or rather, they would be removed from their blessings."
10

Over a period of hundreds of years, the Israelites began to disobey the Creator's commands and statutes and began to fall deeper into sin. This, coupled with taking in foreign wives who came from other nations who brought with them false gods and idolatry, added to their rebellion. Ultimately, the Laws of Moses and the worship of the one true Elohim were abandoned. All in all, Israel failed to observe 70 Sabbath of years or Shmitahs. Because the Creator is righteous and holy, He doesn't tolerate a rebellious and sinful people who openly disregard His ketubah, especially from a wife who has pledged her obedience and faithfulness to her husband.

Because of their disobedience, the Babylonian empire was used by the Almighty to execute judgment upon the southern kingdom of Judah (the Jewish People) in 606 BCE where the Prophet Jeremiah records their captivity for 70 years, one year of captivity for every one year of not observing the Sabbath year or Shmitah. So, while the children of Israel did not allow the land to rest, the Creator allowed judgment to enter their nation thus allowing His land to enjoy her Sabbaths. Mr. Cahn states, "The judgment that fell on the land of Israel in 586 BC was a pivotal event in biblical history, Jewish history, and world history. In it the Temple of Jerusalem would be destroyed and the words of the Hebrew prophets fulfilled." [11]

"And those who escaped from the sword he exiled to Babel, where they became servants to him and his sons until the reign of the reign of Persia, in order to fill the word of יהוה by the mouth of Yirmeyahu, until the land had enjoyed her Sabbaths. As long as she lay waste she kept Sabbath, until seventy years were completed." (II Chronicles 36:20-21)

It is interesting to note that the world is coming up to the 70th year since Israel's rebirth as a nation that was fulfilled on the eve of Shavuot May 14,

1948. Seventy solar years later will bring us to May 2018. Is there a connection with this 70-year prophecy as a possible double prophetic fulfillment especially as it concerns the United States?

The underlining premise of Mr. Cahn's book is that not only does the Creator allow the nation of Israel as a whole to observe the Shmitah year, but also this seems to be a mystery that seems to affect world affairs from the Word Wars to the economic cycles, calamities, and natural disasters. These cycles are deeply rooted in the Jewish Lunar Calendar and their civil year that begins on Tishri 1. Is the Creator trying to get the attention as a nation of turning away from sin or else impending judgment? He further concludes that *the Lord* continues to follow the same seven-year cycle in His dealings with America.

In order to make the case of why the United States seems to be affected by these Shmitahs unlike any other nation on earth, Mr. Cahn treats America as a "Second Israel." The phrase "Second Israel" is an interesting use of words. Is it possible that the United States is a type of second Israel? I think I might be able to shed some light on this by helping identify who Israel is based upon the true context of this word especially with regard to Isaiah chapter nine and the northern kingdom of Israel.

The "Shmitah Release Day"

The *"Shmitah Release Day,"* as I have coined it, was originally a day destined by YHVH to have debt released and for the captives to be set free from their bondage. It was to be a joyous celebration as in a new lease on life. This day was destined to fall on the appointed day of Elul 29 (the eve of Yom Teruah) of the Creator's calendar or the final day of his civil calendar. Years one through six would not suffice. It must fall on the last day of the seventh year or the one day out of 2,520 days (7x360) according to Deuteronomy 15:1, where the end of the seventh year was destined for the

115

release. This cycle would repeat every seven Hebraic years. This is the same pattern observed within a jubilee. Seven times seven or seven sets of Shmitah years that fulfill the requirements in order to bring about the beginning of the 50th Year of Jubilee and it is this *Shmitah Day* that ties it all together. The following image labeled as *50 Years of Jubilee* shows how seven Shmitahs, represented by the small blue boxes, tie into the jubilee and announce the set apart 50th Year that is also a Shmitah of letting the land rest.

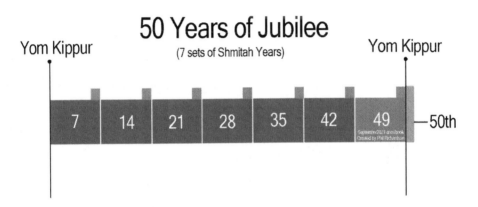

Thus, the key element of Mr. Cahn's second book is *the Shemitah Day* or as I like to identify it as the *"Shmitah Release Day."* Amazingly, it is this *Shmitah Release Day* that can be observed and identified. There is no need to go back thousands of years, like many have done, in order to identify this day within the Shmitah year. The Creator has done it for us so that we may be lined up with his *Appointed Feasts*. He wants us to be lined up so that we can be a light to the nations!

As I have been documenting, pay particular attention to the eve of a major feast day especially in regard to the Fall Feast Days. To clarify, the eve would be just the moment before that feast or up to 24 hours before. In the case of Yom Teruah 2015, the eve of this feast will be Elul 29 that being the Gregorian date of September 14, 2015. This date will represent the final day of the Shmitah on Jewish Civil calendar. This date is a big deal and something to mark on your calendars. You may not fully appreciate this date until I fully address Elul 29 of the Shmitah year.

The Breach

Mr. Cahn has been able to identify the patterns of this remarkable day in his second book. Paraphrasing from his book, 9-11 struck America unexpectantly and was a devastating blow to our way of life as a free and prosperous people. It struck at the heart of our economic (capitalism) and governmental (imperialism) institutions being housed in New York and Washington D.C. It was within just moments after the second plan hit the world trade center that the U.S. Stock market suspended trading and all flights over the continental United States were suspended as well. It was the worst attack on American soil to date.

When the stock market finally opened exactly 6 days later on September 17, 2001, the market would have tanked dropping 684 points with a percent change of 7%. That would have, to date, represented the largest percentage of change drop ever recorded. This event was more of a warning as identified by Mr. Cahn as the first harbinger of a series of nine, known as *the Breach. The Breach,* was the removing of the Creator's hedge of protection off of America. He allowed the events of 9-11 to happen by the removing of that hedge of protection much like He did with ancient Israel in their rebellion. The removing of the hedge of protection was as a direct result of the rebelliousness of the people and the leadership at that time. In the same way, we have rebelled against Him with pride, arrogance and a haughty spirit declaring as a nation, *"The bricks have fallen, but we will rebuild with hewn stone; the sycamores have been cut down, but we will plant cedars in their place."* [12]

We know that the Creator is the same yesterday, today and forever. His laws are set in stone, literally, and are there as a commandment of blessings as long as we obey and follow them. So, is this just a coincidence or is there a second event (witness) that would help shed some light on this event especially with regard to the Shmitah Release Day?

When we look back, we can identify the Sabbath of Years especially with regard to a jubilee period of time that contains seven (7) Shmitah cycles of seven. *The Creator's jubilee cycle* began June 7, 1967 and we can clearly identify these Shmitahs with greater insight. I cover the *"Creator's Jubilee"* in the next chapter. Elul 29, 2001 (the Shmitah Release Day) fell within the 35th Shmitah cycle of this current jubilee that we are experiencing. More precisely, the Shmitah began on Tishri 1 (Yom Teruah) of the year 2000 and finalized on Elul 29 of 2001 (the eve of Yom Teruah). So, the question remains, when would have been the next Shmitah especially in reference to the jubilee cycle?

We find the next Shmitah cycle began on Yom Teruah of 2007 and finalized on the eve of Yom Teruah of 2008 or Elul 29, that being the *Shmitah Release Day*. It would have been on Elul 29 of the Jewish calendar that the U.S. Stock market would have experienced its second largest collapse ever.

Unrestrained greed by the heads of the largest U.S. banks would have ultimately been the ones responsible for this collapse as well as the special interests that serve them. The collapse of the sub-prime mortgage industry to the tune of trillions of dollars would have taken down some of America's largest financial institutions (the too big to fails) if it were not from the aid of the U.S. Government. Ultimately It was the market's reaction to the U.S. Congress' failure to approve the so-called "700 Billion dollar bailout plan" that spooked the market and created such large losses in that day.

By day's end on Elul 29, 2008, the U.S. Stock market corrected 777.7 points by its close, representing 7% of the market on that 7 hour trading day. In other words, the wealth of the American investor and the other investors from around the world had their wealth *"released"* or wiped out on that eve before Yom Teruah instituted by the Almighty as a day destined for either blessings or curses either to the benefit or detriment to the people. I, among many others, believe that this day was divinely orchestrated especially when you factor in the number seven (7) that was prevalent on that day. Keep in mind that the number seven is special to the Creator. It represents Him and He in return leaves His imprint with that number. I do not believe a 777.7 point drop in the market, representing 7% of the market is not coincidental, especially when you factor in that this event happened exactly 7 Hebrew years from the last *Shmitah Release Day* of Elul 29, 2001. The odds of this happening by chance are extremely high. As stated, this day was established for the wiping away of either debt or prosperity (Lev 25:1-7).

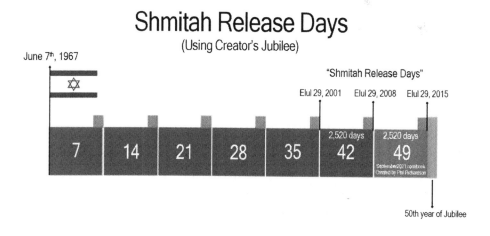

Shmitah Release Days
(Using Creator's Jubilee)

By using the *Creator's Jubilee,* we can view a visual representation of the last two *Shmitah Release Days* of Elul 29 of 2001 and in 2008. See the image titled, *Shmitah Release Days.* It was Elul 29, 2008 (September 29, 2008) that the second greatest stock market crash would have happened. Again, we saw the stock market drop 7% much like it did in 2001, the second in a series of a major crash separated by exactly 2,520 days, or 7 sets of 360 days. Even more striking is the fact that from September 29, 2008 (Elul 29), there would be even greater losses following that Shmitah Release Day and primarily in the month following Tishri.

10/9/2008	-7.33%
10/7/2008	-5.11%
10/15/2008	-7.87%
10/22/2008	-5.69
12/1/2008	-7.70%

Is this the pattern we might expect following this coming Shmitah Release Day on Elul 29, 2015? There is no question that there seems to be a build up of events around the world that may trigger an economic *"release"* and possibly some sort of *"Economic Reset"* of the world's currencies as it is known. By every measurement available, there is a build up of crushing debt to massive levels never seen before and the threat of war has never been so high since the time of the cold war.

The "Shmitah Release Day" and the Connection to Yom Teruah 2015

It is this day, *the Shmitah Release Day,* that ties the nine harbingers together either directly or indirectly. It is this day that is absolutely key in lining up Bible prophecy and the latter day fulfillment of prophecy for it is this day that identifies the *Nation* and that Nation's *City* that controls and influences the economies of the world, that being identified as America and New York City as that Great City. It is America that has had the most influence over the world's economies and for that matter their policies and politics. And what gave America her influence over all of the other nations of the world? I believe that to be the Bretton Woods Conference of 1944, that established the U.S. Dollar as the World's Reserve Currency.

Formally known as the United Nations Monetary and Financial Conference, this United Nations-backed plan was a result of 730 delegates from all 44 Allied nations meeting at the Mount Washington Hotel situated in Bretton Woods, New Hampshire.[13] It would have been at this conference that the delegates would vote on matters dealing with international monetary policy and to set policy in helping rebuild war torn countries by the establishment of the IMF (formally IBRD) and the World Bank. It would be at this conference that the U.S. Dollar would be chosen as the World's Reserve Currency whereby, all other currencies would be pegged to. This act along with pegging the U.S. Dollar to oil (the Petro Dollar), would result in the U.S. Dollar becoming known as the "Almighty Dollar" with the United States having an unfair advantage over every other nation on the planet in terms of economic might, military power and political influence.

Unfortunately, it would be President Nixon in 1971 that would eliminate the gold standard, thus de-pegging this important gold standard from the U.S. Dollar. This monumental act would become the catalysts for a worldwide fiat based currency system of out of control spending, debt build up and debt bubble implosions around the world. The IMF, BIS and World Bank would all take part in helping to destroy national sovereignty of independent nation states through debt creation. This is what we are seeing with Greece, Italy and Portugal, just to name a few. Will these countries be used to bring about the implosion of the entire economic system starting in Europe?

So, we see the United Nations, being home in this *Great City*, as being the vehicle being used to bring about the rise of this *New World Order Global Government* and their strong arm, *the United Nations Security Council* (UNSC). It is the UNSC that is the world's most powerful governing body, setting and enforcing policy for the *"World's Army"* being made up of the fifteen most powerful nations on earth. And, it is these nations that house the largest and most advanced military power on the planet housing a nuclear arsenal able to destroy this planet one thousand times over. I discuss this world governing body in greater detail in chapter eight where I also discuss the connection of "he" lawlessly making a covenant with these powerful fifteen nations under the full governmental authority of the United Nations Security Council. Imagine any one man initiating and setting policy for the *"World's Army!"* That one man might be labeled *"King of the World!"*

The Shmitah is beyond just a mystery. It is but one more tool being used by the Almighty to get our attention! He is purposely revealing his patterns to us in these latter days as a warning of impending judgment and to offer clarity as to His *Signs and Seasons*, cryptic language that identifies His Signs and *Appointed Feasts* of Yom Teruah, Yom Kippur and Tabernacles. Remember, they are His Feasts. Nowhere in Scripture does it state that the feasts are strictly for the Jewish people. This belief is as a result of not properly evaluating who Israel is in context to Scripture. Israel is made up of twelve tribes and the Jewish people come from just one of the tribes, the tribe of Judah.

Thus, the connection to Yom Teruah of 2015 will be this Shmitah Release Day (Elul 29, 2015) that will fall on the Eve of Yom Teruah (September 13, 2015). This is based upon the pattern of the two previous *Shmitah Release Day's* of 2001 and 2008, a period of time that represents the 35th Shmitah and 49th Shmitah of the *Creator's Jubilee* that again, began on Jerusalem's reunification date of June 7, 1967. Keep in mind that according to Leviticus 25:8, the beginning of the 50th year of jubilee will have its beginning at the end of this 49th year. I will reveal more on this in the next chapter.

Why the Connection with America?

Why the deep connection with the United States? As Mr. Cahn has so well documented in his two books, America seems to have a deep connection with Israel and to the heart of the Creator.

Mr. Cahn does not really address this question except to imply that America is the "Second Israel" that is a bit too vague for interpretation. I believe the answer with regard to the deep connection with America might be two-fold. First off, the Isaiah 9:10 prophecy is directly related to the northern kingdom of Israel and not to the southern kingdom of Judah (the Jewish People). This is something not mentioned by Mr. Cahn as it is an easy pill swallowed by most westernized Christians who are simply unaware of the division of the two kingdoms and the prophetic implications of these kingdoms to these latter days. With that said, it is very important to distinguish these two kingdoms and to keep Scripture within its context. The northern kingdom is also known as the House of Joseph (Zechariah 10:6, II Samuel 2:10) and also the house of Ephraim and Manasseh; or just the house of Ephraim. The northern kingdom is also known as Israel. As mentioned, the northern kingdom is made up of the 10 tribes of Israel.

Here is the famous harbinger verse in context with verse nine…

> "And the people shall know, all of them, *Ephrayim* and *the inhabitant of Shomeron*, who say in pride and greatness of heart: "The bricks have fallen down, but we rebuild with hewn stones; the sycamores are cut down, but we replace them with cedars." (Isaiah 9:9-10)

Within the true context of Scripture, Isaiah 9:9-10 clearly identify Ephrayim and the inhabitants of Shomeron. It is Ephrayim and the inhabitants of Shomeron, who say in great pride and greatness of heart that the bricks have fallen down... So, who are these people? Shomeron is identified as the area of Samaria and is derived from the ancient city of Samaria within modern day Israel. It is the region of land that is identified as being north of the Dead Sea encompassing the Sea of Galilee to the Golan Heights incorporating such cities as modern day Jaffa, Jericho, Samaria and Shehem. It is in these areas that identify much of the 10 tribes residing in this area. In contrast, the southern kingdom of Judah incorporated a landmass smaller than the northern area encompassing an area south and west of the Dead Sea inclusive of Jerusalem, Beersheba, Hebron and Lachish.

The context of these verses point to the northern kingdom of Israel, not the southern kingdom of the Jews and the Tribe of Benjamin. So, who then is Ephrayim? Do you recall how Joseph asked his Dad, Jacob, to bless his two boys? The result of Jacob, known as Israel, blessing Ephrayim and Manasseh resulted in an incredible prophecy concerning two great nations, "He (Manasseh) also becomes a people, and he also is great. And yet, his younger brother (Ephrayim) is greater than he, and his seed is to become the completeness of the nations" (Genesis 48:19).

America in Bible Prophecy?

I have heard from many pastors and Bible teachers that American is not mentioned in the Bible. They claim that nowhere in the Scriptures can we identify America. These are the same pastors that would tell me that no man would know the day, the hour, the year or for that matter the decade or century of when Jesus will return back to earth. I disagree with the assertion that America is not mentioned in the Bible, not directly at least.

124

It is my understanding that the reason America is so well connected with the Shmitah and the Creator's blessings stems from this prophecy concerning Ephraim and Manasseh becoming a multitude of nations and great nation in that order and it is also this same reasoning to suggest that we will fall under similar judgments as did the northern kingdom of Ephraim in 722/721 BCE.

So, who are these two nations? Is not prophecy there to be fulfilled? Was it not YHVH who promised that from the seed of Abraham would become a people so great that they would be number greater than the stars? Where there is silence at the pulpit, the Internet shouts, bringing forth knowledge and wisdom and the revealing of mysteries. There is a website that I believe to be accurate in deciphering the seed-lines of Ephrayim and Manasseh and the two great nations they became. I challenge you to visit *britam.org* for further evidence.

Is there a reason that the United States has had such a close spiritual connection with Israel? Is it possible that our forefather's forefathers came out of the northern kingdom that would reunite with the southern kingdom of Judah in these latter days? I believe this to be the case for various reasons!

Yet, there is a deeper question that remains to be asked. If the United Kingdom of Britain and the United States represent these two nations as documented by *britam.org,* then what role will the United States play on the world scene once it is under judgment by the Almighty? Will this Christian Nation that the Almighty has blessed upon measure rebel and morph into a tyrannical "Beast" power? Could it be that the United States is that nation mentioned as the *"beast from the earth"* as recorded in Revelation chapter 13? Is it true that the harbingers are warnings in order to heed the cry to repentance or are the harbingers simply shadow pictures of certain judgment as the context surrounding Isaiah 9:10 prophecies indicate?

This is something that Mr. Cahn does not point out, but rather reassures the reader that America can turn around if we repent as a nation and turn back to the Creator. I actually believe that repentance is the message that should be preached and I give double thumbs up to Mr. Cahn for doing just that. It is certainly a better message than impending doom.

Could it be that the United States in rebellion could morph into Mystery Babylon? Of the prophecies concerning Mystery Babylon (Isaiah 13, 14, 18, 47; Jeremiah 50, 51; Revelation 18), there is no other country on earth that fit the descriptions so well. Christians refuse to notice the 3,000 pound pink elephant in the room, turning a blind eye to conventional wisdom! Since I have opened this can of worms, let me point out just a few of the Scriptures concerning Mystery Babylon and let's see what country could possibly satisfy these descriptions.

"For all the nations have drunk of the wine of the wrath of her fornication, the kings of the earth have committed fornication with her, and the merchants of the earth have become rich through the abundance of her luxury." (Revelation 18:3)

"For she says in her heart, 'I sit as queen, and am no widow, and will not see sorrow.'" (Revelation 18:7)

"The merchants of these things, who became rich by her, will stand at a distance for fear of her torment, weeping and wailing, and saying, 'Alas, alas, *that great city* that was clothed in fine linen, purple, and scarlet, and adorned with gold and precious stones and pearls! For in one hour such great riches came to nothing.' *Every shipmaster, all who travel by ship, sailors, and as many as trade on the sea*, stood at a distance and cried out when they saw the smoke of her burning, saying, 'What is like this great city?'* (Revelation 18:15-18)

126

"For your merchants were the great men of the earth, for by your *sorcery* all the nations were deceived" (Revelation 18:23).

Note that the word for sorcery is pharmacia as in pharmacy. There is not a nation on earth that pump out more pharmacy than the United States.

Within these few verses, we see that this great nation has a great city that is very wealthy whereby the merchants of the world became wealthy. When this city is burned by fire, the shipmasters and merchants that trade by sea, will weep and wail. I believe this great city to be none other than New York City and is why this city plays such an important role in the *Harbinger* and the *Mystery of the Shemitah* books by Johnathan Cahn and it is the *great city* that is home to World Government (The United Nations).

Please see the index for a list of other Scriptures and additional insight. As this is a highly controversial subject, perhaps this should be the subject matter of a future book. I will simply move on to the next topic at hand.

The Israeli and Palestinian Peace Process and the Shmitah

Since 1978, the United States has been at the forefront of the Peace Process between Israel and their Arab neighbors especially with regard to Palestine. This is a deeply divisive subject as most people have an opinion with regard to who should possess the land known in the Bible as the land of Canaan and in modern times as Palestine or Israel. It is quite prophetic that the prophets of old would prophecy regarding this land in the latter years,

"O Elohim, do not remain silent! Do not be speechless, And do not be still, O Ěl! For look, Your enemies make an uproar, And those hating You have lifted up their head. *They craftily plot against Your*

127

people, And conspire against Your treasured ones. They have said, *"Come, And let us wipe them out as a nation, And let the name of Yisra'ēl be remembered no more."* (Psalm 83:1-4)

This verse comes from the 83rd chapter of the book of Psalms, and it is in this chapter where there is a description of a unified multitude of Arab countries that will come against Israel in these later days. This particular chapter is known as the *"Psalm 83 War"* by many prophecy teachers and is a prophecy that has not been fulfilled in the past and one of the first prophecies to be fulfilled according to these teachers. Chapter 83 identifies the nations that will be united as a future coalition to come against Israel in these latter days. This is a prevailing view among the radical side of Islam and the countries that embrace this ideology. It is fascinating to see this underlying theme of "wiping Israel out as a nation" is so well embraced by most if not all Arab countries in our time.

The United States would step up its leadership role in 1978 with the formation of the Camp David Accords in order to tackle this conflict in the Middle East. The Camp David Accords was an effort presented by former President Carter that dealt with the "Palestinian territories" and peace between Israel and Egypt. The second in a series of the peace processes would result in the Madrid Conference of 1991, hosted by Spain and co-sponsored by the U.S. and the Soviet Union. This was an attempt by the international community to revive the Israeli/Palestinian peace process through negotiations involving Israel, the Palestinians and other Arab countries.

The Oslo Accords would be the third in a series of peace talks, which would be directly linked to the Shmitah year. The Oslo Accords would span a period of time from 1993 to 1995 with the Shmitah year falling from 1994 to 1995. The Olso Accords resulted in a set of agreements between Israel and the PLO (Palestinian Liberation Authority). The initial agreements re-

128

sulted in the *Oslo I Accord* being signed by all parties in Washington D.C. in 1993. This would result in the beginning of *the Oslo Process*. This *Oslo Process* would aim at achieving a *"peace treaty"* through two resolutions being passed namely United Nations Security Council Resolution 242 and 338 giving the Palestinians the right of "self-determination." [14] Interestingly enough, the UNSC Resolution #242 was unanimously adopted in November 1967, during a 50th Solar Year of Jubilee that began on September of 1967. UNSC Resolution #338 was adopted in October 22, 1973, during the first Shmitah year of the new jubilee cycle. This resolution called for the ceasefire in the Yom Kippur War according the joint proposal by the United States and the Soviet Union.

Moving forward, the Peace Process would continue its series of Shmitah patterns. The next set of peace summits would result in the 2000 Camp David Summit hosted by then President Bill Clinton. This summit would take place in July of 2000 and was an effort to end the Israeli-Palestinian conflict. The summit ended without an agreement. This Summit would take place just before the Shmitah, which would have its beginning in September of 2000. These talks would, however, lead into the Shmitah with the continuation of talks with the Taba Summit in January of 2001. According to statements issued by the negotiators at the end of the talks, "they came closer to reaching a final settlement than in any previous peace talks." [15]

The next series of talks would be the Annapolis Conference that began on November 27, 2007, and would again take place in an Shmitah year from September 2007 to 2008. This conference would take place at the United States Naval Academy in Annapolis, Maryland, hosted by then President George W. Bush, "The conference aimed to revive the Israeli–Palestinian peace process and implement the 'Roadmap for peace.' " [16] A partial list of over 40 invitees was invited, including China, the Arab League, Russia, the European Union and the United Nations; most of whom accepted the invitation. The conference ended with the issuing of a joint statement from all parties. After the Annapolis Conference, the negotiations were continued."

Almost seven years later would result in another peace process otherwise known as *the Kerry-led Talks* lead by the current Secretary of State, John Kerry from May - July of 2014. Once again, these talks would not result in Israel giving up her land up for so called peace and would end just short of the beginning of the Shmitah year. View the following image, *Shmitah "Peace" Talks*. Notice how all of these *"peace talks"* including the UNSC Resolutions concerning Israel have happened during the Shmitah year that began of the jubilee year of 1967.

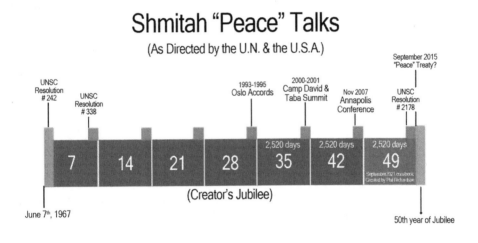

In addition, the harbinger of 9-11 and the greatest market crashes have happened during these Shmitah years as well. Coincidence? I don't think so! Take note of these events landing on the Shmitah years of the Creator's jubilee that can be viewed on the *Shmitah "Peace" Talks* image.

It would be during this final Shmitah year from September 2014 to September 2015, that we would witness some very interesting events take place with regard to Israel. It would be during this final seventh (7th) Shmitah year in the series of seven that we would see a big distancing away from Israel and a big push for a Palestinian State. We would also witness the Obama administration setting policy and diplomacy between Iran and the United States with regard to nuclear energy. This was being established for "good intentions" of course that would open up trade between the two nations.

It was on July 13th, 2015 that Mr. Obama established a 60 day deadline for Congress to approve the measure known as *"The Iran Deal"* that would allow Iran many benefits in exchange for limits on nuclear activities. According to CNN, "In its most simplistic form, the deal means that in exchange for limits on its nuclear activities, Iran would get relief from sanctions while being allowed to continue its atomic program for peaceful purposes." [17] Sixty days forward brings us the September 13th, 2015, the eve of Yom Teruah, that being the *Shmitah Release Day*.

Mr. Netanyahu, while speaking in front of a joint house of the U.S. Congress in March of 2015, stated, "If this regime was not pursuing nuclear weapons, then you'd have a different attitude. But it is pursuing nuclear weapons," [18] he said, citing It's (Iran's) development of ballistic missiles, construction of underground enrichment facilities and refusal to answer questions about the possible military dimensions of its nuclear program." This would be followed by President Obama's "temper tantrum" as stated by John McCain, an obvious reference to President Obama's displeasure with Mr. Netanyahu's speech in front of Congress just prior to his reelection.

In addition, within this 49th Shmitah Cycle we have Pope Francis officially recognizing Palestine as an official State, "This month, the Vatican also effectively recognized the Palestinian State, while stressing that it has long recognized its legitimacy. The Pope himself has made habitual references to "the state of Palestine." The Vatican has expressed its "hope for a solution to the Palestine question" and an end to the conflict "according to the two-state solution." [19]

It is interesting to see these events start to unfold just like the Bible said they would especially to those who are paying attention and know what to look for. Keep an eye on September of this year. Jade Helm is to "conclude" on Yom Teruah and Pope Francis is scheduled to address the U.S. Congress for the first time ever on the Day of Atonement and will, on the following day, be addressing the United Nations on Climate Change with a special emphasis on the Trans Pacific Partnership legislation that will place the control of trade in the hands of a few. These are truly unprecedented times!

As I have laid out, there seems to be a real connection with the designated Shmitah year and the *"Peace" Process* between Israel and their Arab neighbors. The major world players of this *"Peace' Process* repeatedly seem to be Israel, the United States (Presidents) and the United Nations. It will be interesting to see what may happen, if anything, with regard to the peace process before this Shmitah year officially ends this Elul 29, 2015; If not, then I fully expect some type of *"Peace Agreement"* to take place within *the 50th Year of the Creator's Jubilee.* As I will lay out in the next chapter, jubilees represent a heightened layer of judgment. Will the Pope step up his role of "Peace Maker" as stated in the *Saint Malechy's prophecies* concerning Petrus Romanus who will, "Shepherd his sheep during many tribulations?"

Jade Helm 2015

Almost two Shmitah cycles (14 years) have passed since the terrorist attacks of 9-11 and the series of events attributed to the harbingers being fulfilled. As we approach the closing of the Shmitah year cycle this coming eve of Yom Teruah, there are some military exercises taking place, that I believe, may play a major role in the up and coming 50th Jubilee Year that has its beginning on Yom Kippur. I am speaking of Jade Helm 15.

Jade Helm 15 is the name given to these series of military exercises that will be taking place from July 15th to September 15th in seven southern states including Texas, Utah, Arizona, New Mexico, Colorado, Nevada and the southern portion of California. As you might notice, a majority of these states border Mexico. These military exercises will be made up of four branches of the U.S. Military and the scope and size will be quite large having people seriously questioning if these are simply exercises or if this is an opportunity to station troops in the likely event of an economic collapse the fall of this year. One of the striking facts regarding Jade Helm 15 is that it "ends" on September 15, that being Yom Teruah with the 13th/14th being the eve of Yom Teruah or Elul 29 (the Shmitah Release Day) on the Creator's calendar. As I have been documenting thus far, the events falling on either the eve or on the feast days are highly significant especially with regard to this up and coming Fall Feasts.

Of the seven states, Texas and Utah are labeled as "hostile," which prompted a reaction from Texas Governor, Gregg Abbott who has commissioned the State Guard to monitor the training exercises, On Monday, the governor defended his actions. "There was, frankly, an overreaction to the simple fact that someone has to be in charge with gathering and disseminating information," said Abbott, speaking to reporters. "We stepped in to play that role, which is a role to be applauded." [20]

In defense of the Governor from the barrage of the media's bashing, Chuck Norris had a few words regarding these up and coming military drills. In response, Mr. Norris wrote on the conservative website World Net Daily, stating: "Concerned Texans and Americans are in no way calling into question our brave and courageous men and women in uniform. They are merely following orders. What's under question are those who are pulling the strings at the top of Jade Helm 15 back in Washington. The U.S. government says, 'It's just a training exercise.' But I'm not sure the term 'just' has any reference to reality when the government uses it." [21]

Does the government know something we don't? Could it be that these drills will preposition our military and National Guard in key demographic areas in the event our President declares martial law or to at least quell an outbreak caused by a breakdown of our financial institutions? Keep an eye of Jade Helm! The fact that it supposedly "ends" on Yom Teruah speaks volumes to me.

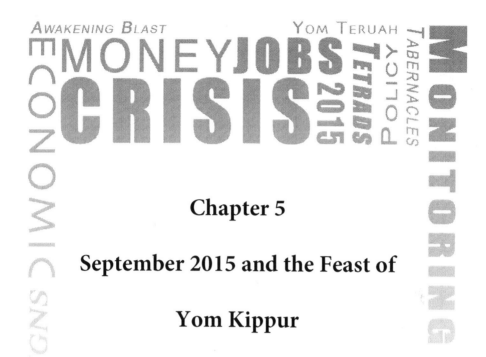

Chapter 5

September 2015 and the Feast of

Yom Kippur

Yom Kippur (Ha-Kadosh) is known to the Jewish people as their holiest day of the year and is the *Appointed Feast* whereby the High Priest (Kohen Gadol) was required by the Almighty to sacrifice bulls and goats and to then sprinkle their blood on the mercy seat of the Ark of the Covenant. It was the belief within Judaism that it was their last chance to change the "Judgment of the Almighty" to one of forgiveness. This act of holding off the judgment from the Creator was simply a temporarily solution of wiping away the sins of the nation.

Yom Kippur is the only High Sabbath feast whereby Israel were required to fast all day, abstaining from food, water and luxuries in order to look deep within their spirit in order to seek repentance. It is also the finale of the *Ten Days of Awe,* essentially the ending of the prophetic time clock of Bible prophecy and of His return in some future year. To the Jew, they believe that YHVH will rule from Jerusalem and to the Christian it will be Yahshua, *the Word of YHVH,* who will rule.

"The Spirit of the Master יהוה is upon Me, because יהוה has anointed Me to bring good news to the meek. He has sent Me to bind up the broken-hearted, to proclaim release to the captives, and the opening of the prison to those who are bound, to *proclaim the acceptable year of יהוה, and the day of vengeance of our Elohim, to comfort all who mourn,"* (Isaiah 61:1-2).

Isaiah 61 is a prescribed Yom Kippur reading in Synagogues all around the world as Jews from all over the world read the same Torah portion for that given High Sabbath and it is the same Scripture from which Yahshua read when He began His ministry. The phrase *"to proclaim the acceptable year of YHVH"* identifies the beginning of a jubilee year of liberty that would be proclaimed on Yom Kippur with the acceptable year continuing until the following eve of Yom Kippur – a 359 day period of time.

Essentially, what Yahshua was proclaiming was that He was the Moschiac (Messiah) on that Day of Atonement as He was the ultimate atoning sacrifice for the covering of sin. That Day of Atonement was all about Him as the prophecy from Isaiah 61 was the prophecy concerning the Messiah.

To recap, the Scriptures indicate that when Yahshua read from Isaiah 61:1-2, that He sat down and all eyes were on Him. He then stated that today "this has come true." He was claiming to be the Messiah! We know that He was "cut short" (Daniel 9:26) of being unable to fulfill the remainder of His purpose. The remainder of the 61st chapter of Isaiah speaks of the bridegroom, "I greatly rejoice in יהוה, my being exults in my Elohim. For He has put *garments of deliverance on me*, He has covered me with the robe of righteousness, as a bridegroom decks himself with ornaments, and as a bride adorns herself with her jewels. For as the earth brings forth its bud, as the garden causes the seed to shoot up, so the Master יהוה causes righteousness and praise to shoot up before all the nations!" (Isaiah 61: 10-11)

136

This verse speaks of deliverance as putting on garments of deliverance (garments of Yeshua). The context is Israel being delivered, but the message I receive ties into His Bride being delivered at the Groom's second coming.

With regard to, *"the acceptable day of YHVH,"* the Strong's Definition for the Hebrew word for "acceptable" is Strong's H7522 and only occurs twice when in reference to YHVH or *The LORD.* Those two Scripture passages are found in Isaiah 58:5 and Isaiah 61:2. The entire chapter 58 is speaking of Yom Kippur and it is this day that identifies *the Appointed Feast* destined as a day of Judgment by the Almighty.

Isaiah 58:1 states, "Cry aloud, do not spare. Lift up your voice like a ram's horn. Declare to My people their transgression, and the house of Ya'aqob their sins." We see from this first verse that Yom Kippur is the day of declaring the sins and wrongdoings on that day of the blowing of the ram's horn or shofar. It is also a day of fasting and of rest, whereby earthly pleasures are foregone in order to afflict the soul. Verse two states, "'Why have we fasted, and You have not seen? Why have we afflicted our beings, and You took no note?' "Look, in the day of your fasting you find pleasure, and drive on all your labourers."

The first four verses identify a time of fasting and then mentions in verse five, *the acceptable day to* יהוה, "Is it a fast that I have chosen, a day for a man to afflict his being? Is it to bow down his head like a bulrush, and to spread out sackcloth and ashes? Do you call this a fast, and an *acceptable day to* יהוה?" It is this day that is the *Appointed Feast* of the Creator for seeking forgiveness as this day is for all people, including Christians, in order to seek forgiveness as it is the Creator's *Mow'ed.* This day has not been "nailed to the cross," as is a common expression, and is still a highly important day whereby the Creator's judgments will take place on this Appointed Day in future years.

137

Hebrews chapter paints a beautiful picture on how Yahshua, being the High Priest, was the ultimate sin offering by the offering of Himself:

"For when, according to Torah, every command had been spoken by Mosheh to all the people, he took the blood of calves and goats, with water, and scarlet wool, and hyssop, and sprinkled both the book itself and all the people, saying, *This is the blood of the covenant which Elohim commanded you.*" And in the same way he sprinkled with blood both the Tent and all the vessels of the service. *And, according to the Torah, almost all is cleansed with blood, and without shedding of blood there is no forgiveness.* It was necessary, then, that the copies of the heavenly ones should be cleansed with these, but the heavenly ones themselves with better slaughter offerings than these. For Messiah has not entered into a Set-apart Place made by hand – figures of the true – but into the heaven itself, now to appear in the presence of Elohim on our behalf, not that He should offer Himself often, as the high priest enters into the Set-apart Place year by year with blood not his own. For if so, He would have had to suffer often, since the foundation of the world. *But now He has appeared once for all at the end of the ages to put away sin by the offering of Himself*" (Hebrews 9:19-26).

Traditionally, Yom Kippur, especially when associated with a Jubilee, was to be a time of liberty if His people who were in obedience. It is liberty that is still available for all people, whether Jew or Gentile especially for those who would respond to His call of Yeshua (Salvation). As we head into the unknown future, it will be Yahshua who will offer true liberty for those who place their trust in Him.

The Foundation of the 70 *weeks*

It is the Book of Daniel that is the key prophetic book in deciphering these latter days. The general understanding among those who study the end times is that Daniel's 70th *week* is a prophetic future seven years that will usher in chaos and great distress among the world's nations and peoples, a period of tribulation. It will be at the end of this terrifying final *week*, where the *King of Kings and Lord of Lords* will place His feet back on the Mount of Olives returning back to earth from heaven as King just recently defeating the Antichrist and the nations that were planning the destruction of Israel and her people along with those Christians who would not submit.

The focus in this chapter will be Daniel chapter 9, verses 24-27. Keep in mind that when you read these four verses, you are stepping back in time approximately 2,400 years ago! At the time of his revelation, the prophet Daniel was deep in prayer confessing his sins and the sins of his people, with a particular heavy heart concerning Jerusalem that laid in waste from its seize and destruction by Babylon. It was at this time that the Angel Gabriel made himself known to Daniel for the purpose to make him *"wise concerning understanding."* The Angel, Gabriel, then spoke to Daniel an amazing prophetic prophecy concerning the arrival of their Messiah in four amazing verses:

24"**Seventy weeks** are decreed for your people and for your set-apart city, to put an end to the transgression, and to seal up sins, and to cover crookedness and to bring in everlasting righteousness, and to seal up vision and prophet, and to anoint the Most Set-apart.

25"Know, then, and understand: from the going forth of the command to restore and build Yerushalayim until Messiah the Prince is **seven weeks** and **sixty-two weeks**. It shall be built again, with streets and a trench, but in times of affliction.

139

26"And *after the sixty-two weeks* Messiah shall be cut off and have naught. And the people of a coming prince shall destroy the city and the set-apart place. And the end of it is with a flood. And wastes are decreed, and fighting until the end.

27"**And he shall confirm a covenant with many** *for one week*. And in the middle of the week he shall put an end to slaughtering and meal offering. And on the wing of abominations he shall lay waste, even until the complete end and that which is decreed is poured out on the one who lays waste."

These four verses are an enigma and deep in mystery concerning the timing of the Messiah's first and second coming. We have approached the time spoken in Daniel 12:4 concerning the opening or unsealing of the books of understanding and knowledge. It is now possible, unlike any other time in history, to fully understand the mystery behind the 69 *weeks* and the final 70th *week* and that is what I plan to explain from this point forward.

It was the 69 *weeks* that was fulfilled by the Messiah's first coming almost 2,000 years ago. Verse 26 makes it clear that He would be cut off as was the case when He was crucified on the cross. Roughly 40 years later in 70 CE, Jerusalem was destroyed under Rome, thus fulfilling verse 26. I will cover verses 24 and 25 in the remainder of this chapter and will cover verse 27 within chapter eight of this book, when I reveal the event that partially fulfilled this prophecy.

In deciphering these few verses, there is a need to discuss the *weeks*. First of all, these weeks are not actual weeks as in 7 days per week, but rather prophetic weeks identifying seven 360-day cycles. The Hebrew word for the word week is shabuwa (Strong's H7620) and is a word that is defined as seven, or a period of seven days or years and *the Feast of Weeks*. The Feast of Weeks, interestingly enough is a period of 49 days that leads up to the Feast of Shavuot, which is the 50th day. Even within the definition of the word, shabuwa reveals a spiritual connection between the Shmitah cycles of 7 years to the Sabbath week of 7 days. The Feast of Weeks is a type of 50 years of jubilee that incorporates the Shmitah cycle of seven years. It is these 7 *weeks* that would be 7 sets of seven years or 49 years (7x7) in totality. And, much like the 50th day of Shavuot, these 49 years lead up to the "50th Year of Jubilee" that begins on the Feast of Yom Kippur according to Leviticus 25:6-8.

Cracking the Mystery of Daniel's 70th *week*!

Understanding and identifying the 69 *weeks* and the 70th *week* or the final seven years of man's rule is absolutely critical in comprehending when the Messiah's return might take place as foretold by the ancient prophets concerning His return.

It was Sir Isaac Newton (1642-1727 CE), one of the greatest mathematicians and scientist of all time who has been acknowledged for his discovery of calculus, the laws of motion, and the laws of gravity based upon the astronomical observations that he made. We find that he was equally passionate, if not more so, with regard to the study of Bible eschatology. It has been said that he dedicated half of his adult life to the study of the enigmatic prophecies contained in the Bible, writing more than one million words and notes on the Bible with a particular focus on the prophecies in the Book of Daniel and Revelation. Toward the end of his life, he would have remained frustrated at his inability to crack the mystery behind the book of Daniel. Upon his death in 1727 CE, those writings and commentaries would be placed in the form of a book and published and given the title, *Observations Upon the Prophecies of Daniel and the Apocalypse of St. John*. [1]

Much like Sir Issac Newton, thousands of scholars throughout the centuries have attempted to crack the mysteries and dates surrounding the 69th and 70th *week* found in Daniel chapter nine. Yet, according to Daniel 12:4, this understanding would be sealed or hidden until the time of the end when many would "diligently search and knowledge would increase."

Another such man, among many, who was able to shed some light on the 69th and 70th *week* prophecy was Sir Robert Anderson who lived from 1841 to 1918 in London, England. He worked in the Scotland Yard as a top investigator and was very detailed in analysis and thought. He wrote a book titled, *The Coming Prince*, where he methodically documented his analysis and knowledge in deciphering this prophecy.

Calculating the dates of the 69 *weeks* that is made up of the 7 *weeks* and the 62 *weeks* is not exactly straightforward and is the reason for the enigmatic nature behind these texts among others. A question I have regarding the division of the *weeks* is why the separation of the *weeks*? Why not just *"69 weeks?"* It is my understanding that this contributes to the enigmatic nature behind the text, but it is actually intentional as you will discover.

In calculating the years of this prophecy, there are two ways to do so that would result in two different answers. One method is by using the solar year of 365.24 days per year and the other involves calculating 360-day cycles.

Using the solar year as a frame of reference, calculating these weeks would result in 483 solar years. Here is the math...

- $(7 \times 7) + (62 \times 7) = (49) + (434) = 483$ SOLAR YEARS

Calculating the actual years is a bit more complex than just using the solar year. In his book, *The Coming Prince*, Mr. Robert Anderson defines the 360-day year that is in question and an important consideration in deciphering this prophecy. In the sixth chapter of his book, he writes:

"Daniel's prayer referred to seventy years fulfilled: the prophecy which came in answer to that prayer foretold a period of seven times seventy still to come. But here a question arises which never has received sufficient notice in the consideration of this subject. None will doubt that the era is a period of years; but of what kind of year is it composed? That the Jewish year was lunisolar appears to be reasonably certain. If tradition may be trusted, Abraham preserved in his family the year of 360 days, which he had known in his Chaldean home. The month dates of the flood (150 days being specified as the interval between the seventeenth day of the second month, and the same day of the seventh month) appear to show that this form of year was the earliest known to our race. Sir Isaac Newton states, that 'all nations, before the just length of the solar year was known, reckoned months by the course of the moon, and years by the return of winter and summer, spring and autumn; and in making calendars for their festivals, they reckoned thirty days to a lunar month, and twelve lunar months to a year, taking the nearest round numbers, whence came the division of the ecliptic into 360 degrees.' And in adopting this statement, Sir G. C. Lewis avers that "all credible testimony and all antecedent probability lead to the result that a solar year containing twelve lunar months, determined within certain limits of error, has been generally recognized by the nations adjoining the Mediterranean, from a remote antiquity." [2]

What Mr. Anderson did was to multiply the years x 360-day cycles in order to find the total amount of days. The 360-day cycle is the time frame used in prophetic dates within the Scriptures. As an example, the book of Revelation 11:3 and 12:6 describes 1,260 days or 42 months that would account for 30 days per months and 360 day/year (30x12). In addition,

Genesis 7 & 8 offer clues resulting in 30 days per month as this was the calendar system used in ancient times stretching from Israel, Babylonia, Assyria and Egypt. As a result of incorporating the 360-day cycles, the resulting prophetic calculations would be:

- 483 SOLAR YEARS X 360-DAY CYCLES OR = 173,880 DAYS
- 173,880 DAYS / 365.2422 DAYS/YR. = 476.0677 YEARS OR 476 YEARS & 25 DAYS

The result of these calculations show the corrected 476 prophetic solar years compared to 483 solar years, a mere difference of 7 years.

Another way of looking at this is (49 + 434) 360-day cycles or (17,640 days) + (156,240 days) = 173,880 days. Take notice of the **17,640** days as this will become extremely significant from this point forward!

So, instead of using the solar year of 483 years, Sir Robert Anderson shows why it is necessary to use the prophetic time of 476 years and 25 days for this prophecy. Now that we have the prophetic years, we now need to identify the edict that set this prophecy in motion. It was Sir Robert Anderson who identified the events that lead to the edict being given by Artaxerxes as recorded in Nehemiah chapter 2:1, "And it came to pass in the month of Nisan, in the twentieth year of King Artaxerxes,…" The Scripture indicates that it would have been the 20th year reign of Artaxerxes, the prince of Persia that would have been the time period of when this edict was given to Nehemiah in the first month of Nisan.

History identifies Artaxerxes Longimanus as that Persian King who reigned over that kingdom for 40 years from a period of time from 464 to 424 BCE. According to these dates, his 20th year reign would have taken place in 444 BCE or right around that time frame. Mr. Anderson documents this time as 445 BCE, while others such as the Jewish Encyclopedia

144

and other sources place this date at 444 BCE. The verse in question is verse 25,

"Know, then, and understand: from the going forth of the command to restore and build Yerushalayim until Messiah the Prince is seven weeks and sixty-two weeks"

Thus, from the time of the edict from Artaxerxes Longimanus, for the purpose of rebuilding and restoring Jerusalem until *"Messiah the Prince,"* is simply a matter of subtraction. Since there is no actual zero between the common era, we need to subtract 1 from the equation.[3]

- (445-476) -1 = -32 OR 32 CE

Sir Robert Anderson calculated the date, 32 CE. It was 32 CE in the month of Nisan that many Pastors identify the time when Yahshua was entering Jerusalem, just before Passover. It was in Jerusalem where the people began to sing, *"Hoshiana! Blessed is he..."* It would have been this prophetic event of Yahshua entering Jerusalem that would have qualified for the fulfillment of the 69 *weeks*. Here is the scriptural reference for this:

"On the next day a great crowd who had come to the festival, when they heard that יהושע was coming to Yerushalayim, took the branches of palm trees and went out to meet Him, and were crying out, *"Hoshia-na! Blessed is He who is coming in the Name of יהוה, the Sovereign of Yisra'ĕl!"* And יהושע, having found a young donkey, sat on it, as it has been written: *"Do not fear, daughter of Tsiyon, see, your Sovereign is coming, sitting on the colt of a donkey."* (John 12:12-15)

It would have been the prophecy from Zechariah 9:9 that would have been the fulfillment at that moment further revealing Yahshua as the one spoken by the prophets.

"Rejoice greatly, O daughter of Tsiyon! Shout, O daughter of Yerushalayim! See, your Sovereign is coming to you, He is righteous and endowed with deliverance, humble and riding on a donkey, a colt, the foal of a donkey."

On a side note, the Hebrew word for Hossana is Hoshiana (Strong's H3467) and means to be saved or delivered as in being saved from within a battle. It is a desperate cry for help, a last ditch effort to be saved from the only one who can save. The root word for this definition is Yasha and is a verb denoting action as in to be liberated, to be saved, to be deliver, and to give victory and is very close to his Messianic name of Yeshua that means salvation. The other part of the word is na' (Strong's H4994) and is used as a desperate prayer. It is this word, Yasha na', that describes Yahshua/Yeshua as being the only one that can save. It will be at the end of this age when that desperate cry, Hoshia-na, will once again be heard from the Jewish People from around the world at their greatest hour of need.

The common belief within Christianity is that Yahshua was crucified between 28 CE to 34 CE. There are many theories and opinions as to these dates, but there is only one correct answer. It is of the opinion of Sir Robert Anderson that this date was the year 32 CE. If this were the case, then the 7 plus 62 week prophecy would fit perfectly from 445 BCE to 32 CE.

However, I believe for different reasons that this date might be off a year or two. If the edict given was closer to 444 BCE as stated in the Jewish Encyclopedia, then this date would have been 33 CE, and if off by another year, then this date would have been 34 CE. According to Torah Calendar, this would have been the year that Yahshua was crucified, since that Passover would have fallen on a Wednesday, thus qualifying for the full 3 days and 3 nights and His resurrection on the first of the week between sunset Saturday night and sunrise Sunday morning. In any event, Yahshua fulfilled this prophecy and He is the Messiah spoken of by the prophet Daniel.

What is significant and worth noting is that this 360-day cycle was used in his calculations and resulted in the fulfillment of the 69 week prophecy as noted. And, it is this 360-day cycle that is in play today.

The "360-day cycle" can be observed today, if you know what to look for. This cycle creates certain patterns that can be observed and is the reason why I strongly believe it to be divinely orchestrated by the Creator. It is this 360-day cycle that points to Daniel's 7 *week* as a double prophetic fulfillment of Bible prophecy and, it is this 7 *weeks* or 49 years, that once completed will usher us into the 70th *week* or final 7 years according to Daniel chapter nine. These are exciting times in which we live, as we are that last generation to witness Bible prophecy coming to pass before our very eyes.

I really want to nail this point down before I move forward. As stated, this 360-day cycle is so compelling and profound that the only logical conclusion is that this 360-day cycle is divinely orchestrated! It is set apart from any other time or even any other calendar system available today. It does not incorporate intercalation, of adding an additional month roughly every two to three years in order to balance the lunar months to the solar year and it is for this reason that this 360-day cycle is completely independent from the solar year. If we are to have any hope in understanding the timing of these latter day prophecies, then we need to get in tune with the Creator's frequency! *The 360-day cycle is His Frequency!*

The *Creator's Jubilee* and the Connection to Yom Kippur 2015

I have briefly mentioned the jubilee cycle in chapter two of this book and elsewhere and will now be going into greater depth. To summarize, the solar jubilee is made up of 50 solar years being made up of 365.24 days per year. The other jubilee that I have been able to identify is based upon the Creator's 360-day cycle and is what I have termed as the *"Creator's Jubilee."*

As discussed in chapter two, the solar and *Creator's Jubilee* can be observed especially in relation to June 7th 1967, when the spiritual dominion manifested into the physical with Jerusalem being taken back by force by the Israeli Army, the day after *The Six Day War*. This victory over Jerusalem, once again, began the countdown timer of the prophetic clock as it had worked just prior to the death of the Messiah almost 2,000 years ago. It would have been that period of time just after the death of Yahshua that this prophetic clock would have ceased right in line with the prophecy, *"And after the sixty-two weeks Messiah shall be cut off and have naught."*

This analogy of the prophetic clock is intimately tied to Jerusalem and the Daniel seven *week* prophecies. As you will discover, the Shmitah, Jerusalem and *the Creator's Jubilee* are all tied together. But, before I get into this special jubilee, I need to address that solar jubilee once more.

As noted in Leviticus 25: 8-10, "'And you shall count seven Sabbaths of years for yourself, seven times seven years. And the time of the seven Sabbaths of years shall be to you forty-nine years. 'You shall then sound a ram's horn to pass through on the tenth day of the seventh month, on the Day of Atonement cause a ram's horn to pass through all your land. 'And you shall set the fiftieth year apart, and proclaim release throughout all the land to all its inhabitants, it is a Jubilee for you. And each of you shall return to his possession, and each of you return to his clan."

To recap, what we find in these verses is the mentioning of the Shmitah year (Sabbath of years) and how seven Shmitah years becomes *"forty-nine*

148

years." It is at that point in the seventh month and the 10th day (Yom Kippur), that the shofar is blown proclaiming the jubilee, which is the beginning of the 50th Year of Jubilee. This 50th Year of Jubilee would begin on Yom Kippur and would end the following eve of Yom Kippur, 359 days later. I realize that I am being redundant, but I really want you to grasp the jubilee cycles as they are key to understanding the times in which we live. Please note that one cannot separate the Shmitahs from the jubilee as they are intimately tied together. This is why the Shmitah cycle is such a big deal and adds to the confirmation of what is written in this book.

As mentioned, there is the more common solar jubilee cycle that can be observed throughout history and that has been identified on the key years of 1917, 1967 and 2017. What I am going to discuss now is a more in depth look into *the Creator's Jubilee.* This is a special, set apart jubilee cycle that still meets the definition of the jubilee in Leviticus 25:8-11. It is this jubilee that is made up of the Creator's set apart 360-day cycles that is much different from the typical solar year jubilee.

Through my research, I have been able to pick up on certain patterns through this 360-day cycle especially as it pertains to Jerusalem. If I were to pick out a line from the 25th verse of Daniel chapter nine, it would read as follows, *"...to restore and build Yerushalayim until Messiah the Prince is seven week."* My focus here will be on this section of Scripture. If I were to rephrase this Scripture in my own words, it might read: "With the restoring of Jerusalem on June 7th, 1967 into the hands of the Jewish people, until the Messiah Yahshua is 49 years (seven *'weeks'*)."

This is a bit of a stretch, but I want you to visualize the possibility of a double prophetic fulfillment of Daniel's Seven *weeks* that had it's beginning exactly on June 7, 1967.

What I would like to do now is to identify these 360-day cycles. Using Leviticus 25:8-11 as our standard, I have been able to observe forty nine

149

360-day cycles beginning on June 7, 1967. Likewise, these same cycles can be divided by seven producing seven sets of 2,520 days. See the following chart, "Creator's Jubilee."

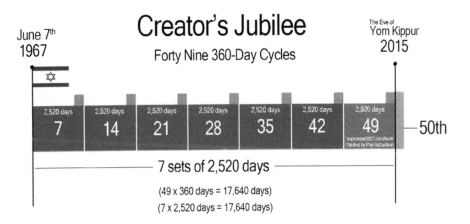

You will notice that these 7 weeks of years (7 x 2,520 days) or (49 x 360-day cycles) would equal 17,640 days and would be the exact amount of days of the *Daniel 7 weeks* of years as identified by Sir Robert Anderson. With the starting date of June 7, 1967 as being the re-unification date of Jerusalem and counting out 7 sets of weeks or 7 sets of 2,520 days (17,640 days), we come out to a future date of September 23, 2015 that being the eve of Yom Kippur . In order to check the accuracy of this date, all that would need to be done is to add this information to *timeanddate.com* and the results would look like so.

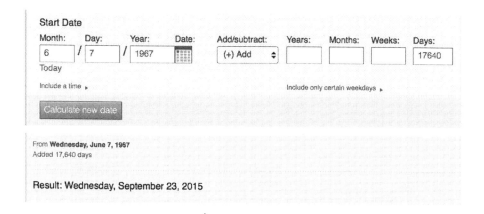

Again, the possible combinations are as follows:

- 49 YEARS X 360 DAY CYCLES = 17,640 DAYS
- 7 YEARS X 2,520 DAYS/ YEAR = 17,640 DAYS
- SEVEN WEEKS = 7 X 2,520 = 17,640 DAYS

Dividing these days by the solar years would result in the following: 17,640 days / 365.2422 = 48.2967 days or 48 years & 108 days.

Placing 48 years and 108 days into *timeanddate.com* would result in September 23rd, 2015 as well.

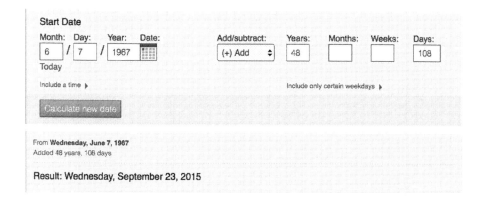

151

What about the Creator's calendar? What Hebraic day on His calendar would this date fall on? All that would be needed at this point would be to go to Torah Calendar and select 2015 and the 7th month. The result will take you to the month of Tishri in 2015. As you will notice, September 23, 2015 will fall on the eve of Yom Kippur, being the 9th day of the 7th month. See the following image from *Torah Calendar*.

3rd Day	4th Day	5th Day	6th Day	Sabbath
Yom Shli-shi	Yom Re-vi-i	Yom Ham-i-shi	Yom Shi-shi	Sha-bat
Monday sunset until Tuesday sunset	Tuesday sunset until Wednesday sunset	Wednesday sunset until Thursday sunset	Thursday sunset until Friday sunset	Friday sunset until Saturday sunset
Rosh Chodesh First Visible Crescent Moon seen at sunset on 15 Sep	**1** Yom Teruah Day of Trumpets Rosh Hashanah Civil New Year Rosh Hashanah 15 Sep 2015 C.E. sunset to 16 Sep 2015 C.E. sunset Day: 2,191,466	**2** Yamim Noraim Days of Awe 16 Sep 2015 C.E. sunset to 17 Sep 2015 C.E. sunset Day: 2,191,467	**3** Yamim Noraim Days of Awe 17 Sep 2015 C.E. sunset to 18 Sep 2015 C.E. sunset Day: 2,191,468	**4** Yamim Noraim Days of Awe Shabbat Shuvah Va-Yelech 18 Sep 2015 C.E. sunset to 19 Sep 2015 C.E. sunset Day: 2,191,469
7 Yamim Noraim Days of Awe 21 Sep 2015 C.E. sunset to 22 Sep 2015 C.E. sunset Day: 2,191,472	**8** Yamim Noraim Days of Awe Fall Equinox 23 Sep, 08h:21m UT 22 Sep sunset to 23 Sep sunset Day: 2,191,473	**9** Yamim Noraim Days of Awe 23 Sep 2015 C.E. sunset to 24 Sep 2015 C.E. sunset Day: 2,191,474	**10** Yom Kippur Day of Atonement Yamim Noraim Days of Awe Yom Kippur 24 Sep 2015 C.E. sunset to 25 Sep 2015 C.E. sunset Day: 2,191,475	**11** Ha 'azinu 25 Sep 2015 C.E. sunset to 26 Sep 2015 C.E. sunset Day: 2,191,476

Notice where September 23, 2015 falls. This, again, is the exact 7 *weeks* of Daniel's 7 *week* prophecy and meets the definition of Leviticus 25:8-11, that describes seven sets of *Sabbath years* that would be 49 completed years. It would be at the completion of the 49 years and at the beginning of the 50th year that the shofar would be blown announcing *the 50th Year of Jubilee* within the 7th lunar month.

This is absolutely profound! Please note that the (forty-nine) 360-day cycles are 49 prophetic years and do not need to be solar years to qualify.

Isn't our Creator, YHVH, incredible! This shows His orderly and precise nature as the Creator and points to His *Appointed Feast of* Yom Kippur.

The Double Prophetic Fulfillment of Daniel's 7 weeks

Ladies and Gentlemen, what began on June 7, 1967 and that will conclude on the eve of Yom Kippur 2015 is a Double Prophetic Fulfillment of Daniel's Seven weeks or 49 prophetic years. What becomes clear is that this Day of Atonement (Yom Kippur) on September 24, 2015 will qualify as Daniel's 70th week prophecy or the remaining final 7 years of 360-days (2,520 days).

But, as I have discovered, this full 2,520 days (70th *week*), will be shortened by one 360-day cycle leaving a balance of 2,160 days or 6 full prophetic "days" of the week (6 x 360-day cycles). This will become much more clear to you as I discuss this in more detail on why this is the case in the 8th and 9th chapter of this book. For now, please see the following graph that highlights what we have discussed thus far.

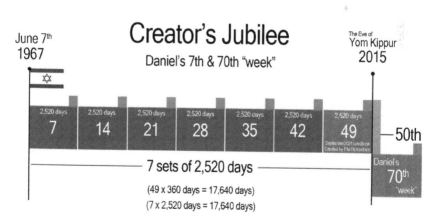

It is this *Creator's Jubilee* that would be the connection to the eve of Yom Kippur 2015.

In order to be as accurate as possible, September 24, 2015 falls on Yom Kippur and it is Yom Kippur that officially begins *the 50th Year of Jubilee* with the sounding of the shofar. So, in reality, *the Creator's full 50 Years of Jubilee* would be a period of time from June 7, 1967 to the eve of Yom Kippur 2016.

Verse 26 of Daniel chapter nine indicates that Messiah would be cut off at the end of the 69 *weeks* and this is what happened in 32 to 34 CE. When He was cut off, the prophetic time clock stopped and Bible prophecy was placed on hold until the turn of the 20th century when the Jewish people would begin to return to their homeland and, as stated, this prophetic time clock would start ticking on June 7th, 1967.

The Creator gives warnings before He judges. I believe one of these warnings has to do with timing. If we know His timing, then we can make preparations and our focus and mission would have greater purpose. If we are not in tune with his frequency, then we are going to miss *His Appointed Times*. This is what I believe that *the Creator's Jubilee is* all about. It is about warning, timing and purpose. And the purpose of the dual prophetic fulfillment of the *Creator's Jubilee* would be to point to the 70th *week* or the final 7 years of man's rule on earth otherwise known as the tribulation.

The other verse that plays into the final 70th *week* would be verse 27, "And he shall confirm a covenant with many for one week. And in the middle of the week he shall put an end to slaughtering and meal offering. And on the wing of abominations he shall lay waste, even until the complete end and that which is decreed is poured out on the one who lays waste."

There are many theories within Christianity on just this verse alone. For instance, who is "he" that confirms a covenant with the many? Could the "he" be referring to Yahshua when He was cut off in the middle of the week or could it be a type of dual prophecy of the two? I have my own

154

theory regarding this verse and I believe there is a dual prophecy at work here. I believe that this was partially fulfilled last year as far as the confirming a covenant with the many, but not for the seven years, which completes the prophecy. I discuss this in the 8th chapter of this book; however, I believe that this seven-year covenant that did not happen last year, may happen this year between the eves of Yom Teruah to Yom Kippur of 2015. This up and coming covenant will be between Israel and the Palestinians and/or other Arab countries that will involve the United Nations and/or America. This may be proven true or untrue by the end of September. Keep an eye on what transpires this September!

I have included a visual representation of these two jubilees, one being the common solar jubilee and the hidden *Creator's Jubilee* along with the 70th *week* of Daniel. Please see the image, "The Two Jubilees."

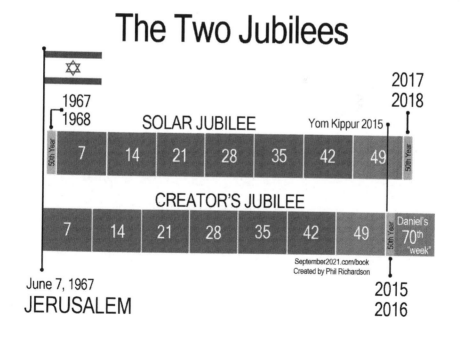

Take notice that the 50th year of the *Creator's Jubilee* falls on Yom Kippur 2015 and ends Yom Kippur 2016, while the 50th year of the more common solar jubilee begins Yom Kippur 2017 and finishes Yom Kippur 2018. The beginning of the 50th Year of the solar jubilee also lines up with a great sign that will have take place just 10 days earlier on Yom Teruah 2017. It is in chapter seven, where I go over what I have coined as *the Mid-Tribulation Sign*. This is the Great Sign seen in the heavens that was identified by John the Revelator and that was last seen by man 3,865 years ago. This knowledge would not have been possible without computers and the star gazing software made available in just the past eight years or so.

I have included a conceptual graph, "Daniel's final 70th week." See below!

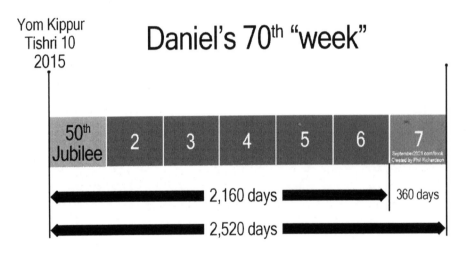

This final 70th *week* will have it's beginning exactly on Yom Kippur 2015 that coincides with the beginning of the 50th Year of the *Creator's Jubilee* as shown. I have only accounted for 6 years and not the logical 7 years of Daniel's 70th *week*. So, instead of adding the 2,520 days (7 years x 360 days/year), I am only adding 2,160 days (6 years x 360 day cycles), a difference of one 360-day cycle.

There is a very good reason for this difference of one 360-day cycle as I will be covering this more in depth in the 8th chapter where you will be introduced to the Metonic lunar cycle, the 86 moons verses 87 moons and a certain covenant that was made with 15 powerful nations.

It is my belief that the 6,000th year since creation will begin on Tishri 1 of the Jewish Civil Calendar, that being Rosh Hashanah and/or Yom Teruah 2015. This is also part of the reason that the Almighty has allowed us to understand and to identify the patterns of his jubilee, *the Creator's Jubilee,* to announce the beginning of the Seventh Millennium for it is the belief of many prophecy experts that the beginning of Daniel's 70th *week* would usher in the 7th millennium and this is what we indeed find with the only exception of the beginning of the 7th millennium happening one 360-day cycle past the start of Daniel's 70th week (explained in detail in the final chapter of this book). Interestingly enough, one of the idioms associated with Yom Teruah is the *"Birthday of the World"* or *"Ha Yom Harat Olam"* in Hebrew. It is this belief among the Jewish people that the Creator created the world on the "First of Tishri" translated from the Hebrew, Aqleph b' Tishri, as "In the Beginning" the opening words in Genesis 1:1, "In the beginning Elohim created the heavens and the earth."

As you might be noticing, I am slowly adding to these graphs so that I might communicate to you as effective as possible because of the depth of these topics and the profound implications behind them.

I will continue this into the following chapter as I will tie the Lunar Moon Tetrads into this graph as well as you will discover the concrete patterns of the Creator as these *Blood Moon Tetrads* represent "distinguished marks" that highlight His jubilee with the "Super Blood Moon" appearing for the whole world to see on the eve of Tabernacles 2015.

The Pope, the U.S. and the UN

I couldn't help but to comment with regard to the planned visit by Pope Francis (Petrus Romanus) to the United States on none other than Yom Kippur 2015. Currently, he is planning to speak to both houses of the U.S. Congress on that day, unprecedented, as he will be the first Pope ever to address the U.S. Congress. If that were not unprecedented enough, he will on the following day, address the World Governing Body of Global Government, known as the United Nations.

It was House Speaker John Boehner (R-Ohio), himself a Catholic, who made the announcement:

"That day (September 24, 2015), His Holiness will be the first pope in our history to address a joint session of Congress," Boehner said at his weekly news conference. "We're humbled that the Holy Father has accepted our invitation and certainly look forward to receiving his message on behalf of the American people." [4]

Even President Obama is looking forward to this meeting as he praised Pope Francis Thursday at the National Prayer Breakfast. "Like so many people around the world, I've been touched by his call to relieve suffering and to show justice and mercy and compassion to the most vulnerable," Obama said. "He challenges us to press on in what he calls our 'march of living hope.' And like millions of Americans, I am very much looking forward to welcoming Pope Francis to the United States later this year." [5]

Of course this is a stark contrast to his cold shoulder Israeli Prime Minister Benjamin Netanyahu received from President Obama when Mr. Netanyahu addressed both houses of Congress on March 3, 2015. It is interesting to see both power players of the world (The Vatican and the U.S.) embrace each other, yet shun Israel.

Keep an eye on Pope Francis who will be at the UN helping to push forward the *Sustainable Development Agenda* that will take place from September 25th to 27th in 2015. This new Sustainable Agenda will focus on climate change and more specifically on economics, agriculture, education and gender equality. The result of this agenda may lead to the excuse to micromanage virtually every aspect of our lives for the "good of the planet." I have noticed that the Vatican is a big supporter of pushing forward climate change legislation. As a matter of fact, the head of the UN, the Secretary-General, meet with Pope Francis at the Vatican on April 28, 2014 to discuss this goal and he (the Secretary-General) was in agreement that, "science and religion are not at odds on climate change." [67] Something to keep an eye on!

Yes, Bible prophecy is indeed taking place before our very eyes. As I have documented and continue to document, it will be the Fall Feast Days of Yom Teruah, Yom Kippur and Tabernacles that are absolutely relevant to the prophetic fulfillment of Bible prophecy in these latter days before the return of the Messiah. Take note on what key events happen on the major Fall Feast days or on their eve in the coming years.

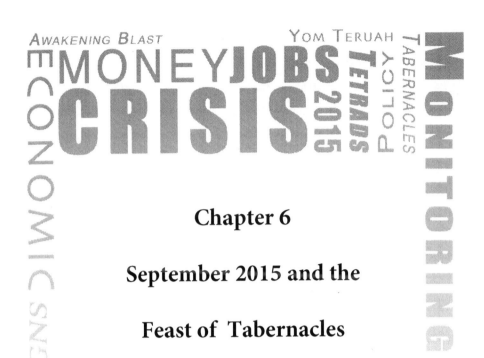

Chapter 6

September 2015 and the

Feast of Tabernacles

Up till now, I have discussed the connections to the Fall Feast Days of the eve of Yom Teruah, having the connection to the Shmitah Release Day of Elul 29, 2015, and of the connection to the eve of Yom Kippur being the final day of Daniel's 49 prophetic years or what I call the Creator's Jubilee. Now I am going to discuss the connection to the eve of Tabernacles 2015. All three of these connections is what I refer to as the *Three Pillar Foundation.*

A Deeper look into Tabernacles

The scriptural reference for the Feast of Tabernacles is found in Leviticus 23:39-43,

" 'On the fifteenth day of the seventh month, when you gather in the fruit of the land, observe the festival of יהוה for seven days. On the first day is a rest, and on the eighth day a rest. 'And you shall take for yourselves on the first day the fruit of good trees, branches of palm trees, twigs of leafy trees, and willows of the stream, and shall rejoice before יהוה your Elohim for seven days. 'And you shall observe it as a festival to יהוה for seven days in the year – a law forever in your generations. Observe it in the seventh month. 'Dwell in booths for seven days; all who are native Yisra'ĕlites dwell in booths, so that your generations know that I made the children of Yisra'ĕl dwell in booths when I brought them out of the land of Mitsrayim. I am יהוה your Elohim.' "

From the Scriptures above, the Feast of Tabernacles falls on the 15th day of Tishri, just 5 days after Yom Kippur and 15 days after Yom Teruah. There are two high Sabbaths that are required to be observed, the first and the eighth would be high Sabbath days, with the eighth day being the known as *The Last Great Day*. We also see that the Feast of Tabernacles is to be observed into the 7th millennium and all future generations. We see this recorded in Zechariah,

"And it shall be *that all who are left from all the gentiles* which came up against Yerushalayim, shall go up from year to year to bow themselves to the Sovereign, יהוה of hosts, *and to observe the Festival of Booths*. And it shall be, that if anyone of the clans of the earth does not come up to Yerushalayim to bow himself to the Sovereign, יהוה of hosts, on them there is to be no rain. And if the clan of Egypt does not come up and enter in, then there is no rain. *On them is the plague with which יהוה plagues the gentiles who do not come up to observe the Festival of Booths.* This is the punishment of Egypt and the punishment of all the gentiles that do not come up to observe the Festival of Booths" (Zechariah 14:17-19)

161

This passage of Zechariah is in reference to the 7th millennial reign when Yahshua reigns as King within Jerusalem over all the surviving governments of the world. It will be the Messiah that will cause and allow plagues on all gentile nations who do not obey the Festival of Tabernacles. So much for the idea that the feasts are just for the Jews.

Another dimension we see of this feast was that the Israelites were to live in temporary structures known as booths so that all future generations would know that the Creator brought them out of Egypt. Even to this day, those Jews who observe this feast live in Booths for seven days. This was and still is a time when the Creator is honored with the fruit of the fall harvest of grapes and other harvests. It is a reflection of his supplication for the Israelites once they entered Sinai. In addition, this final feast is still the most joyous of the feast and is celebrated with lively singing, dancing and feasting for seven days. A great time of celebration, dancing and joy.

The Significance of Tabernacles in Our Time

According to Messianic Rabbi Johnathan Cahn, "The rabbis saw Tishri and the high holy days of autumn as focusing on the kingship of God, His rule, His power, His sovereignty, and His dominion. The sounding of the shofar during the Feast of Trumpets was, among other things, the proclaiming of the Lord as King and Sovereign over the world, over the nation, and over the lives of His people." [1] We see that this is a common theme among the Jewish Rabbis today, that the Almighty will reign with man, proclaiming Kingship over all people. The common view within Christianity is that it will be Yahshua who will be proclaimed *Lord and King* over the Sovereigns of the world; whereas, the ancient Scriptures indicate that it will be YHVH that will rule on earth. As stated, once you realize that Yahshua is the *Word of YHVH*, then you start to realize that the ancient prophecies are speaking of Him.

162

Right now, Yahshua has not been pronounced King, but is the Mashiach (Messiah) Elect, meaning that He will receive his crown as King on the same day He marries his Bride as is one of the idioms associated with Yom Teruah. Thus, in order for the Messiah or Prince to be pronounced King, He first needs to marry His Bride and in order to marry His Bride, His Father must send his son to *snatch* his bride at the Father's *Appointed Feast*!

These future events are clearly shadow pictures of good things to come. It is my belief, that in some future Tabernacles, the Great Wedding Feast will take place after the Bridegroom and Prince becomes a Husband and King in one day. This Great Wedding Feast will be a Feast of all Feasts for all of those who have been invited by the Father. It will be on some future Yom Teruah that the Messiah marries His Bride where they will be proclaimed King and Queen.

The timing of this future event is not completely clear to me, but here is an interesting perspective of this future Tabernacles as quoted from *sweetmanna.org,* "Those that think the wedding supper of the Lamb will be when Messiah returns to earth with His bride, I believe could be mistaken, because when Messiah and His wife return to earth with the armies of heaven it will be for the purposes of judgment. With His second coming, He is not seen as a joyous bridegroom coming for His bride with the merry making of His male companions, but rather as a mighty warrior. He is seen as *The King of Kings and the Lord of Lords* riding on a white horse with a rod of iron to rule the nations. There will be a supper, but of another kind." [2]

So, it is understood that the shadow picture of the seven feast days of Tabernacles is the reflection of the seven days of *the Great Wedding Feast* made available to those who but their faith and trust in Yahshua. It is this seventh Feast of Tabernacles that is a culmination of the holy day season that begins with the month of Elul in preparation of the seventh month of

Tishri, a time of self examination and repentance with the reminder from the sound of the shofar, a day of Teruah and the warning blasts. Here are these shadow pictures of these Fall Feast days starting in the month of Elul listed from from *hope-in-israel.org,* [3]

- MONTH OF ELUL -- 30 DAYS -- WARNING TO EXAMINE OURSELVES AND COME TO DEEPER REPENTANCE
- ROSH HASHANAH -- DAY OF BLOWING -- PICTURES FINAL WARNINGS OF GOD SYMBOLIZED BY TRUMPETS OF REVELATION, CALL TO REPENTANCE
- DAYS OF AWE -- FINAL WARNINGS TO PREPARE TO MEET THE MESSIAH
- YOM KIPPUR -- MESSIAH RETURNS, AND JUDGES THE WORLD
- FEAST OF SUKKOT -- SEVEN DAYS OF JOYOUS EXUBERANCE AND FEASTING -- SYMBOLIZING MILLENNIAL KINGDOM OF MESSIAH, AND "WEDDING FEAST" OF MARRIAGE AND LAMB
- HOSHANA RABBAH -- LAST GREAT DAY OF SUKKOT -- SYMBOLIZES "GREAT WHITE THRONE JUDGMENT, WHEN ALL WHO EVER LIVED RECEIVE OPPORTUNITY FOR SALVATION

The Blood Moons

When I think of Tabernacles, I can't but help make a connection to Genesis 1:14,

"And Elohim said, "Let lights come to be in the expanse of the heavens to separate the day from the night, and let them be for signs and appointed times, and for days and years,"

As discussed, the feast days are the Appointed Times of the Hebrew word for Mow'ed. The English translators translated it as seasons, yet this is a poor translation as explained in the first chapter of this book. The Hebrew word for signs is Owth and part of the definition is as a *distinguished mark* as in a reference point in time and space. It is this one Scripture that identifies the calendar system we are to use that should be based upon the celestial movement of the stars, sun and the moon with the priority given to the moon cycle.

All of the seven feasts, with the exception of Shavuot, First Fruits and Yom Kippur, are directly linked to either lunar or solar activity and to the *"Signs"* that the moon and the sun exhibit based on their celestial relationship to one another. In order to bring clarity to this verse and to make my point, when I read Genesis 1:14, I read and interpreted it in my mind as follows:

"And Elohim said, "Let lights come to be in the expanse of the heavens from the stars and constellations and from the sun and the moon, that separate the day from the night, and let the constellations, the sun and the moon, be for signs, solar and lunar eclipses, distinguished marks, *Appointed Feasts*, and for days and years." (Phil's Version)

Of the feasts, the Feast of Yom Teruah is the only feast that is directly associated with solar eclipses and the sighting of the crescent moon that may take up to two days (Tishri 1 & 2) for its sighting and thus is known as the feast where *"No Man Knows The Day or The Hour,"* still said by Rabbis in Israel today, an obvious idiom used by Yahshua in describing this feast and the connection to the Ancient Jewish Wedding that I discussed in the first chapter of this book.

The Feast of Passover and Unleavened Bread are directly linked to the lunar moon cycle falling on Nisan 14 and Nisan 15, respectively, as well as the Feast of Tabernacles falling on Tishri 15. It is the middle of the lunar month when the moon is considered full and the beginning of the lunar month when it is said to be dark or new. For simplicity reasons, I will be using Passover to describe the lunar eclipse cycles that we have been observing.

Thus, it is only the Feast of Passover in the spring and the Feast of Tabernacles in the fall that highlight the full lunar moon cycles as distinguished marks and *Appointed Feasts* in reference to time and space and the Creator's prophetic time clock.

This brings me to discuss the *"Tetrad Blood Moon"* that we are in the midst of. So, what are these so called *Tetrad Blood Moons?* Before I answer this, I need to back up and identify these Tetrads since the time of Yahshua, when He was on this earth.

A blood moon is another way of describing a total lunar eclipse of the moon. The term *Blood Moon* is given as its description because of its red-like appearance when the moon is within the full umbra of the earths shadow known as a total lunar eclipse. According to the lunar eclipse NASA website, lunar eclipses are mostly identified as either Penumbra, Partial or Total (Umbra). The penumbra describes an eclipse where the moon falls on the outer shadow of the earth, while the partial falls on the partly shaded area beyond the umbra. It is the umbra that is given special attention as it is the eclipse of the moon that falls within the dark, central part of the earth's shadow and it is the umbra where the longer wavelengths from the sun's light (red and orange) refract on the moon giving the moon its deep red appearance as being like blood, and so the term *Blood Moon.*

Moon Appears as Blood in Total Eclipse
Earth's Umbra & Penubra Shadows

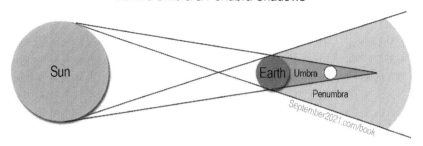

There are a few references within the Bible to these *Blood Moons*. One such reference is Joel 2:31-32 that reads, "The sun is turned into darkness, and the moon into blood, before the coming of the great and awesome day of יהוה. "And it shall be that everyone who calls on the Name of יהוה shall be delivered."

It is my understanding that the description of these blood moon in Joel will happen when the earth's atmosphere is scorched and may or may not be in reference to this final lunar event of the tetrad. The reason for this is that, the sun is turned into darkness. This up and coming Yom Teruah will be a partial eclipse of the sun, but will only be seen in Antarctica, and not seen by close to 99.9% of the world's population. I believe this prophecy in Joel refers to a time when the sun and moon appear as described simultaneously and is not necessarily a reference to September 2015. For the sake of simplicity, I will continue to refer to the lunar eclipses as blood moons, but just keep in mind the distinction of the blood moon in Joel 2:31.

The "Tetrad Blood Moons"

Up till now, I have described the lunar eclipses, but not the tetrads. The tetrads are rarer and are made up of four consecutive total lunar eclipses, in which the moon moves within the earth's umbra or earth's complete shadow. This event is so rare that it has only happened 171 times in the past 6,000 years. Generally speaking, these tetrads occur near the spring and in the fall in back to back years.

2014 to 2015
"Hebraic Tetrad"

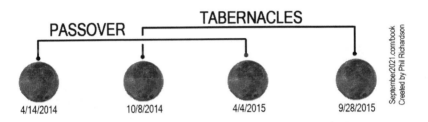

What is even rarer and much more significant is when these tetrads fall in the month of Nisan and the month of Tishri on the eve, or day of Passover and Tabernacles back to back for two years in a row. This is a very rare event and has been documented to have happened only three times in the past 100 years. As a matter of fact, it is so rare that we are now in the midst of the Ninth *Hebraic Tetrad* since the birth of Yahshua. The *Hebraic Tetrad* we are now experiencing happened on Passover 2014 (4/4/14), Tabernacles 2014 (10/8/14), Passover 2015 (4/4/15) and will conclude on Tabernacles 2015 (9/28/15) or more exactly on the eve of Tabernacles 2015. This final *Blood Moon* of the series will be a super moon meaning that the moon will be at its closest point to earth in its elliptical orbit around the earth and is the reason it has been given the name *"Super Blood Moon."* It will be this final lunar moon of the series that will be seen by a vast majority of the world including Israel. I have included a snap shot of this final blood moon event from the *Torah Calendar Google Earth Eclipse Viewer.*

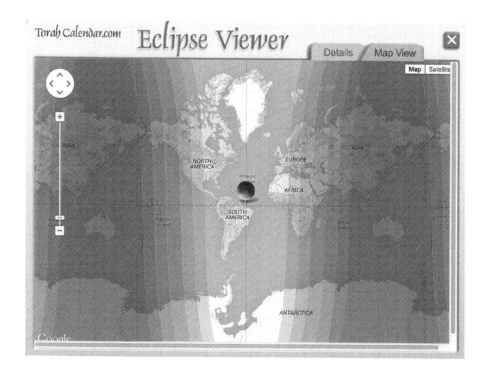

You will notice that a majority of the world will experience this final blood moon as far west as Alaska to as far east as central China representing the majority of the world's population and all of the key nations that will play a major role in fulfilling Bible prophecy inclusive of the United States, Israel, the Arab countries, China and Russia.

Torah Calendar has some good reference material when it comes to these *Blood Moon Tetrads*. One of them is a pdf file they produced titled, *Four-BloodMoons.pdf*, and subtitled as *Total Lunar Eclipse Tetrad 171 and Civil Year 6,000*. This pdf is detailed with regard to all of the lunar Tetrads since creation until the year 7,000 and contains 16,875 lunar eclipses in total for that period of time.

Torah Calendar goes as far as to actually identify and number the 2014 to 2015 tetrad as being tetrad # 171 since creation, as the title suggest, and it is this tetrad #171 that may represent both Judgment and Liberty, whereas the last two *Hebraic Tetrads* represented Liberty with the return of the land to the Jewish people. According to the *FourBloodMoons.pdf*, "These 9 lunar tetrads occurred in the years: 162-163 C.E., 795-796 C.E., 842-843-C.E., 860-861 C.E., 1428- 1429 C.E., 1475-1476 C.E., 1493-1494 C.E., 1949-1950 C.E. and 2014-2015 C.E., which is Lunar Tetrad 171."

To simplify, I will identify the last four Hebraic Tetrads and show you their connection to the Jewish people. As confirmed by NASA, the lunar tetrad that fell on the Feasts of Passover and Tabernacles, back to back, took place in 1493/94 CE. It would have been just prior to this time that the Jewish people would have been under extreme persecution as a result of being exiled from Spain based upon the decree from Ferdinand and Isabella.[4] It was this decree that forced hundreds of thousands of Jews to flee to the four corners of the earth with tens of thousands losing their lives. It was this shameful act, under the authority of the Roman Catholic Church via the Spanish Inquisition and the governmental authority of Spain, that caused this atrocity and not Christianity as is so widely publicized.

From the 1493/94 Hebraic Tetrad, there would be a separation of over 450 years until the next Hebraic Tetrad that would occur in 1949/50. It was during this time, when Israel was reborn as a nation on May 14, 1948 on the eve of Shavuot fulfilling the prophecy of the nation Israel being reborn in one day according to Isaiah 66:8. So, we have seen thus far, the Hebraic Tetrad highlighting the scattering and re-gathering of the Jewish People with the focus on the actual land and of the Jewish people.

The next set of Hebraic Tetrads would fall in 1967/68, again, Passover to Tabernacles, back to back. It would be during this tetrad that Jerusalem would be brought back in control of the Jewish People on the highly significant day of June 7, 1967, following the 6 Day War, where Israel, against all odds, defeated their Arab enemies. If you want to discover divine intervention with regard to the Jewish People and Jerusalem, then there is no better example than the *Miracles* that happened during those 6 days. It would be Passover 1967 when the first Blood Moon in the series would fall just 42 days prior to the re-capturing of Jerusalem, thus placing the rebuilding of Jerusalem within the tetrad.

Forty-six years later would result in the next set of Hebraic Tetrads that would fall on Passover to Tabernacles, back to back, in 2014 to 2015. Three Blood Moons in the series would have taken place with the final Super Blood Moon to occur on the eve of Tabernacles this year.

Here are some screen shots from the NASA website showing these *Hebraic Tetrads*.

The 1949/1950 Tetrad

1949 Apr 13	04:11:25	Total	121	1.425	03h26m 01h25m	Americas, Europe, Africa
1949 Oct 07	02:56:55	Total	126	1.224	03h43m 01h13m	Americas, Europe, Africa, w Asia
1950 Apr 02	20:44:34	Total	131	1.033	03h10m 00h27m	e S America, Europe, Africa, Asia, Australia
1950 Sep 26	04:17:11	Total	136	1.078	03h30m 00h44m	Americas, Europe, Africa, w Asia

The 1967/1968 Tetrad

1967 Apr 24	12:07:04	Total	121	1.336	03h23m 01h18m	Asia, Australia, Pacific, Americas
1967 Oct 18	10:15:48	Total	126	1.143	03h39m 01h00m	Asia, Australia, Pacific, Americas
1968 Apr 13	04:48:01	Total	131	1.112	03h14m 00h49m	Americas, Europe, Africa
1968 Oct 06	11:42:35	Total	136	1.169	03h34m 01h03m	Asia, Australia, Pacific, Americas

The 2014/2015 Tetrad

171

2014 Apr 15	07:46:48	Total	122	1.291	03h35m 01h18m	Aus., Pacific, Americas
2014 Oct 08	10:55:44	Total	127	1.166	03h20m 00h59m	Asia, Aus., Pacific, Americas
2015 Apr 04	12:01:24	Total	132	1.001	03h29m 00h05m	Asia, Aus., Pacific, Americas
2015 Sep 28	02:48:17	Total	137	1.276	03h20m 01h12m	e Pacific, Americas, Europe, Africa, w Asia

With regard to the 2014/2015 tetrad, it is this final tetrad that has partially fallen in the midst of the 48th & 49th 360-day cycle that happens to be a Shmitah year. It will be this final Super Blood Moon that will fall within the 50th year of jubilee, just four days after Yom Kippur, the day that *the Creator's 50th Year of Jubilee* is announced. See the image below for a visual representation of these three *"Hebraic Tetrads."*

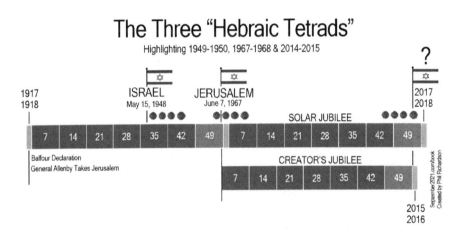

The Three "Hebraic Tetrads"

Highlighting 1949-1950, 1967-1968 & 2014-2015

What you might have noticed is the relationship of these final three Hebraic Tetrads to the land of Israel and to Jerusalem, the Creator's Holy City. Notice how the final two Hebraic Tetrads correlate with the Creator's Jubilee as discussed in the last chapter. It is almost as if the Hebraic Tetrads create a distinguished mark as in quotation marks around the 49 prophetic years (Daniel's 7th *week*) or known by myself as the Creator's Jubilee.

Also, if that were not spectacular enough, I believe that the 1949 to 1950 Tetrad that began on Tabernacles of 1949, may offer a clue to when we might see some conflict in Israel. Is it possible that in much the same way that the 1967 to 1968 and the 2014 to 2015 Tetrads highlights the Creator's Jubilee, that the 1949 to 1950 and the 2014 to 2015 Tetrads may highlight conflict in Israel? Whereas the re-birth of Israel fell exactly 333 days before the first Tetrad of Passover 1949, could it be that Israel will take back more land roughly the same amount of days after Tabernacles of 2015? If we were to calculate exactly 333 days forward from Tabernacles 2015, then we would come to Elul 26 or the 26th day of the sixth month of 2016.

What I find fascinating is that the Parashah reading would be #51 and #52 according to Torah Calendar.[5] The two Hebrew words for this day are Nitzavim and Va-Yelech that means *You Are Standing* and *And He Went* in that order. These two readings are from chapters 29 through 31 of Deuteronomy, and are generally read in Synagogues close to the beginning of the Fall Feast days.

According to Torah Calendar, "Va-Yelech was the Parashah on the first Sabbath in the Physical Universe. Moses was 120 years old when he gave us Va-Yelech. It is 120 Jubilee years from Creation until the Messiah's reign. In the first reading (עליה, aliyah), Moses told the Israelites that he was 120 years old that day, could no longer go out and come in, and God had told him that he was not to go over the Jordan River. God would go over before them and destroy the nations ahead of them, and Joshua would go over before them, as well." [6]

I find this rather remarkable that Deuteronomy chapter 31 mentions that Moses was 120 years old and would not be permitted to enter the promised land, yet Joshua (Yahshua's name in English) would go before them along with the Almighty to destroy the nations. We see this prophecy being repeated today as the Almighty will defend Israel at the end of the 120 Jubilees (120 years), crushing their enemies in order for Israel to enter the promised land (more land) along with Yahshua destroying their enemies at the battle of Armageddon.

The "Blood Moon Tetrads" Announce the 70th week

So, we see these blood moon signs in the heavens have been given to us in these latter years as a warning and as a distinguished mark by the Creator. We know that the Creator sits outside of time and is omnipotent and omnipresent according to Scripture. Everything that I have been able to observe with regard to the Almighty has everything to do with purpose, order, and intelligence. It is this element of Divine Order that I have been able to observe thus far with these graphs. The purpose is ultimately the fulfillment of prophecy that continue to occur and will continue until all is complete.

If I were to paint an analogy for you, I would use the illustration of the Creator, who is outside of time, standing in front of a huge white board that represents 7,000 years of time, placing his distinguished marks of four large red dots, identified as these Tetrad Blood Moon, on this board ever so carefully as to highlight the re-birth of the Jewish People from the dry bones, the re-birth of Israel as a Nation, the re-birth of Jerusalem, and a distinguished mark being placed in the year 6,000 (September 2015) that would signify his 50th year of Jubilee and the final 70th *week* of the prophecy with the imminent return of the Messiah at the end of that *week*. And, I picture him placing these tetrads in such a way that would represent perfect order, purpose and intelligence.

It is clear to me that these Hebraic Tetrads are not there by chance! What the facts show is that the first two blood moons of 1967 highlight June 7,

1967 with the dominion of Jerusalem being transferred back to the Jewish people. What we see with the last two blood moons of 2015 is that they once again highlight Jerusalem and the completion of the (49) 360-day cycles or 49 prophetic years that will usher in *the Creator's 50th Year of Jubilee* beginning on Yom Kippur 2015 as noted on the graph following the 49th year. It is Yom Kippur 2015 that will officially bring in Daniel's final 70th *week* or the final 7 years. Please see the graph for further analysis.

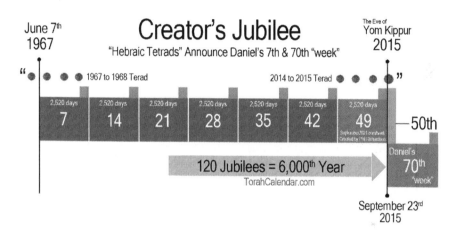

To sum up my point, it is as if these final two Blood Moon Tetrads act as a *distinguished mark* as the Creator Himself is using them as "quotation marks" in order to highlight His divine Jubilee. As we have learned, it not only highlights the Creator's Jubilee, but Daniel's *Seven weeks* as a double prophetic fulfillment of Bible prophecy, *both being one and the same.*

In addition, I believe that Yom Teruah 2015 will also be the start of the Civil Year 6,000; whereas, the year 6,001 will begin the 7th millennium. This can be verified by visiting Torahcalendar.com and viewing for yourself. I believe they are off one year as they have not lined up with the Creator's Jubilee, as stated. This knowledge was simply not known back in 2008 when their site was established.

The Final Super Blood Moon and the Connection to Tabernacles 2015

I am using the term Super Blood Moon to identify this final blood moon in September 2015 that will be at its closest point to earth giving the moon its large appearance in the sky of up to 15% larger than normal. It will be this final Super Blood Moon of the 171st tetrad that will complete the connection to Tabernacles 2015, and it being the 9th Hebraic Tetrad since the time of Yahshua with the number nine representing Judgment. The question I have, will this final blood moon represent liberation as well, considering that the other two Hebraic Tetrads represented a return of Israel and Jerusalem to the Jewish People? It is possible that this final blood moon in the series may represent both judgment and liberation as Scripture seems to indicate this idea such as what we find in Daniel 12:1 and other similar Scriptures.

Is it possible that this Super Blood Moon will signify the rebuilding process of the Jewish Temple on Mount Moriah located in Jerusalem? Could it at least represent the beginning of animal sacrifices that will need to take place in order for Bible prophecy to be fulfilled? I believe that either one of these events may come to pass before this final blood moon is witnessed on earth.

It will be this final Super Blood Moon whereby heaven will announce to the world this second to last great warning sign seen in the sky. I say second to the last because the great warning sign of all signs will take place on Yom Teruah 2017. I go into great detail on this *Great Sign* in the next chapter. This, of course, rules out any asteroids or UFO's that may be seen in the sky in the final 70th *week* and does not take into account the greatest sign of all signs, that being the sign of the coming of the son of man from among the clouds, accompanied by the armies in heaven, ready to wage war against those nations who dare come against Israel at the end of the 70th *week*. My point is that He is returning to judge the nations. Be very leery of a Messiah that comes in Peace only or someone who comes across as offering the solution to mankind's problems especially with regard to the coming financial crises. This same *"messiah"* will then force all to receive a mark on the right hand or on the forehead. The True Messiah will come back as a conquering king who will slaughter the armies of the Antichrist and will not simply be a man of *peace;* however, with that said, He will eventually set up a kingdom of Shalom (True Peace) ruling over all the nations by force represented by the rod of iron. For a more in depth understanding of this topic, read revelation 19:11-21.

The Three Pillar Foundation

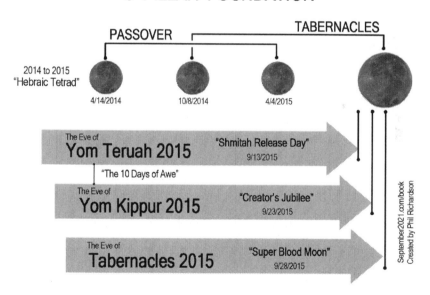

Now that I have identified all three events as they relate to the Fall Feast Days of 2015, I would like to connect all three in a graph titled, *the 3 Pillar Foundation,* so that you can see their relationship to one another. I have done so by showing this critical period of time we are about to enter.

What you will notice is that the 49th Shmitah ends on the eve of Yom Teruah as we enter the 6,000th year the following day on Yom Teruah being the New Year of the civil calendar also known as Rosh Hashanah.

There then is a ten day countdown of the 10 Days of Awe starting Tishri 1 and finalizing on Tishri 10 of Yom Kippur. One day prior will be the eve of Yom Kippur that will be the final day of the 49th 360-day cycle. Thus, Yom Kippur will announce the beginning of the *Creator's 50th Year of Jubilee* and also the beginning of the 70th *week*. And, it will be the final *Super Blood Moon* that will be the major sign to all the world that we have entered not only the 70th *week*, but also heralding towards the beginning of the 7th millennium.

These three significant events of 2015 lining up with the eve of the Fall Feast days is not by chance or coincidence but rather points to divine order and purpose. The purpose, as stated, is to announce the return of the true Mashiach back to earth who will be the ultimate fulfillment of the Fall Feast Days that represent good things to come for those who call upon His name.

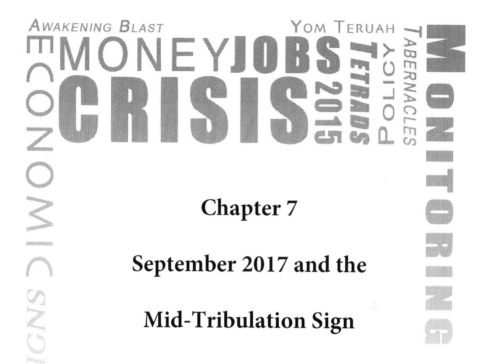

Chapter 7

September 2017 and the

Mid-Tribulation Sign

When studying this topic, I am amazed on how the enemy has blinded this current generation from seeking the signs that the Creator has declared would be displayed in the heavens. A sign is meant to offer guidance or to act as a warning much like one would observe a *Do Not Enter* sign while driving. That sign is there to help us and to give us clarity for the purpose of the preservation of life. In much the same way, the Bible makes it clear *"Signs"* would be visible in the heavens and this is what we see in September 2017.

As discussed in the past chapters, the heavenly host of stars are there partially for signs as in a distinguished mark and/or a warning sign. Additionally, they are for specific Appointed Times or *Appointed Feast* as is their correct translation.

We see other references to the stars or constellations that can be found in the Book of Job 38: 31-32, "Can you bind the cluster of the Pleiades, or loose the belt of Orion? Can you bring out Mazzaroth in its season? Or can you guide the Great Bear with its cubs? Do you know the ordinances of the heavens?" The Hebrew word Mazzaroth is in direct reference to "the 12 signs of the Zodiac and their 36 associated constellations" according to the definition by Strong's concordance H4216 of that word. The word for season as in "Mazzaroth in its season" is not Mow'ed, but rather "eth" that is in reference to the solar seasons such as spring, summer, winter and fall. It is clear that the Creator is identifying the constellations in this passage.

The Mazzaroth goes back since the beginning of man and tells a story within these twelve constellations that speaks of Israel and the coming of their Messiah as a humble servant and then as a conquering king. The enemy has turned this amazing story of the Messiah coming to redeem mankind into what is known today as the Zodiac that is filled with witchcraft and the occult. And, it is for this reason that Christians stray away from this topic not realizing that the enemy has hijacked the story of the Messiah that has been written in the stars, and now is seen as a taboo and something we shouldn't dare study nor are we encouraged to do so.

When you realize that this has been the plan of the enemy, as I have, then you will begin to search out what *he doesn't want you to discover*. This discovery as I came to realize has more to do with the timing of the Messiah's return. It is this timing that the enemy wants to blind you from and he has done a good job even in changing our perception.

Look, the Virgin Conceives and Gives Birth to a Son

Since my focus is on the Messiah's second return, I would like to focus on just two of these constellations, that being the *Virgin* (Bethula in Hebrew) known today as Virgo and *the Lion from the tribe of Judah* (Ariel in Hebrew) known today as Leo. It were these two constellations that the Maggi were looking at as a sign of Messiah's first coming as a humble servant to be born from a virgin as is hinted in the ancient writings of the book of Isaiah 7:14, "Therefore יהוה Himself gives you a sign: Look, the maiden conceives and gives birth to a Son, and shall call His Name Immanu'ĕl." This along with the prophetic words from Genesis regarding a future King,

"Judah is a lion's whelp; From the prey, my son, you have gone up. He bows down, he lies down as a lion; And as a lion, who shall rouse him? The scepter shall not depart from Judah, Nor a lawgiver from between his feet, Until Shiloh comes; And to Him shall be the obedience of the people." (Genesis 49:9-10)

The writings of the Prophets gave the Maggi an indication or a sign when the Messiah would arrive the first time and possibly the second time as you will discover.

There is a very interesting documentary/movie, *The Star of Bethlehem* that was directed by Stephen McEveety (*The Passion of the Christ*) and presenter Rick Larson that accurately identifies the signs of what the Maggi were looking for as a confirmation in order to make their long trip from the East to worship and give gifts to the newly born *King of the World*. In this documentary, they highlight the constellation Virgo and Leo and one very interesting *"roaming star"* known today as the planet Jupiter (Ha Tzaldiq in Hebrew). To the ancients, the planets within our solar system were known as roaming stars because of their appearance as stars. These roaming stars were used as *signs* specifically when they interacted within the constellations from our perspective on Earth. According to the documentary, it was Jupiter, the King Planet, that "triple crowned" Regulus, the King Star, that initiated the Maggi's long journey. Regulus is situated right at the heart of the Lion (Leo) and is attributed to Kingship, power and rulership in many cultures. In Arabic, it means, *the Heart of the Lion*, whereas to the Babylonians it was called Sharru that meant *The King,* with a deeper meaning of *The star that stands in the breast of the Lion: the King.* [1]

As indicated, Jupiter is known as the *King Planet* not only to the ancients but also in our current age. It is known as the king planet primarily because it is the largest planet within our solar system, hence the name Jupiter after the pagan god of Jupiter. Jupiter is a gas giant king that would be able to hold over 1,000 earths. Jupiter is also unique in that it orbits around the sun every 11.83 years or roughly 12 years and its orbital path is at such distance from earth that it takes on retrograde motion. From earth, the phenomena of retrograde motion as it applies to Jupiter takes on an unusual almost impossible path where it appears to stop its course and move backward, stop again and then begin to move forward once again. This can be observed by viewing this phenomena through *Stellarium.* I have done this and have noticed Jupiter's remarkable movements through the constellations. What is remarkable about this software is the ability to go back thousands of years and forward thousands of years into the future in order to observe the *signs* in the heavens. I have done so and I was able to document how the King Planet, Jupiter, made its way towards the constellation of Leo, known to the ancients as the *Lion of Judah* within the Mazzaroth.

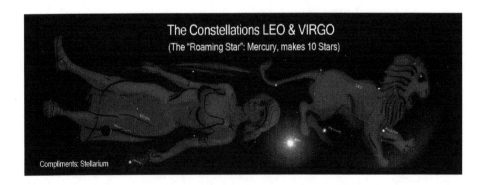

The Constellations LEO & VIRGO
(The "Roaming Star": Mercury, makes 10 Stars)

Compliments: Stellarium

What is interesting is that the Constellation Leo sits above the Constellation Virgo otherwise known as the *Virgin*. As the sun journeys across the sky over a one year period of time, it will pierce all twelve constellations within the Mazzaroth. Right around the month of August, the sun will appear to go through the Constellation Leo and then will make its approach to the Constellation Virgo right around the month of September followed by the moon that will make her appearance towards the feet of Virgo. Since the Lion sits above the *Virgin's head*, it can be said that Leo crowns the head of the Virgin. This becomes very interesting once one realizes that the Constellation Leo is represented by just nine stars.

What becomes very interesting is when the King Planet, Jupiter, interacts within these two constellations especially Regulus, the *King Star* that is located on the right paw of the Lion within the constellation of the Lion of Judah. Regulus is one of the largest stars ever discovered and it is for this reason it is known as the King Star especially to the ancient astronomers and wise men of Babylon. It was the Prophet Daniel who was promoted as the administrator over all of the wise men of Babylon,

> "Then the king promoted Daniel and gave him many great gifts; and he made him ruler over the whole province of Babylon, and chief administrator over all the wise men of Babylon" (Daniel 2:48).

The Ancient Babylonians kept systematic records of the patterns and movement of the roaming stars and constellations known as the *Astronomical Diaries* that were very accurate and complete. Author, N.M. Swerdlow of his book, *The Babylonian Theory of the Planets* states, "Indeed, the Diaries, originally extending from the eighth or seventh to the first century, are by far the longest continuous scientific record, or should we say, the record of the longest continuous scientific research, of any kind in all of history, for modern science itself has existed for only half as long.

And of course it is the Diaries, or the records from which the Diaries were compiled, that provided the observations that were later used as the empirical foundation of the mathematical astronomy of the ephemerides, in which the same phenomena of the moon and planets recorded in the omen texts were reduced to calculation." [2] My point is that the Prophet Daniel and the ancient Babylonians were very aware of the *Signs* in the heavens by having the most accurate means and methods at their disposal.

The Creator gave Daniel his position as head of the Chaldeans and wise men in order to bring clarity to the Maggi and to us today. Undoubtedly Daniel left instructions to future generations such as the Maggi who were well aware of the timing of the Messiah being born of a virgin. As recorded in Daniel 9:25,

"Know therefore and understand, That from the going forth of the command To restore and build Jerusalem Until Messiah the Prince, There shall be seven weeks and sixty-two weeks; The street shall be built again, and the wall, Even in troublesome times."

The Maggi had a really good idea when the Messiah was to be born. They understood that from the command to restore Jerusalem, there would be 49 years (*7 weeks*) and 434 years (*62 weeks*) for a total of 483 years. As discussed, because of the 360-day cycle, the solar years amounted to 476 years. Regardless of the actual year, the time frame was what they needed and they also knew what sign to look for, that sign being *the Virgin giving birth to the King.*

"Therefore יהוה Himself gives you a sign: Look, the maiden conceives and gives birth to a Son, and shall call His Name Immanu'ĕl." (Isaiah 7:14)

184

The Roaming King Planet

What I am about to explain is a double prophetic fulfillment of Bible prophecy, one in the celestial realm and the other in the physical realm. With regard to the celestial realm, the sign given would be for the Virgin (maiden) to give birth to the King child, that being Immanuel or God with us.

First off, this sign is from the Creator, YHVH, himself. This was the sign the Maggi were looking for. Now, let me break this down in more detail!

Once every 11.83 years, the King Planet, Jupiter, crosses the birth canal of the constellation of the Virgin while the Constellation of the Lion of Judah is crowning her head. Again, this happens ONLY ONCE every 11.83 years. One year prior to this event, Jupiter can be seen *crowning* or crossing over Regulus, the king star in the Constellation of the Lion of Judah. This becomes a phenomenon, when from our perspective on earth, Jupiter *triple crowns* Regulus because of retrograde motion. It was this triple crowning that the Maggi were looking for in order to begin their long journey towards the West, knowing that the King would be born from the Virgin in both a celestial sense and a physical sense of the word as a double prophetic fulfillment. We see a reference to Jupiter as recorded in Matt 2:6, "Then Herodes, having called the Magi secretly, learned exactly from them what time the star appeared." The implication here is that the star was a roaming star since all other stars are fixed in space.

While researching this topic on *Stellarium* one night, I went back an additional 2 sets of 12 year cycles to the years 14 to 13 BCE and to 26 to 25 BCE. What I noticed was that these two sets of years displayed the same type of patterns with regard to Jupiter triple crowning Regulus. The events that transpired in November 26 BCE to June 25 BCE were so profound that I knew this sign got the Maggi's attention. What I noticed was an amazing display of Mars, Jupiter and Saturn taking retrograde motion

185

around Regulus that would have been a sign as a type of first witness. The second witness would have taken place in 14 to 13 BCE with the grand finale of Messiah's birth happening 3 to 2 BCE with the triple crowning of Regulus by Jupiter. By the way, I have noticed these dual witnesses even within my own research such as the two *Shmitah Release Days,* the *two Confirmations* that I have yet to cover and others.

Revelation Chapter 12 and Yom Teruah

"AND A GREAT SIGN WAS SEEN IN THE HEAVEN: A WOMAN CLAD WITH THE SUN, WITH THE MOON UNDER HER FEET, AND ON HER HEAD A CROWN OF TWELVE STARS. AND BEING PREGNANT, SHE CRIED OUT IN LABOUR AND IN PAIN TO GIVE BIRTH." (REVELATION 12:1-2)

Most prophecy "Gurus" attribute Revelation 12:1-2 to Yahshua being born of a virgin almost 2,000 years ago and/or the 12 stars representing each tribe from the tribe of Israel with the tribe of Judah represented by the virgin, Mary giving birth to Immanu'ĕl, but they are misguided for various reasons, which I will explain.

It is clear from the context of this verse that this sign was seen in the heaven. Within the Book of Revelation, John was presented with the challenge of describing major world events to the best of his ability after his open vision, whereby he was literally taken outside the barriers of time into the future. This event only could have happened by the consent of the Almighty as we know that the Almighty is outside of time, seeing the beginning and the end at one instance. We now know that time is a variable that can be slowed down and stopped as it reaches the speed of light as Albert Einstein explained in his *Theory of Relativity.*

If you read the first few verses of Revelation chapter 12 within its context, it becomes clear that this sign would be seen from the sky, which is made up of the constellations and the planets. As indicated, the sign of the virgin giving birth as a woman who is clad with the sun, with the moon under her feet clearly identifies the Constellation Virgo as it is known today. The event where she is clad with the sun, with the moon at her feet only happens once per year around the month of September on the specific day of Yom Teruah.

It is during Yom Teruah when Virgo is clad or clothed with the sun. It is at this point that the moon is hidden or dark as the sun is positioned relatively behind the moon. This is the reason the moon is dark. This can be easily viewed by again viewing this on your computer by using the software. It is this visible sighting of the crescent of the moon that officially begins Yom Teruah and we see this on the software when the moon is moving closer to the feet of the Constellation Virgo. The moon makes its journey to the virgin's feet one day later typically on Tishri 2 of the Lunar Calendar.

The event that makes this event even more spectacular has to do with Jupiter, the roaming King Planet. The possibility of viewing Jupiter within the Constellation of Virgo can only be done once every 11.83 years. The possibility of viewing Jupiter being "Birthed" is even rarer, happening roughly only one-third of the time during Yom Teruah because Jupiter is either deep in the womb or far away, meaning that the odds of this sign happening is just once every thirty six years (1:36). The Virgin's celestial birth canal is made up of 4 stars within the constellation of Virgo. For a better understanding of this, please refer to the following picture taken from *Stellarium.*

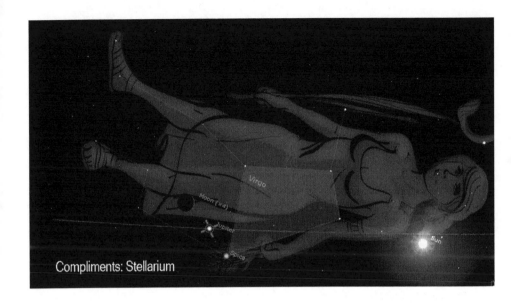

Compliments: Stellarium

Notice that this picture shows the Constellation Virgo being clothed with the sun, the moon moving towards her feet while the king planet, Jupiter, is being born out of her celestial birth canal. I have highlighted her celestial womb being made up of the four stars as shown. Again, the rarity of this sign seen in heaven happening is approximately once every 36 years. However, there is one other very important aspect of this prophecy and that has to do with her crown of 12 stars.

Crowned with 12 Stars

It's the crowning of the 12 stars that makes this an extremely rare event and truly a Great Sign as described by the Apostle John! As discussed, the Constellation Leo is made up of nine stars and as such always has nine stars. What would make this prophecy a fulfillment would be to witness Jupiter being born across the virgin's celestial birth canal while being crowned with 12 stars. So where would the other stars come from? If we consider that the 9 planets that make up our solar system were roaming stars, much like Jupiter, then we can see that this *Sign* would be fulfilled if just 3 of these 9 stars were within the constellation of Leo. This is truly a rare event especially when Jupiter is being born that again can only happen approximately once every 36 years. I proved this to myself one night by painstakingly going year by year back in time while using the *Stellarium* program. My process for this was to highlight Jupiter in a flashing red and to make the Constellation Virgo the default frame of reference by setting the date to September timeframe within the software. I then advanced the years one by one until I witnessed Jupiter born in that time frame. Virgo needed to be clothed with the sun, with the moon moving towards her feet on or near Yom Teruah when the moon can be seen taking on light from the sun or the crescent within the software. What I discovered was simply amazing!

A Sign Last Seen 3,865 Years Ago

From my vantage point of May 2015 and working backwards in time, I was able to see just how rare this sign was. About eight months prior to this, I made a video documenting these events by taking snap shots of these events on the program every time Jupiter was born or being born. I was able to go back 200 years to 1800 CE and forward 200 years to 2200 CE. I was able to identify this event just once in the near future. I uploaded this video to YouTube for all to watch on my website. I will cover this in detail later on.

By going back in time, year after year, it wasn't until 1850 BCE when I noticed all of the requirements of this sign happening all at once. In other words, Jupiter being born out of her womb, while *the woman* was being crowned with a garland of 12 stars above her head within the Constellation of Leo, at the same time the woman was being clothed with the sun and the moon under her feet. This is the only time this event has ever happened and it happened 3,865 years ago! LET THAT SINK IN... 3,865 YEARS! This is truly a *Rare and Great Sign!*

189

So, this begs the question, when will this sign be seen again? The answer is much sooner than we realize or would like to believe! When I made my original video on this, I did a countdown from 2200 CE down to September 2014. More of a drum roll, if you will. What was discovered (I do not take credit for this discovery) is that this event will occur only one other time in the not too distance future. To note, we would have never had this knowledge without the advancement of computers, software and the internet. Indeed the Book of Daniel chapter 12 is being *unsealed* as we are in the *Time of the End*!

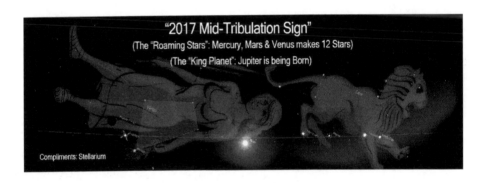

The picture above titled, *"2017 Mid-Tribulation Sign"* satisfies all of the requirements of Revelation Chapter 12:1-2. In addition, if my theory is correct, then tribulation would begin this Yom Teruah to Yom Kippur of 2015. Logically, this sign would be indicative of a mid-tribulation event because it falls in the twelfth chapter of the book of Revelation with the Book of Revelation being written in chronological order starting with chapter 1 and ending with chapter 22 and with chapters 6 through 18 describing the events of the 7 years of tribulation.

Chapters 6 through 9 identify a loss of life of up to 75% of humanity during that period of time. This means that from the period of time from Yom Teruah 2015 to Yom Teruah 2017, there may be a sizable loss of life that would take place, but more than likely not the 75% as stated in these passages as I believe the 7 seals represent (seven) 360-Day cycles. It is my belief that loss of life as indicated in the Book of Revelation progressively gets worst as each seal is loosened. I discuss more of this in the final chapter of the book.

I believe the Creator is giving us this sign in the heavens not only as a warning, but to highlight the actual prophetic time of these latter days as I have tried to the best of my ability to lay out within this book. Not only does this sign's future date of September 21, 2017 highlight the *Appointed Feast* of Yom Teruah, but we also have this Great Sign of all time, being a *Mid-Tribulation Sign*. This sign may pass the 2014 to 2015 Tetrad Blood Moon's order of importance due to the dire consequences associated with this sign! Notice how all of this knowledge and revelation is quickening as we approach the beginning of the Seventh Millennium!

Birthed at 41 weeks

In order to add icing to the cake and to validate this 2017 sign, I would like to highlight Jupiter's retrograde motion, in particular just prior to this future sign. I have shown you that the Constellation Virgo has a celestial birth canal represented by 4 stars with one of those stars being Spica. Those 4 stars form an irregular trapezoid that is representative of her womb. What is remarkable is that as Jupiter is traveling through the Constellation Virgo, it crosses into her celestial "womb" on November 20, 2016 and moves forward, and then backwards and then forward again and finally crosses through the birth canal on September 9, 2017. When I go to *TimeandDate.com* and place those two dates, it gives me a total duration of 41 weeks and 6 days or 9 months and 20 days. According to the American College of Obstetricians and Gynecologists, "In humans, birth normally occurs at a gestational age of about 40 weeks, though a normal range is from 37 to 42 weeks." Thus, the 2017 sign in the heavens literally shows the celestial gestational period of Jupiter being in the womb within the normal period of a human baby. Incredible! And what a confirmation!

According to the ancient cultures, the constellation Virgo, before it was Virgo, meant "a virgin holding a branch and a seed that will be gloriously beautiful." This reminds me of the Scripture from Genesis 2:15 which says,

> "And I put enmity between you and the woman, and between your seed and her Seed. He shall crush your head, and you shall crush His heel."

This verse describes her Seed (Notice the capitalization) coming to crush the serpent's head. This verse was partially fulfilled when her Seed, describing the Messiah, came to crush sin and the penalty of death while His second advent will complete this prophecy as He will come to destroy the corrupted power structures of world government.

As you might have noticed, the Virgin is holding a branch in her hand that is represented as the Branch of Jesse within the Scriptures from whom the Seed comes from or of that lineage flowing from Jesse to David and down the line until Joseph and Mary both coming from that line although Joseph was not his earthly father. Her Seed is represented within the constellations by the star Spica, meaning a seed of corn from the Greek. It is this Seed and Branch that the *King Planet* crosses before it is born on Yom Teruah of 2017. The ancient cultures that recognized the constellations as describing the coming Messiah, identified this Seed as gloriously beautiful.

Interestingly enough, a few verses from Revelation 12:1-2 identifies the child being birthed.

"And she bore a male child who was to shepherd all nations with a rod of iron. And her child was caught away to Elohim and to His throne." (Revelation 12:5)

John is clearly describing Yahshua here. John, being one of the 12 disciples, alludes to the fact *"The Word that became flesh"* (The Word of YHVH) came into the world the first time as a humble servant as referenced by the child who was caught away to the Father in Heaven. John recognized that the Prophets spoke of a conquering King who would save those Jews and Gentiles who would be grafted into the olive tree of Israel through him who, "would shepherd all nations with a rod of iron." In essence, Yahshua will come back to take the dominion away from Lucifer and will transfer that dominion back to himself that was lost at the original sin of Adam. This act will officially drive a sword into the sovereignty of the rule of man since it is Lucifer who is the ruler of the governments and political systems of this world.

Does this Sign Point to the Rapture?

There is one other interesting angle I would like to address regarding the male child being caught away to Elohim and that would be the Greek word harpazo, which is the word that describes being snatched by force and is the same word used in 1 Thessalonians 4:17 where we get the word rapture.

"Then we, the living who are left over, shall be **caught away** together with them in the clouds to meet the Master in the air – and so we shall always be with the Master. So, then, encourage one another with these words" (1 Thessalonians 4:17).

Part of the mystery behind the texts is to make spiritual connections with the meaning behind the Greek or Hebrew words being used. The connection I make is the potential of the Bridegroom coming for the Bride on this *Appointed Feast* of Yom Teruah because of the possibility of this word in so describing being caught away. This makes sense to me because the Bride needs to be purified and made clean and that seems to be made possible when she is refined in the refiner's fire of tribulation. To me, the promise of a pre-tribulation rapture has become as American as apple pie, meaning that the pre-rapture theory has been ingrained in our Christian culture as we Americans do not want to suffer or experience hardship and thus, we claim this theory for ourselves.

The Scriptures indicate that we are not appointed to wrath by the Creator, but the Scriptures also indicate that if you truly follow Yahshua, then you will experience many trials and tribulations. My intuition tells me that the Bride needs either one or two years of tribulation in order to be purified, but with that said, I also realize that according to the *Ancient Jewish Wedding,* the bridegroom comes for his bride and takes her back to his Father's house to spend 7 days (7 years or less) at the Great Wedding Feast. It is in the final chapter of this book, where I discuss the beginning of the 7th Millennium, the resurrection of the righteous and the marriage of the Lamb.

At this point, I would like to point to a few outside sources that point to September of 2017 as being a very interesting point of time to focus on.

Rabbi Judah Ben Samuel's 800 Year Old Prophecy Points to September 2017

The 2017 to 2018 Solar Jubilee, as you will discover, have much to do with the prophecy of Rabbi Judah Ben Samuel. Because this prophecy is from an exterior source outside of the Bible, and due to my inability to fully document its authenticity beyond being mentioned in the Jewish Encyclopedia dated 1909 CE, I will tread lightly on this subject; however, because it fits so well with what is written in this book and the connections I have been

194

able to make along with an accurate account of the jubilee cycles, I find it more trustworthy for these reasons. If I were to look at it from its historical context from 1917 to the present, the prophecy does an amazing job at highlighting the 50 year jubilee cycles.

Apparently, this is at least an 800 year old prophecy from a Rabbi Judah Ben Samuel who lived from 1140 to 1217 CE in Regensbug, Germany. His true name was Judah HeHasid who wrote three books by the titles, Sefer Hasidim (Book of the Pious), Sefer Gematriyot (a book on astrology) and Sefer Hakavod (Book of Glory), so we are dealing with a real individual and author. The latter book is now lost and few quotations have remained by subsequent authors. According to an original post by WND, [3] It was during this time that this curious and mystical Rabbi began to publish his biblical calculations that he called the Gematria and his astronomical observations as well. It was from this that he published the following:

Rabbi Judah ben Samuel - *"When the Ottomans (Turks) - who were already a power to be reckoned with on the Bosporus in the time of Judah Ben Samuel - conquer Jerusalem they will rule over Jerusalem for eight jubilees. Afterwards Jerusalem will become no-man's land for one jubilee, and then in the ninth jubilee it will once again come back into the possession of the Jewish nation - which would signify the beginning of the Messianic end time."*

Prophecy of the 10 Jubilees

of Judah Ben Samuel

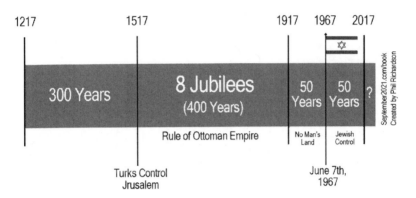

This is graphical representation of that quote. You will notice that there are a total of 10 jubilees represented by this prophecy starting in 1517 and ending in 2017.

To review, a full jubilee is 50 years with the final year being the *50th Year of Jubilee* that would always fall on Yom Kippur after 49, full years. These jubilees are further composed of seven Shmitah cycles plus the 50th year that is also a Shmitah year of allowing the land to rest as mandated by the Creator.

Leviticus 25:8-9 states, "'And you shall count seven Sabbaths of years for yourself, seven times seven years. And the time of the seven Sabbaths of years shall be to you forty-nine years. 'You shall then sound a ram's horn to pass through on the tenth day of the seventh month, on the Day of Atonement cause a ram's horn to pass through all your land.'"

History tells us that the Ottoman Turks conquered Jerusalem in 1517 CE. They ruled over Jerusalem for 400 years or 8 jubilees (8 x 50) until General

Allenby of the British military walked into Jerusalem by foot out of respect for the holy city and seizing Jerusalem on Hanukkah on December 11, 1917. Coincidently, this was roughly one month later from the Balfour Declaration (November 2, 1917), which initiated the process of setting up a Jewish State in the land of Canaan. Both the Balfour Declaration and the seizing of Jerusalem happened during the Jubilee 50th year cycle that had it's beginning on Yom Kippur (YK) 1917 and continued one year later to YK 1918. Exactly 50 years later would have been the preceding jubilee cycle of YK 1967 to YK 1968. Coincidently, 50 years later would place the future jubilee cycle from YK 2017 to YK 2018.

The prophecy continues to state that Jerusalem would become a "no-man's land" for one jubilee from a period between 1917 to 1967 and this is exactly what we see from that period of time as the City was divided until it was transferred back in the control of the Jewish nation on June 7th, 1967. Interestingly enough, the prophecy states that it would come into the possession of the Jewish nation in the ninth jubilee. According to my calculations, the ninth jubilee began on Yom Kippur 1917 and finalized on Yom Kippur 1967. The Jewish nation took back control of Jerusalem just 4 to 5 months prior to the beginning of the final 10th jubilee, according to the prophecy.

It goes on to state that when Jerusalem finally comes back into control of the Jewish nation, then this would "signify the beginning of the Messianic end time!" According to my research and what is being documented within this book, I highly agree with this final statement of this prophecy. In my view, the beginning of the Messianic end time began the final 50 year countdown until Yom Kippur 2015 and Yom Kippur 2017. The prophecy implies that Yom Kippur 2017 to Yom Kippur 2018 will conclude the 10th Jubilee of this prophecy. The question remains is what is the Messianic end time, as stated in this prophecy? As stated previously, I believe June 7th, 1967 was the day that began the prophetic time clock of the

Creator's final jubilee as well as the Solar Jubilee. These two Jubilees are separated by a two year period of time and both have everything to do with understanding this prophecy and the answer to the beginning of the *Messianic End Time* and the beginning of the *Messianic Age*.

Saint Malechy's 870 Year Old Prophecy and Pope Francis, the Final Pope!

There is yet another prophecy that I am using to help identify the times in which we live. This would be the ever so *popular Saint Malechy's Prophecy* that was made popular by Tom Horn and Chris Putnam in their book, *Petrus Romanus* published on March 2013. I was aware of this prophecy before their book came out and was highly anticipating reading this book, that I promptly ordered on Amazon. I had formulated my own opinion of this prophecy and I was able to make a connection with the 8 kings of the book of Revelation chapter 17 and ended up writing an article on this subject matter just prior to the identity of Pope Petrus and the resignation of Pope Joseph Ratzinger.

The *Prophecy of the Popes* as they have come to be known, are a series of 112 short, cryptic Latin Mottos or phrases that identify all 112 future Roman Catholic Popes from a beginning point that began with Pope Celestine II who reigned from 1143 to 1144 CE. The latin motto's of Saint Malechy were first published in a book titled, *Last Judgment* (Lignum Vitae) written by Arnold de Wyon (Wion) and published in 1595 CE that is remarkably still available and thus can be verified.

Author Wion attributes these 112 short prophecies to Saint Malachy, the 12th century Archbishop of Armagh, Ireland. The book documents all of the latin mottos that were fulfilled very accurately up to 1595 as well as the latin mottos beyond 1595, naming all 112 cryptic latin mottos. There is some debate as to the authentic nature of these prophecies, but I believe the book should speak for itself especially now looking back to its original publication 420 years ago.

Pope #1 of the prophecy, Pope Celestine II was followed by 73 other popes prior to the year 1595 CE, that being the publishing date of Wion's book. This would mean that beyond the year 1595 CE., the prophecy would need to identify a maximum of 38 future popes. A complete list of all of these popes with their contributing latin mottos and fulfillments are listed on the Wikipedia website titled, *Prophecy_of_the_Popes.* I will highlight a few of these popes and their mottos so you can become familiar with these patterns.

The latin phrase that stands out to me is "Religion Destroyed" and is attributed to Pope #104 of the prophecy, Pope Benedict XV (Giacomo Della Chiesa). This pope reigned from 1914 to 1922 while WWI was raging. The motto, *Religion Destroyed* is an accurate depiction of the tens of millions of Russian Christians who were killed during the Russian Revolution of 1917. This was a time of great political change and persecution.

Another of the mottos fulfilled was the one that described John Paul II. His motto reads, "From the labour of the sun / Of the eclipse of the sun". What is interesting is that Pope John Paul II, the 110th pope of the prophecy, was born (May 18, 1920) and buried (April 8, 2005) during solar eclipses that happened on those two days of his birth and burial. Additionally, it is well known that John Paul II was the one pope who did the most traveling and thus the connection to laboring in the sun.

Pope #111, Pope Benedict XVI (Joseph Ratzinger), had the motto, "Glory of the olive". A possible fulfillment of this could have been Benedict's choice of his papal name stemming from the Saint Benedict of Nursia, founder of the Benedictine Order, of which the Olivetans are one branch.

Last but not least would identify Pope Francis as #112, the current and final pope according to the 900 year old prophecy. The latin motto attributed to this current pope is the longest of the mottos by far and the most profound by a long shot. So you may be asking, what does the final motto say? I thought you would never ask! Here it is with the Latin and English translation.

"In persecutione extrema S.R.E. sedebit. Petrus Romanus, qui pascet oves in multis tribulationibus, quibus transactis civitas septicollis diruetur, & judex tremendus judicabit populum suum. Finis."

"In the final persecution of the Holy Roman Church, there will sit, Peter the Roman, who will pasture his sheep in many tribulations, and when these things are finished, the city of seven hills will be destroyed, and the dreadful judge will judge his people. The End."

There are two ways to read the opening sentence. Does the opening verse imply that those who make up the church, will be persecuted or does it imply that the one who will persecute, would be made up of the church (ie. The Vatican)? Something to think about! The motto mentions Peter the Roman. A Roman by the name of Peter doesn't seem to line up with Pope Francis. Or does it? If we look further, we discover that the current Pope's birth name is Jorge Mario Bergoglio, an Italian name from Italian (Roman) parents.

Author, Tom Horn sees a significance in Bergoglio naming himself after Francis of Assisi, an Italian, or Roman, priest whose original name was Francesco di Pietro (Peter) di Bernardone, literally, "Peter the Roman." Horn goes on to say, " 'Petrus Romanus' in the prophecy implies this pope will reaffirm the authority of the Roman Pontiff over the Church and will emphasize the supremacy of the Roman Catholic Faith and the Roman Catholic Church above all other religions and denominations, and its authority over all Christians and all peoples of the world."

Next, we see a mention of many tribulations during his reign. Keep in mind that Pope Francis as of June 2015, is 79 years old and that John Paul II was only 84 when he died. The implication is that these tribulations must happen soon or at least within the next 10 years just based on his age alone. The other thing we see is that this pope will offer comfort to his sheep and possibly the world during this time. The motto goes on to say that in the end, the city of seven hills will be destroyed. This lines right up with the book of Revelation, whereby it will be a city of seven hills that will be destroyed as well. This does speak of Rome, known as the city of seven hills or mountains, but could also speak of other cities such as Tehran, Jerusalem, Moscow, Mecca and Istanbul that are also known as having 7 hills. From my perspective, the implication is that Rome will be destroyed towards the end of tribulation.

Finally, we see a dreadful judge to judge his people and the world. This obviously speaks of Yahshua coming as a Great Conquering King in the clouds with the trumpets blasting along with his saints prepared for battle against the antichrist and the world's armies.

Despite the objections from those who would like to discredit this prophecy, I do embrace it and believe it is legitimate partly due to the book associated with is prophecy that is 420 years old and that can be validated as well as the connection I have been able to make in regard to the *Saint Malechy' Prophecies* and how they tie into the eight kings of Revelation Chapter 17 and the, "beast that was, and is not, and yet is" as referenced from Revelation 17:8. I originally wrote an article about this a few years back and was able to make an exact connection with the popes who, after the 1929 Lateran Treaty, became kings once their tiny institution (The Vatican) became the smallest recognizable independent nation on earth. The fact of the matter is that Pope Francis is the 8th pope since the Lateran Treaty of 1929 and # 112 of the Saint Malechy's Prophecy. You can read more by reading my article [4] on this.

AWAKENING BLAST   YOM TERUAH
MONEYJOBS
ECONO CRISIS
ECONOMIC SIGNS
TABERNACLES
POLICY
MONITORING
TETRADS 2015

Chapter 8

September 2014 and the Final 2,550 Days

My Aha Moment

So far, we have discussed events taking place this coming September 2015. However, there was one event that began on the eve of Yom Teruah of 2014 that would set off a chain of events with regard to Bible prophecy being fulfilled in the near future. A vast majority of prophecy gurus, pastors and prophecy students missed it completely, yet the implications are monumental. Before I get into this, I need to go back and re-visit the day I had a major revelation that I have termed as my "Aha" Moment.

Back in June 2014, I made the decision to begin writing a book that was to be titled *Countdown: September 2015*. In this book, I was going to discuss the patterns and connections associated with the eve of the major Fall Feast days of 2015 and the Mid-Tribulation Sign of 2017, much like I have done in the last four chapters of this book. At that time, I had no revelation of any future years beyond 2017. My goal was to finish writing this book by September of 2014 and get it published.

While writing my book, I got stuck on my understanding of the 1260, 1290 and 1335 days of Daniel chapter twelve. While searching on the internet, I came across a website that I had visited once before, but did not make the spiritual connection. This time, it made perfect sense to me and became a major milestone of my understanding and revelation, as I was able to make concrete connections to the final seven years of man's rule on this earth. The date of my "Aha" Moment was August 19, 2014. It was on this date when I came across Gavin Finley's webpage, *endtimepilgrim.org*, for the second time. More specifically, it was a webpage within his main site, where he identified some amazing connections that he had made with regard to the 1260 and 1290 days. The first time I visited his site, I was just learning and being accustomed to the Hebraic understanding of my Christian Faith, so I could not fully grasp his revelation with regard to the Fall Feast Days of Yom Teruah, Yom Kippur and Tabernacles and how they tie into Daniel Chapter 12. However, the second time was more like a fireworks display of understanding and revelation. It was as though I was able to begin placing together the pieces of the gigantic puzzle known as Bible prophecy. On August 19, 2014, this puzzle became to take shape.

Based on this new revelation, one particular day, among many, stuck out as being a monumental day. This day was September 24, 2014 or more importantly, the eve of Yom Teruah. For the next 90 minutes, I began to search for clues as what might happen on that day as this day was still a little more than one month away. Eventually, I came across a certain someone who would be heading the chairmanship of the world governing body known as the United Nations. It was at that moment that I realized that I would need to abandon my book and set up a webpage [1] revealing all of this new revelation and announcing on my website banner, "The Antichrist to Confirm a Covenant with the Many from September 24 to 26 of 2014." It would be at that time that I would intensely begin to write pages and articles on my website of this new revelation, produce graphs and timeline charts using Photoshop and finally producing videos and uploading to Youtube just prior to the September 24th deadline. It would have been on September 22, 2014, just two days prior to my deadline, that I would have uploaded these videos to YouTube [2] in order to document what is written here.

A Closer Look into the Final 2,550 Days

In the sixth chapter of this book, I laid out the lunar tetrad moons otherwise known as the Hebraic Tetrad of 2014 to 2015 and how they represent a sign or distinguished mark and more specifically, how they highlight Daniel's final seven *weeks* as a double prophetic fulfillment of Scripture with the re-unification of Jerusalem on June 7, 1967 as discussed. For the purpose of this chapter, I will be highlighting the final 2,550 days (1260+1290) of Daniel chapter twelve and will be pointing out the significance of those 2,550 days to two significant Fall Feast days that coincide with the Metonic Lunar Cycle.

The twelfth chapter of the book of Daniel is highly prophetic for the time we are living in at this moment in time. It describes three future time periods being 1260, 1290 and 1335 days. Here are their key references from the Bible:

"And I heard the man dressed in linen, who was above the waters of the river, and he held up his right hand and his left hand to the heavens, and swore by Him who lives forever, that it would be for *a time, times, and half a time*. And when they have ended scattering the power of the set-apart people, then all these shall be completed."

"And from the time that which is continual is taken away, and the abomination that lays waste is set up, is *one thousand two hundred*

204

and ninety days. "Blessed is he who is waiting earnestly, and comes to the *one thousand three hundred and thirty-five days."* (Daniel 12:7, 11-12, emphasis added)

We see from these verses, that there are three timeframes represented: time, times, and half a time, which is 1,260; 1,290 and 1,335 days. Note that these days are based upon the lunar Hebraic calendar of 360 days per year and not the Gregorian solar calendar of 365.24 days per year.

Sir Robert Anderson even makes mention of this in his book, *The Coming Prince*, where he writes, "Now this seventieth week is admittedly a period of seven years, and half of this period is three times described as "a time, times, and half a time," or "the dividing of a time;" (Daniel 7:25; 12:7; Revelation 12:14) twice as forty-two months; (Revelation 11:2; 13:5) and twice as 1,260 days. (Revelation 11:3; 12:6) But 1,260 days are exactly equal to forty-two months of thirty days, or three and a half years of 360 days, whereas three and a half Julian years contain 1, 278 days. It follows therefore that the prophetic year is not the Julian year, but the ancient year of 360 days." [3]

Over the years, I have read different opinions of what these three periods of time might represent; however, it was not clear to me until I came to Gavin Finley's website that second time, that it made complete and perfect sense. What I discovered on that day was that these three timeframes fit perfectly between the feast days! As discussed in chapter two, the 1,260 plus 1,290 days comes to 2,550 days that fit perfectly between the Feast days of Yom Teruah and Yom Kippur over a span of seven Hebraic years plus 30 days. So, from the sighting of the new moon on Yom Teruah (Tishri 1), we add 2,550 days and it will conclude on a future Yom Kippur (Tishri 10), separated by roughly seven years. Please see the graph from Mr. Gavin Finley's website that opened up this understanding for me.

The Fall Feasts of Israel

**The _Feast of Trumpets_ will mark
day one of the 70th Week of Daniel;
Seven years later the _Day of Atonement_
will usher in the last day of this age.**

Tishrei 1 <- - - - - - - - 7 years - - - - - - - - > **Tishrei 10**
Tishrei 1 <- - - - 86 moons + 10 days - - - > **Tishrei 10**
Tishrei 1 <- - 7 Biblical yrs. + 30 days - - > **Tishrei 10**
Tishrei 1 < - - - (7 x 360) + 30 days - - - - > **Tishrei 10**
Tishrei 1 <- - - - - 2520 + 30 days - - - - - > **Tishrei 10**
Tishrei 1 <- - The 70th Week + 30 days - > **Tishrei 10**
Tishrei 1 <- - - 1260 + 1260 + 30 days - - > **Tishrei 10**
Tishrei 1 <- - - - - 1260 + 1290 days - - - - > **Tishrei 10**
Tishrei 1 <- - - - - - - - 2550 days - - - - - - > **Tishrei 10**

Feast of Trumpets or Rosh Hashanah	Day of Atonement or Yom Kippur
Tishrei 1	Tishrei 10
Year X	Year X + 7

You can see that Mr. Finley does a great job at breaking down a 2,550 day period of time that begins exactly on Tishri 1 and ends on Tishri 10 just about 7 years later. Here are some additional ways of saying this!

- 1260 + 1290 = 2,550 DAYS
- 1260 + 1260 + 30 = 2,550 DAYS
- 1260 + 1260 + THE "30 DAYS OF TESHUVAH" = 2,550 DAYS
- 7 HEBRAIC YEARS (2,520 DAYS) + 30 DAYS = 2,550 DAYS
- TISHRI 1 (YOM TERUAH) + 2,550 DAYS = TISHRI 10 (YOM KIPPUR)

206

- ROSH HASHANAH + 2,550 DAYS = THE DAY OF ATONEMENT
- 86 MOON CYCLES + 10 DAYS = 2,550 DAYS
- 86 MOON CYCLES + THE 10 DAYS OF AWE = 2,550 DAYS

As discussed, the final day of the 2,550 days, does not always fall on Yom Kippur due to the synodic month making up 29.5306 days. Because of this, there is a conflict with aligning 12 moon cycles in one solar year. For instance, 12 moon cycles would amount to 354.37 days (12 x 29.53), while 13 moon cycles would amount to 383.90 days (13 x 29.53). The solar year, being 365.24 days, falls between the 12th and 13th moon cycle, an obvious problem with lining up the seasons and the times for planting and harvesting.

The Metonic Lunar Cycle and the 86 Moons versus 87 Moons

With regard to ancient Israel, they were under instruction to balance the lunar cycles with the solar seasons in order that their barley, wheat and grape harvests would line up year after year and for season after season. To keep things simple, these instructions come from Exodus 13:10, instructing Israel to observe the Festival of Unleavened Bread by offering the first fruits of the barley offering to YHVH on that *Appointed Feast* and to observe the rule of the equinox based upon Genesis 1:14 with the relationship of the moon to the sun.

It wasn't until 359 C.E., that Hillel II established and standardized the Jewish Calendar system by incorporating the Metonic lunar cycle. It was this Metonic lunar cycle that was based upon the writings of Meton of Athens, a Greek astronomer and mathematician who lived in the fifth century BCE. It was Mr. Meton who observed that nineteen solar years are almost equal to 235 lunar moon cycles. As a matter of fact, the cycle is so close, that it only accounts for a few hours (0.08 days x 24 hours/day) difference over a span of nineteen years.[4]

- 235 SYNODIC MONTHS = 6,939.688 DAYS
- 19 GREGORIAN YEARS = 6,939.608 DAYS

It is this Metonic lunar moon cycle that is observed and standardized today within the Jewish Calendar in order to keep the lunar months in sync with the solar year. In order to accomplish this, an extra month is added roughly every three years otherwise known as intercalation. This extra month within the Jewish Calendar system is identified as Adar II added after the month of Adar.

The Metonic Lunar Cycle always follows a pattern within its 19-year cycle. The embolism years fall on year 3, 6, 8, 11, 14, 17, and 19 of the cycle. Torah Calendar acknowledges the Metonic cycle, but takes it another step further by incorporating the "rule of the equinox" through the command to intercalate. We find this reference on their website:

"Intercalation on the Creation Calendar is based on a mathematical rule called the rule of the equinox. The occasional addition of Month 13 can be thought of as adding a leap month for some Hebrew Years and is required to keep the agricultural festivals of יהוה in their seasons. The command to intercalate by the rule of the equinox can be deduced from the instructions in Genesis 1:14 in which the sun and the moon are to determine years, and from Exodus 13:10 in which the Festival of Unleavened Bread is to be kept in its season from year to year."[5]

As I was saying, the 2,550 days does not always fall on Yom Kippur. The Metonic Lunar cycle of adding an additional month roughly every 3 years in order to keep in sync with the solar year, results in an additional two lunar months being added over a 2,550 day period of time. Likewise, because of the Metonic lunar cycle, there would be seven year cycles that would result in the addition of three lunar months that would push it beyond the 2,550 days to 2,579/2,580 days.

The Metonic cycle that we are currently in began in 1997/98 and will end in 2016/17 according to Mr. Finley.[6] This cycle also lines up with Jewish calendar system [7] as well. Within this nineteen year cycle, the 2,550 day cycle starting on Yom Teruah and ending exactly on Yom Kippur will take place 7 times out of 19 times, a 37% chance of it happening. On the flip side, the chances against this happening would be 63%. Ultimately, what Mr. Finley believes as to when Daniel's 70th week will begin is the difference between 86 moons and 87 moons! Keep in mind that the difference between Yom Teruah and Yom Kippur is ten days. Another way of saying this might be...

- (86 MOONS + 10 DAYS = 2,550 DAYS) OR ((86 X 29.53) +10)= 2,550 DAYS (37% CHANCE)

On the other hand, there is a 63% chance that this phenomena would not line up. So, in any given 12 years of the 19 year Metonic cycle, there would be a total of 87 moons. Another way of looking at this might be...

- (87 MOONS + 10 DAYS = 2,579/2,580 DAYS) OR ((87 X 29.53) +10) = 2,579/2,580 DAYS (63% CHANCE)

To recap, the amount of moon cycles from any given Tishri to Tishri over a seven year period of time either results in 84 moons + 2 extra intercalary months OR 84 moons + 3 intercalary months, an amount of 86 moons verses 87 moons. In order to satisfy the requirements for 2,550 days (1260 +1290), which would begin on Yom Teruah (Tishri 1) and end 2,550 days later on Yom Kippur (Tishri 10), there would need to be 86 moon cycles and not 87 moon cycles.

- (84 MOONS + 2 INTERCALARY MONTHS) = **86 MOON CYCLES = 2,550 DAYS**

Based upon the findings of Mr. Finley with regard to the Metonic Lunar Moon Cycle, the four most likely dates, in his words, of "the 70th *week* prophecy" beginning within the next ten years based upon the phenomena of the 86 moon cycle of 2,550 days (1260+1290) beginning on Yom Teruah (YT) and ending on Yom Kippur (YK) would be:

- YT 2014 TO YK 2021
- YT 2017 TO YK 2024
- YT 2019 TO YK 2026
- YT 2022 TO YK 2029

I would like to clarify that the above dates would qualify for the start and finish of the 2,550 days and would not necessarily qualify for the 70th week prophecy as claimed by Mr. Finley on his website and on his graphs. The 2,550 days lining up with the final 7 years of the 70th week of Daniel's prophecy is a good assumption. I will explain in detail why these two time periods are actually separated by one year in just one moment.

But first, all of these dates can be easily verified by going to Torah Calendar and finding the future dates of Tishri 1 for the years 2014, 2017, 2019, 2022 and then adding 2,550 days using timeanddate.com for determining the future Gregorian year and date. I have done this for you!

The following future dates **DO** line up with Torah Calendar and thus Would qualify for the final 2,550 days :

- YT (9/24/2014) +2,550 DAYS = YK (9/17/2021)
- YT (9/20/2017) +2,550 DAYS = YK (9/13/2024)
- YT (9/17/2020) +2,550 DAYS = YK (9/11/2027)
- YT (9/26/2022) +2,550 DAYS = YK (9/19/2029)

While, these following dates, DO NOT line up with Torah Calendar and thus **WOULD NOT** qualify for the final 2,550 days:

- YT 2015 TO YK 2022
- YT 2016 TO YK 2023
- YT 2018 TO YK 2025
- YT 2019 TO YK 2026
- YT 2021 TO YK 2028

As you may have noticed, there seems to be a slight conflict with *Torah Calendar* and the Metonic Lunar Moon Cycle. The Metonic lunar cycle from YT 2019 to YK 2026 does not line up with *Torah Calendar,* while YK 2020 to YK 2027 does line up with *Torah Calendar,* but is not reflected in the Metonic Lunar cycle.

I believe the difference is as a result of how *Torah Calendar* calculates the moon phases as these calculations might be slightly different from the Metonic lunar cycle. *Torah Calendar* uses the most advanced lunar and solar data from Jet Propulsion Laboratory (JPL) and other reliable sources that have an accuracy of + - 30 minutes in 4,000 years, according to their website. *Torah Calendar* also accounts for the Spring Equinox lining up on the Feast of Unleavened Bread or after.

In any event, you can clearly see at least three dates line up with both Torah Calendar and the Metonic Lunar cycle and as a result act as a type of double confirmation:

- YT (9/24/2014) +2,550 DAYS = YK (9/17/2021)
- YT (9/20/2017) +2,550 DAYS = YK (9/13/2024)
- YT (9/26/2022) +2,550 DAYS = YK (9/19/2029)

Here is a graph taken from Mr. Finley's website that covers a ten year period of time from 2013 to 2023. Keep in mind, that he is qualifying these times as the 70th *week* and as stated, it is better to qualify the following start dates as the beginning of the final 2,550 days and not the beginning of the *70th week.*

Number of moons in 7 Years beginning on Rosh Hoshanah 2013	2013-2014 13 moons Passover ECLIPSE	2014-2015 12 moons	2015-2016 12 moons	2016-2017 13 moons	2017-2018 12 moons	2018-1019 13 moons	2019-2020 12 moons	87 moons (Fails to qualify for 70th week)
Number of moons in 7 Years beginning on Rosh Hoshanah 2014	2014-2015 12 moons 3 Holy Day ECLIPSES	2015-2016 12 moons	2016-2017 13 moons	2017-2018 12 moons	2018-1019 13 moons	2019-2020 12 moons	2020-2021 12 moons	86 moons ☑ (Qualifies for the 70th week)
Number of moons in 7 Years beginning on Rosh Hoshanah 2015	2015-2016 12 moons 2 Fall Feast ECLIPSES	2016-2017 13 moons	2017-2018 12 moons	2018-1019 13 moons	2019-2020 12 moons	2020-2021 12 moons	2021-1022 13 moons	87 moons (Fails to qualify for the 70th week)
Number of moons in 7 Years beginning on Rosh Hoshanah 2016	2016-2017 13 moons; & TOTAL SOLAR ECLIPSE 8/21/17 crossing the USA!	2017-2018 12 moons	2018-1019 13 moons	2019-2020 12 moons	2020-2021 12 moons	2021-1022 13 moons	2022-2023 12 moons	87 moons (Fails to qualify for 70th week)
Number of moons in 7 Years beginning on Rosh Hoshanah 2017	2017-2018 12 moons	2018-1019 13 moons	2019-2020 12 moons	2020-2021 12 moons	2021-1022 13 moons	2022-2023 12 moons	2023-1024 12 moons	86 moons ☑ (Qualifies for the 70th week)
Number of moons in 7 Years beginning on Rosh Hoshanah 2018	2018-1019 13 moons	2019-2020 12 moons	2020-2021 12 moons	2021-1022 13 moons	2022-2023 12 moons	2023-1024 12 moons	2024-2025 13 moons	87 moons (Fails to qualify for 70th week)
Number of moons in 7 Years beginning on Rosh Hoshanah 2019	2019-2020 12 moons	2020-2021 12 moons	2021-1022 13 moons	2022-2023 12 moons	2023-1024 12 moons	2024-2025 13 moons	2025-1026 12 moons	86 moons ☑ (Qualifies for the 70th week)
Number of moons in 7 Years beginning on Rosh Hoshanah 2020	2020-2021 12 moons	2021-1022 13 moons	2022-2023 12 moons	2023-1024 12 moons	2024-2025 13 moons	2025-1026 12 moons	2026-2027 13 moons	87 moons (Fails to qualify for 70th week)
Number of moons in 7 Years beginning on Rosh Hoshanah 2021	2021-1022 13 moons	2022-2023 12 moons	2023-1024 12 moons	2024-2025 13 moons	2025-1026 12 moons	2026-2027 13 moons	2027-2028 12 moons	87 moons (Fails to qualify for 70th week)
Number of moons in 7 Years beginning on Rosh Hoshanah 2022	2022-2023 12 moons	2023-1024 12 moons	2024-2025 13 moons	2025-1026 12 moons	2026-2027 13 moons	2027-2028 12 moons	2028-1029 12 moons	86 moons ☑ (Qualifies for the 70th week)
Number of moons in 7 Years beginning on Rosh Hoshanah 2023	2023-1024 12 moons	2024-2025 13 moons	2025-1026 12 moons	2026-2027 13 moons	2027-2028 12 moons	2028-1029 12 moons	2029-2030 13 moons	87 moons (Fails to qualify for 70th week)

Mr. Finley doesn't take into account *Torah Calendar* or other lunar calendar systems, but simply relies on the Metonic Lunar Cycle for his analysis. What I find particularly interesting is that Mr. Finely has placed the next likely time of the *"70th week"* (2,550 days) beginning on Yom Teruah 2017 and ending on Yom Kippur 2024 as evident by this date being highlighted in yellow. Prior to September 2014, Mr. Finley had highlighted Rosh Hashanah of 2014 as being the likely start of the *"70th week"* (2,550 days). As incredibly bright and spiritually gifted as Mr. Finley is, even he missed the significance of what transpired on September 24, 2014. Rosh Hashanah (Yom Teruah) of 2014 still qualifies for the final 2,550 days, as you will discover, with the still future Feast of Yom Teruah 2015 qualifying for the 70th week.

A Closer Look at the 1,335 Days

At this point, you can certainly see how the addition of the 1,260 days and the 1,290 days point to the feast days, but what about the third time frame of the 1,335 days that is found in Daniel 12:12? Does this point to the feast days as well? Let's take a look!

The 1,335 days is a period of time that equates to roughly 3.7 Hebraic years. If we begin on Yom Teruah of any given year and count out 1,335 days we will come to Shavuot. When we account for intercalation, we will come to the Feast of Shavuot in some years, while not in other years. Again, the Metonic lunar cycle would play into this. By using *timeand-date.com* and *Torah Calendar*, we see how the intercalation of the 13th month will effect the 1,335 days from either falling on Shavuot or falling one month behind this feast day. On the Creator's Calendar, the 1,335 days will either fall on the 5th/6th of the second month or the 5th/6th of the third month. In order for the 1,335 days to land on the Feast Day of Shavuot, it must fall within the third month of the spiritual year. I have double checked the years from 2014 to 2019 on *Torah Calendar* to determine possible future fulfillment's of this prophecy. See the following:

- YT **9/24/2014** + 1,335 DAYS = SHAVUOT 5/21/2018 (3RD MONTH)
- YT 9/14/2015 + 1,335 DAYS = SHAVUOT 5/11/2019 (3RD MONTH)
- YT 9/1/2016 + 1,335 DAYS = 4/28/2020 (NOT SHAVUOT) (2ND MONTH)
- YT **9/20/2017** + 1,335 DAYS = SHAVUOT 5/17/2021 (3RD MONTH)
- YT 9/9/2018 + 1,335 DAYS = 5/6/2022 (NOT SHAVUOT) (2ND MONTH)
- YT 8/30/2019 + 1,335 DAYS = 4/26/2023 (NOT SHAVUOT) (2ND MONTH)

So, as you might have noticed the 1,335 day prophecy points exactly from Yom Teruah to Shavuot, while the (1,260 +1,290) day prophecy point exactly from Yom Teruah to Yom Kippur. It is logical to believe that the 2,550 days and 1,335 days tie together through their common bond of beginning on Yom Teruah in certain years. Those years, as identified, would be only two within the next 6 years. Those two years in common would be:

- THE EVE OF YOM TERUAH 2014 (9/24/2014)
- THE EVE OF YOM TERUAH 2017 (9/20/2017)

Logically, it seems that the chances are rather high that either this past Yom Teruah 2014 or the future Yom Teruah 2017 will play into the start of the 2,550 day count down. See the following graph for a better understanding of these two dates.

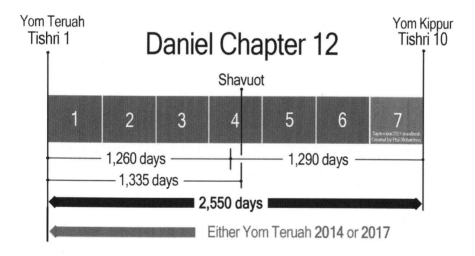

The questions remains whether or not this would have begun on the eve of Yom Teruah 2014 (September 24, 2014) or the future date of the eve of Yom Teruah 2017 (September 20, 2017)? Still, this supposition is still inconclusive and more evidence needs to come forward in order to confirm this start date for the final 2,550 days.

President Obama and the Connection to Yom Teruah 2014

It would have been on August 19, 2014, while searching for approximately 90 minutes with regard to the significance of September 24, 2014 (the eve of Yom Teruah), that I would discover that President Obama would be heading the United Nation Security Council (UNSC) on September 24, 2014 according to the internet news site I had discovered during my frantic search for facts.

As soon as I read the headline, "President Obama to lead the UNSC Meeting," my mind instantaneously made a connection to the first time he had done this exactly five solar years prior on September 24, 2009. The first time he headed the chairmanship of the UNSC, he was there to direct an agenda for nuclear disarmament.

"For only the fifth time in its history, the United Nations Security Council met at the level of heads of state on 24 September 2009, the subject at hand, nuclear nonproliferation and disarmament. United States President Barack Obama chaired the meeting, the first time a U.S. president had led a session of the Council. Mr. Obama opened the meeting by presenting to the 15-member Security Council a draft resolution, the contents of which had been agreed upon in earlier consultations. The Council swiftly and unanimously passed the measure — resolution 1887 — followed by remarks from Mr. Obama, U.N. Secretary-General Ban Ki-moon, the members of the Council and others." [8]

Setting an agenda and passing a resolution (Resolution 1887) to reduce the amount of nuclear warheads and to disarm potential threats is a great accomplishment and is essential for our very survival as a species along with *true* worldwide peace. What was striking about that day, was not about the resolution to reduce nuclear arms, but rather the lawless means of how it took place. Before I get into this, I need to discuss how the UNSC functions. According to the official United Nations website:

"Under the Charter, the Security Council has primary responsibility for the maintenance of international peace and security. It has 15 Members, and each Member has one vote. Under the Charter, all Member States are obligated to comply with Council decisions."

The Security Council takes the lead in determining the existence of a threat to the peace or act of aggression. It calls upon the parties to a dispute to settle it by peaceful means and recommends methods of adjustment or terms of settlement. In some cases, the Security Council can resort to imposing sanctions or even authorize the use of force to maintain or restore international peace and security.

"The Security Council also recommends to the General Assembly the appointment of the Secretary-General and the admission of new Members to the United Nations. And, together with the General Assembly, it elects the judges of the International Court of Justice." [9]

Under the UN Charter, the functions and powers of the Security Council are:

- TO MAINTAIN INTERNATIONAL PEACE AND SECURITY IN ACCORDANCE WITH THE PRINCIPLES AND PURPOSES OF THE UNITED NATIONS;
- TO INVESTIGATE ANY DISPUTE OR SITUATION WHICH MIGHT LEAD TO INTERNATIONAL FRICTION;
- TO RECOMMEND METHODS OF ADJUSTING SUCH DISPUTES OR THE TERMS OF SETTLEMENT;
- TO FORMULATE PLANS FOR THE ESTABLISHMENT OF A SYSTEM TO REGULATE ARMAMENTS;

217

- TO DETERMINE THE EXISTENCE OF A THREAT TO THE PEACE OR ACT OF AGGRESSION AND TO RECOMMEND WHAT ACTION SHOULD BE TAKEN;
- TO CALL ON MEMBERS TO APPLY ECONOMIC SANCTIONS AND OTHER MEASURES NOT INVOLVING THE USE OF FORCE TO PREVENT OR STOP AGGRESSION;
- TO TAKE MILITARY ACTION AGAINST AN AGGRESSOR;
- TO RECOMMEND THE ADMISSION OF NEW MEMBERS;
- TO EXERCISE THE TRUSTEESHIP FUNCTIONS OF THE UNITED NATIONS IN "STRATEGIC AREAS";
- TO RECOMMEND TO THE GENERAL ASSEMBLY THE APPOINTMENT OF THE SECRETARY-GENERAL AND, TOGETHER WITH THE ASSEMBLY, TO ELECT THE JUDGES OF THE INTERNATIONAL COURT OF JUSTICE.

Of the 15 members that make up the UNSC, the United States, China, France, Russia and the United Kingdom account for five permanent members and have remained permanent members since its inception back in January of 1946.

The other ten nations are considered non-permanent members and are elected for a period of two years based upon a vote by the General Assembly. Each member state or nation chairs the 15-member UNSC on a rotating monthly basis regardless of its membership statues. The person representing their particular nation state is known as the "President," so any person who "chairs" the UNSC regardless of status is known as the "President of the United Nations Security Council." In most cases, these "Presidents" have been and are United Nations Ambassadors that represent their particular nation state. As a matter of fact, the Charter's rules state, "A representative of each of its members must be present at all times at UN Headquarters so that the Security Council can meet at any time as the need arises." [10] Throughout the course of a year, their can be hundreds of situations or conflicts that arise that would need to be addressed within the Security Council in the form of official meetings. To date, the council has met over 7,450 times to discuss and address conflicts that arise.

According to statements from the official UN website, "The Permanent Representative (ambassador) of the state that holds the presidency is usually the president of the Council, but if an official from the state who is higher in authority than the Permanent Representative (such as a foreign minister, prime minister, or head of state) is present in the Council, the higher official is the president. For example, in January 2000, a month in which the United States held the "Presidency" of the Security Council, U.S. Vice President Al Gore, headed the United States delegation to the United Nations for a few days. As a result, Gore was the "President" of the Security Council during this time." [11]

For an accurate and complete list of all of the "Presidents" that have ever chaired the United Nations Security Council, please visit the database in Wikipedia under the search term (Presidents of the UNSC). There, you will find the complete list of all who served as "Presidents" of their respected nation states. Concerning the United States and their long history at the UN, all of the "Presidents" have either been State Senators, US ambassadors to the UN, Secretary of States, Secretary of the Treasurer and former Vice President, Al Gore, as being the highest position next only to the President of the United States up until 2009, when President Obama became the first "President" of the UNSC to ever sit as chairman of the world's most powerful legislative body on the planet.

Most Presidents of the United States would never think of chairing this position as to prevent the public perception of the Presidency becoming a monarchy (King) or dictatorship. Aside from the stigma of appearing as King, holding two offices while President is unconstitutional and an impeachable offense if the media were to run with that story, which they won't. According to Article 1 Section 9 of the US Constitution:

219

"No Title of Nobility shall be granted by the United States: And no Person holding any Office of Profit or Trust under them, shall, without the Consent of the Congress, accept of any present, Emolument, Office, or Title, of any kind whatever, from any King, Prince, or foreign State." [12]

Instead of U.S. Ambassador to the UN, Susan Rice, taking the gavel and despite the Constitution, President Obama took it upon himself to Chair the UN Security Council. In doing so, he became "President" of the UN, holding two Nobility titles at the same time, an unprecedented move by any President of the United States. You might think this is no big deal, but our founding fathers placed and established safeguards that were written into the Constitution in order for this Republic to remain a Republic and not to morph into a Monarchy or a different form of government for which it was never intended. Our form of Government is unique among the world governmental systems, which guarantees individual rights to all and even to the poorest and weakest among us. It is because of the Constitution and our Bill of Rights, with the enforcement of the rule of law, that the citizens of the United States have become the most envied in the world with regard to their high living standards and the right to free expression. Ultimately, it is the Creator who is the guarantor of our rights as it is quite clear in Romans 13:1 that citizens are subject to the government we elect, *"Let every soul be subject to the governing authorities. For there is no authority except from God,..."* No one is placed into office that the Creator has not allowed. Thus, as proven by history, governments are either a source of blessings or curses against its citizens. **Either instruments of Freedom or Tyranny!**

What Mr. Obama willfully did back in 2009, would be considered by many, including myself, as "lawless" especially by a former Illinois Constitutional Attorney who would clearly know better. By holding a title of Nobility under the United Nations, he was in fact, operating under the full authority of the United Nations and allowing himself to make decisions, to set the agenda and to influence legislation that would result in resolutions being mandated after a vote by the committee, which was the case in September 2009.[13] He would legally and lawfully be a "King" if he passed and directed legislation as "President of the UNSC." But, there is more going on here than meets the eye.

Despite these UN Resolutions, we have witnessed, and are witnessing, a Middle East that has become more and more unstable especially as a result of the rise of ISIS and ISIL. Regardless of how many resolutions are past by the UN, there continue to be a further breakdown of the rule of law in the Middle East. According to Newsmax, "In light of the Middle East meltdown we are witnessing right before our eyes, it is quite clear that the U.N. Security Council has failed in its mission to maintain international peace and security; to investigate the situations that have led to international frictions; to recommend methods of adjusting such disputes; to formulate plans to regulate armaments in this troubled region; to determine the existence of threats to peace, recommend actions to be taken to cease aggressions; and to exercise the trusteeship functions of the United Nations in "strategic areas." [14]

In spite of the nuclear nonproliferation agreements being passed that would target such countries as Iran from developing nuclear weapons, Mr. Obama has made it his mission that Iran posses the means to develop nuclear energy in order to increase commerce and thus, violating the edicts of the UNSC Resolutions that he chaired. It was Senator Coats that stated, " The administration's tactics in the negotiations with Iran were flawed from the outset, beginning with its backing down on the demand that Iran stop enriching uranium (a demand that was contained in six U.N. Security Council resolutions passed between 2006 and 2010). ..."We were misled by that illusion. Today, 20 years after the nuclear agreement with North Korea, negotiated by the Clinton administration, that country now has an estimated 20 nuclear warheads. And the Chinese experts tell us that the

North Koreans will have more than 40 by the end of next year and an effective ICBM intercontinental ballistic missile, to put those weapons on." [15]

If you are able to read through the lines, then you start to realize that the United States selectively enforces these mandates based upon the administration's agenda. Regardless of the Presidents affiliated party, whether Republican or Democrat, the Presidency has been sliding closer and closer to a dictatorship no thanks to the executive orders that have been stacking up since John F. Kennedy and all future Presidents regardless of party affiliation in order to be used at that right moment. In the end, we get the government we vote for!

The "President" of the United Nations

As I was saying, back on August 19, 2014, when I discovered that President Obama was again going to preside over the UN Security Council, I knew that it was significant for reasons I have laid out and the fact that September 24, 2014 would land on the eve of Yom Teruah. It would also be that significant day that would start the final 2,550 days, as I discovered just moments before. I knew that it would again result in an act of lawlessness as what had happened just five years prior.

It was at this moment that I realized that I would need to completely abandon my book and to place what was revealed to me online, revealing this new revelation to all who would visit my website. I chose the domain, september2015.com because of the divine connections coming to a head in that future time. Over the course of two to three weeks, I would write content, post articles and put together timeline graphs showing these Divine Connections to future Fall Fest Days by using Photoshop and finally uploading YouTube videos as documented. I would openly state on my website banner, the following: *The Anti-Christ to Confirm a Covenant*

222

with the Many, from September 24th to 26th 2014, a three day window from the eve to the second day of Yom Teruah 2014.

In my zeal, I would have also sent handwritten letters and graphs to the top Hebrew Roots teachers/pastors in America about three weeks prior to this event. Understanding the significance of what has about to take place, and because the seven years of tribulation fit so well within that 2,550 day timeframe, I thought for sure that the seven years of tribulation would start Yom Teruah 2014. In addition, I theorized that Mr. Obama might enact a "Peace" Deal between Israel and Palestine and/or other Arab countries much like past U.S. Presidents have attempted to do so since 1978 especially during years falling on the Shmitah, as I have documented, with this Shmitah cycle beginning on Yom Teruah 2014 and ending on the eve of Yom Teruah 2015, the Shmitah Release Day.

Ultimately, as it turned out, none of those events took place as stated. What did take place, however, is that Mr. Obama did lawlessly preside over the United Nations Security Council for a second time (2nd witness) that would result in the passage of UNSC Resolution #2178, the sixth time in the history of the UNSC that all Heads of State were present at the meeting and who would vote on legislation under the authority of the world body—the United Nations.

You must realize that the chances of the United States being selected to chair the UNSC in September is very rare. September is significant because the month of Tishri (when the Fall Feasts take place) generally fall in that month. As a matter of fact, from 2015 to 2021, all the Fall Feasts from Yom Teruah to Tabernacles will fall within September with the exception of Tabernacles of 2017 falling in the month of October according to *Torah Calendar*.

To make my point, I have documented all of the times that the United States has been chosen to chair in the month of September. What I have discovered is that since 1946, the United States have chaired the UNSC in the month of September just four times: 1965, 1997, 2009 and 2014.[16] The chances of it chairing from now to 2021 is pretty slim because of these arbitrary months of rotation.

The UN Security Council is unique in that it is the strong arm and military might of the United Nations and, thus, the power structure of World Government housed in that *Great City* – New York City. It is amazing to me to see the rise of this Mystery Babylon in these latter days.

It was Ancient Babylon where the Bible makes an account of all the people being united in language, economy, religion, thought and military. Eventually, their pride and arrogance would reached to heaven, as represented by the Tower of Babel and it would be at that moment where the Creator would divide the people and their language. We again see the world being united as in the days of Ancient Babylon in one language, economy, religion, thought and military. Everything is in place! All it would take now is for these "terrorist" to bring the world to her knees and the rise of the *New World Order* would be complete. The question remains as to whether or not Mr. Obama will be a part of this plan.

A Covenant with the Many

It would have been the eve of Yom Teruah 2014 (September 24th, 2014) that the "President of the UNSC," (Mr. Obama) would have directed a Resolution calling for the destruction of terrorist groups. UNSC Resolution #2178, "Threats to International Peace and Security caused by Terrorist Acts," is legislation that would declare war on ISIS, ISIL, Al Qaida and other rogue terrorist organizations. This resolution was passed unanimously, under the leadership of the "President" of the UN Security Council, who along with 15 of the world's most powerful militaries, made a Covenant to declare war on terrorist. Just the permanent members of this vote, being made up of the United States, Russia, China, England and France, would harness enough military might to fulfill the events as described in the Book of Revelation.

As stated under the UN charter, one of the functions of the UNSC is to "take military action against an aggressor." And under the Charter, all Member States are obligated to comply with Council decisions meaning that they would all be unified in their objective to declare war on "terrorism." One man possessing the power and authority of directing agenda, setting policy and heading the passage of Resolutions has too much power for any one man to posses especially when that one man is already head of the most powerful nation and military might on the planet. Something to consider! One thing is for sure, Mr. Obama gets things done and is able to set policy and pass resolutions with other leaders of the most powerful countries of the world. Some might even call him, "King of the World."

One other aspect of this event that I would like to highlight has to do with the play on words. It would have been on the following day on September 25, 2014 that I would have for the first time, watched the video of Mr. Obama heading the UNSC just one day prior. What I noticed was the play on words. When you watch the video, you will notice that the plaque that represents the position and name of the country is placed on the table with the representative of that country sitting behind this plaque. On that day, the plaque read, *"The President of the United States."* This is deceptive and most people would never have caught on that this title as it is reserved for any representative who presides over the chair of the United States. Back in 2009, if US Ambassador to the UN, Susan Rice, were to have chaired that seat, then she would have been given the title, *The President of the United States.* This goes for any person who chairs this position regardless of rank or title inclusive of Senators, Ambassadors or even former Vice President Al Gore. They all receive this title. My point is that Mr. Obama was passing legislation for World Government and was doing so under the full authority of the United Nations. At that moment, he in fact, was acting under a *Title of Nobility* for the United Nations!

With regard to deception, I have noticed that Wikipedia does not even mention Mr. Obama's name for September 2014 within their long and complete list of "Presidents" of the UNSC. But, instead they name Samantha Powers, the official United States Ambassador to the United Nations. This is incorrect because according to the UN's own website, "The Permanent Representative (ambassador) of the state that holds the presidency is usually the president of the Council, but if an official from the state who is higher in authority than the Permanent Representative (such as a foreign minister, prime minister, or head of state) is present in the Council, the higher official is the president." So, according to the stated policy of the United Nations, it would have been the official who is higher in authority, who would have been the "President" and in this case this would have been Mr. Obama.

However, they do mention his name in 2009, which makes me think that his name was deliberately left out to keep Bible students from making this connection. See the snap shots taken from the Wikipedia [17] website below...

March 2009	Libya	Ibrahim Dabbashi[76] and Abdurrahman Mohamed Shalgham[77]
April 2009	Mexico	Claude Heller[78] and Patricia Espinosa[79]
May 2009	Russia	Vitaly Churkin[80] and Sergey Lavrov[81]
June 2009	Turkey	Baki Ilkin[82] and Ahmet Davutoğlu[83]
July 2009	Uganda	Ruhakana Rugunda[84] and Sam Kutesa[85]
August 2009	United Kingdom	John Sawers[86]
September 2009	United States	Susan Rice,[87] Barack Obama,[88] Rosemary DiCarlo,[89] and Hillary Rodham Clinton[90]
October 2009	Vietnam	Lê Lương Minh[91]
November 2009	Austria	Thomas Mayr-Harting[92]
December 2009	Burkina Faso	Michel Kafando[93]

And for September 2014...

March 2014	Luxembourg	Sylvie Lucas[163]
April 2014	Nigeria	Joy Ogwu[164]
May 2014	Republic of Korea	Oh Joon[165]
June 2014	Russian Federation	Vitaly Churkin[166]
July 2014	Rwanda	Eugène-Richard Gasana[167]
August 2014	United Kingdom	Mark Lyall Grant[168]
September 2014	United States	Samantha Power[169]
October 2014	Argentina	María Cristina Perceval[170]
November 2014	Australia	Gary Quinlan[171]
December 2014	Chad	Mahamat Zene Cherif[172]

Some may think it is a big stretch to compare the event that transpired on September 24, 2014 with Daniel 9:27.

"And he shall confirm a covenant with many for one week. And in the middle of the week he shall put an end to slaughtering and meal offering. And on the wing of abominations he shall lay waste, even until the complete end and that which is decreed is poured out on the one who lays waste."* (Daniel 9:27)

First off, there are some assumption made with regard to this verse and there are a few prominent opinions as to who "he" is referring to. Two of the most prominent theories is that "he" refers to either Yahshua/Jesus or the Antichrist. After all, it was Yahshua who was cut off after his 3-1/2 year ministry in the midst of the week or 7 years and it would have been Yahshua that would have been the atoning sacrificial lamb. There are some within the Hebrew Roots movement that believe Yahshua's ministry was 70 weeks or 1.3 years long as is the position held by Michael Rood. I see the significance of this viewpoint, but I personally don't hold to this belief system.

The other theory states that it will be the Antichrist who will confirm a covenant with many for one week. The assumption is that this will initiate the 70th week (7 years) of Daniel's 70th week prophecy, the final 7 years of man's rule on this earth, which is a good assumption to make. It will be in

227

the midst of this week or 3-1/2 Hebraic years (1,260 days), that "he" will put an end to slaughtering and meal offerings and it would be at this time when "he" will perform the abomination in the set apart place as referred to by Yahshua in his Oliviet Discourse recorded in Matthew 24:15, *"So when you see the 'abomination that lays waste,' spoken of by Dani'ĕl the prophet, set up in the set-apart place..."* It will be this final act of defiance that will unleash the Creator's wrath on the world of unbelievers. The *"abomination of desolation"* as it is also called is the final act of rebellion by the Antichrist that will legally qualify for the judgement by the Almighty.

There is debate as to what this abomination might be, but most believe "he" will stand in the newly built Jewish Temple and will demand to be worshipped much like the Creator is worshipped. My view is slightly different! I believe that there is no need to re-build the Jewish Temple because there is already a temple there known as the Dome of the Rock and/or the El Aqsa Mosque, that sits on the holy place being Mount Moriah that is an abomination as being in the same spot or close to the same spot as was the "Holy of Holies" within Herod's Temple. The Dome of the Rock has been a "temple" to the Muslims since 691 CE and an abomination to the Jewish People ever since. This, again, is the 3,000 pound pink elephant sitting in the room that no one seems to be noticing. It is very likely that it is this "temple" where "he" will stand demanding worship. In order for this to be fulfilled, there must be a sacrificial system set up on Mount Moriah for the Jewish People, this being their desire in order to fulfill the prophecies in Daniel concerning the sacrificial system.

What I have found is that Bible prophecy is often times fulfilled much differently than our minds are capable of understanding and often there are double or even triple prophetic fulfillments from a single Bible verse as is the case with the double prophetic fulfillment of Daniel's seven weeks prophecy as discussed in chapter 5.

Do you recall the separation of time from the comma in Isaiah 61:2, *"to proclaim the acceptable year of* יהוה, *and the day of vengeance of our Elohim, to comfort all who mourn"* and what it signified? The space/comma that separates *"year of* יהוה, *and the day of vengeance of our Elohim"* is a space that represents a period of time of almost 2,000 years as this day of vengeance is still awaiting its future fulfillment through Yahshua.

Now, let's take a look at part of the prophecy of Daniel 9:27, "And he shall confirm a covenant with many for one week." If we were to apply the same reasoning, then it would read, *"And he shall confirm a covenant with many* (confirming a covenant, UNSC Resolution #2178, with 15 powerful nations and "he" possibly make a peace treaty between Israel and other Arab countries from Yom Teruah to Yom Kippur of 2015) *for one week."* I realize that there are assumptions and it seems like a stretch, which it is. There is no way for any of us to fully comprehend on how this will transpire and who "he" might end up being, but if you have read this far, then you have already made some connections to September 2015. As you will discover, this will begin to make more sense in the next and final chapter.

Russia to Chair the UNSC in September 2015 and Will Approve a Palestinian State!

While we are on the subject of the "Presidents" of the UNSC, I find it interesting that Russia is scheduled to be "President" of the UNSC in the month of September 2015. I do not know at this time, which representative will preside over the UNSC, but it will more than likely result in the 7th emergency meeting of the Heads of State meeting at the UNSC, with Russia setting policy this time around instead of the United States. See the following image ...

Dates	State	Name
January 2015	Chile	Cristian Barros[173]
February 2015	People's Republic of China	Liu Jieyi[174]
March 2015	France	François Delattre[175]
April 2015	Jordan	Dina Kawar[176]
May 2015	Lithuania[177]	Raimonda Murmokaitė
June 2015	Malaysia[177]	Dato Ramlan Ibrahim
July 2015	New Zealand[177]	Gerard van Bohemen
August 2015	Nigeria[177]	
September 2015 (scheduled)	Russia[177]	
October 2015 (scheduled)	Spain[177]	
November 2015 (scheduled)	United Kingdom[177]	
December 2015 (scheduled)	United States[177]	

With regard to Russia, they have held this position in the month of September five other times in the years 1947, 1966, 1969, 1986, 1990 and of course is scheduled this coming September 2015. As you can see, there really is no rime or reason with the selection of this position.

"In September of this year, the UN Security Council is expected to vote on a UN resolution to establish the Palestinian state. France is already working on a proposal to give formal UN Security Council recognition to the Palestinians. The resolution would declare that a divided Jerusalem is the capital of both Israel and a Palestinian state. In addition, the new document would set the 1967 borders as the baseline for future negotiations to establish the final borders between the two nations," the Russian News Agency Pravda.Ru reports. [18]

They continue, "France will most likely submit the resolution for a vote after the 70th session of the UN General Assembly begins on September 15. For the time as many as 136 countries have recognized a Palestinian state, but the United States has always blocked recognition by the UN Security Council. This time may be different though, because there are quite a few indications that Barack Obama actually plans to back the French resolution in September. If that happens, and the UN Security Council approves this resolution, it is going to have enormous implications for all of us."

So, we see that a representative from Russia will become the "President" of the UNSC on Yom Teruah 2015 that will decide in favor of a Palestinian State, although this is yet to be seen. It will be this resolution that will divide Jerusalem unless the President of the United States, Barack Obama, vetos this French legislation, "If the United States does not veto the French resolution later this year, it will almost certainly pass. So right now, the only thing standing in the way of a Palestinian state is Barack Obama. And considering the fact that he is probably the most anti-Israel president in our history, that is a very sobering thought." [19]

As you can see it will be the "70th" session of the UN General Assembly. Mark my words, the United Nations will play and are playing a Key role in the fulfillment of Bible prophecy in the coming years.

The other point I would like to make has to do with the coalition of nations identified as the Gog and Magog Coalition headed up by non other than Russia. Keep in mind that the chances of Russia chairing the UNSC in September of 2016 to 2021 is slim, although they have chaired this position in September 1966 and September 1969, just three years apart. So it is possible, just not probable.

It is this future coalition that is mentioned in the Bible as recorded in the Book of Ezekiel 38 & 39. With Russia scheduled to head the UNSC as "President" of the UNSC, will that Representative from Russia create a coalition known in Scripture as the Gog and Magog Coalition? Here is the verses associated with this future prophecy yet to be fulfilled.

"Now the word of the Lord came to me, saying, "Son of man, set your face against Gog, of the land of Magog, the prince of Rosh, Meshech, and Tubal, and prophesy against him, and say, 'Thus says the Lord God: Behold, I am against you, O Gog, the prince of Rosh, Meshech, and Tubal. I will turn you around, put hooks into your jaws, and lead you out, with all your army, horses, and horsemen, all splendidly clothed, a great company with bucklers and shields, all of them handling swords. Persia, Ethiopia, and Libya are with them, all of them with shield and helmet; Gomer and all its troops; the house of Togarmah from the far north and all its troops—many people are with you." (Ezekiel 38:2-6, NKJV)

"Prepare yourself and be ready, you and all your companies that are gathered about you; and be a guard for them. *After many days* you will be visited. *In the latter years* you will come into the land of those *brought back from the sword and gathered from many people on the mountains of Israel, which had long been desolate; they were brought out of the nations, and now all of them dwell safely.* You will ascend, coming like a storm, covering the land like a cloud, you and all your troops and many peoples with you" (Ezekiel 8:1-9 NKJV).

These Scriptures identify Russia and a coalition of other nations (Iran, Ethiopia, Libya, Turkey and other geographical close nations) coming against Israel in the latter years being brought forth from the sword and gathering back to the mountains of Israel, which had long been desolate. This prophecy is clearly identifying Israel at this time in world history and speaks of no other time prior. Many prophecy teachers identify that the Psalm 83 War must come first along with the destruction of Damascus prior to the Gog and Magog War.

There is no way to know if a coalition will be formed under the chairman-ship of the UNSC this September; However, if Israel will not submit to the demands of the United Nations Security Council's decision, then we could see a coalition being put together to deal with the problem especially with Russia at the helm, yet this leads me to speculate on another additional pos-sibility.

With regard to resolution # 2178, is it possible that this coalition of nations (the nations who passed this resolution) will attack ISIS when they eventu-ally infiltrate Israel, much like the ongoing bombing campaigns being waged in Iraq and Syria against ISIS? Will this powerful alliance of 15 na-tions commence their bombing campaign in Israel in order to "destroy" ISIS? Some of you know where I am going with this! And, isn't it inter-esting that despite the best efforts of the UNSC and the military cam-paigns against ISIS and other terrorist groups, that these terrorist groups are remarkably growing in strength and size? How can this be especially when the most powerful nations are waging war against them with the on-going bombing campaign? Once again, there is more here than meets the "All-Seeing" eye!

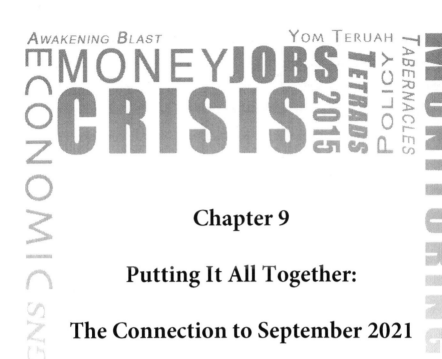

Chapter 9

Putting It All Together:

The Connection to September 2021

"And He came to the Ancient of Days, and they brought Him near before Him. And to Him was given rulership and preciousness and a reign, that all peoples, nations, and languages should serve Him. His rule is an everlasting rule which shall not pass away, and His reign that which shall not be destroyed." (Daniel 7: 13-14)

The common belief within Christianity of end times eschatology closely follow these seven events:

Event # 1 - The Antichrist rises to power through diplomacy and uses his position of power for his own gain through craftiness and deception and is the one who negotiates a seven year peace covenant on behalf of Israel.

Event # 2 - The Antichrist soon afterwards take peace away from the earth as he is given more power from the World Community.

Event # 3 - The Rapture of the church happens just before tribulation begins. The start of tribulation is the beginning of the much anticipated final 70th week of Daniel.

Event # 4 - World War III erupts and leads to massive death and worldwide famine and the Antichrist implementing the mark of the beast system, whereby, no man is able to buy or sell without that mark.

Event # 5 - Increase distress among the nations lead to widespread persecution of Jews and Christians and those who refuse to take the chip (mark) will be put to death.

Event # 6 - After 3-1/2 years, the Almighty releases his wrath on an unbelieving world through a great earthquake, the sun not giving its light, the moon appearing as blood, the stars falling from heaven and other supernatural events.

Event # 7 – Right at the end of the seven years, with the atmosphere scorched with darkness, all those left on earth are caught by surprise as Jesus returns in a flash of light, which illuminates the entire globe and places His feet back on the Mount of Olives in Jerusalem.

There is more to this obviously but, these seven steps represent a good overview, nonetheless. I will now tie everything together in this final chapter.

Thus far, we have been able to make some amazing connections with regard to the Creator's Jubilee, the solar jubilees, the Shmitahs, the 120 jubilee cycle, the 6,000th year, the 2,550 days from Yom Teruah to Yom Kippur, the Mid-Tribulation Sign of 2017 and so much more! But, one thing that seems to be lacking are two or more confirmations (witnesses) of what has been presented thus far. There is a verse in the Bible that seems to indicate this idea, "…out of the mouth of two or three witnesses shall every word be established" (II Corinthians 13:1).

The Confirmation and Double Confirmation of June 7, 1967 and September 24, 2014

Back on August 19th, 2014 when I came across Gavin Finley's website and made the connection to the final 2,550 days starting on Yom Teruah 2014 and ending on Yom Kippur 2021, I then had enough information to begin checking dates by using *timeanddate* and by using *Torah Calendar* in order to see how the Gregorian dates lined up with the feast days especially as they relate to the eve of the Fall Feast days. What I discovered was absolutely mind blowing!

Starting with June 7th, 1967, I began to add the days of the 49 years of the *Creator's Jubilee* that being 17,640 days with the 2,550 days that I had just discovered would begin in a little more than one month from my vantage point in August 2014. I knew that the eve of Yom Kippur 2015 was key as being the moment before the beginning of the *Creator's 50th Year of Jubilee* as the total number of days were 17,640 days, exactly the amount of days of the *7 weeks* of Daniel and as documented by Sir Robert Anderson.

Likewise, moments before I discovered that the eve of Yom Teruah 2014 (September 24, 2014) would also play a significant role considering that the mid-Tribulation Sign would appear on Yom Teruah 2017 and thus could not be the start of the 7 years of tribulation simply because this sign was a mid-tribulation sign as I have documented for you in chapter seven of this book.

With this new revelation, I simply started adding the days together via *timeanddate.com* by selecting "What date is it in X Days?" I then selected June 7th, 1967 and added 19,830 days being made up of 17,640 days plus 2,550 days, less 360 days. The result was the following:

Date calculator: Add to or subtract from a date

This service enables you to add or subtract days, months and years to a date to calculate a past or future date.
Design changes: What is new and why?

Start Date

Month:	Day:	Year:	Date:	Add/subtract:	Years:	Months:	Weeks:	Days:
6	7	1967		(+) Add				19830

Today

Include a time ►   Include only certain weekdays ►

Calculate new date

From **Wednesday, June 7, 1967**
Added 19,830 days

Result: Tuesday, September 21, 2021

The result is September 21, 2021. When I confirmed this future date of September 21, 2021 on *Torah Calendar*, I was amazed to see that it landed on the eve of Tabernacles as this future date fell on the 14th day of the seventh month of Tishri. See the screen shot of the 7th month of Tishri 2021 from the Torah Calendar website below for a confirmation of this keeping in mind that Sukkot is Tabernacles.

3rd Day	4th Day	5th Day	6th Day	Sabbath
Yom Shli-shi	Yom Re-vi-i	Yom Ham-i-shi	Yom Shi-shi	Sha-bat
Monday sunset until Tuesday sunset	Tuesday sunset until Wednesday sunset	Wednesday sunset until Thursday sunset	Thursday sunset until Friday sunset	Friday sunset until Saturday sunset
		1 **Yom Teruah** Day of Trumpets Rosh Hashanah Civil New Year Yom Teruah 8 Sep 2021 C.E. sunset to 9 Sep 2021 C.E. sunset Day: 2,193,651	**2** Yamim Noraim Days of Awe 9 Sep 2021 C.E. sunset to 10 Sep 2021 C.E. sunset Day: 2,193,652	**3** Yamim Noraim Days of Awe Shabbat Shuvah Ha'azinu 10 Sep 2021 C.E. sunset to 11 Sep 2021 C.E. sunset Day: 2,193,653
	Rosh Chodesh First Visible Crescent Moon seen at sunset on 8 Sep			
6 Yamim Noraim Days of Awe 13 Sep 2021 C.E. sunset to 14 Sep 2021 C.E. sunset Day: 2,193,656	**7** Yamim Noraim Days of Awe 14 Sep 2021 C.E. sunset to 15 Sep 2021 C.E. sunset Day: 2,193,657	**8** Yamim Noraim Days of Awe 15 Sep 2021 C.E. sunset to 16 Sep 2021 C.E. sunset Day: 2,193,658	**9** Yamim Noraim Days of Awe 16 Sep 2021 C.E. sunset to 17 Sep 2021 C.E. sunset Day: 2,193,659	**10** **Yom Kippur** Day of Atonement Yamim Noraim Days of Awe Yom Kippur 17 Sep 2021 C.E. sunset to 18 Sep 2021 C.E. sunset Day: 2,193,660
13 20 Sep 2021 C.E. sunset to 21 Sep 2021 C.E. sunset Day: 2,193,663	**14** **Eve of Sukkot** Tabernacles Set Up Today Joshua 5:13-6:5 Matthew 16:24-17:9 Eve of Sukkot 21 Sep 2021 C.E. sunset to 22 Sep 2021 C.E. sunset Day: 2,193,664	**15** **Sukkot** Tabernacles Day 1 Sukkot Day 1 **Fall Equinox** 22 Sep, 19h:21m UT 22 Sep sunset to 23 Sep sunset Day: 2,193,665	**16** **Sukkot** Tabernacles Day 2 Sukkot Day 2 23 Sep 2021 C.E. sunset to 24 Sep 2021 C.E. sunset Day: 2,193,666	**17** **Sukkot** Tabernacles Day 3 Sukkot Sabbath 24 Sep 2021 C.E. sunset to 25 Sep 2021 C.E. sunset Day: 2,193,667

I was simply amazed to see that simply adding 19,830 days from June 7th, 1967 resulted in the future date of the eve of Tabernacles/Sukkot 2021. As I was discovering, dates or major events falling on the eve of the feast days was highly significant especially with regard to the future Fall Feast Days.

I then began to plug in other dates to see what else I might discover and in order to verify this date with a second "witness." The next obvious choice was to place the then future date of September 24, 2014, being the eve of Yom Teruah, in the *timeanddate* website and adding 2,550 days from that date. The result was Electrifying! See the following screen shot of this revelation:

238

Date calculator: Add to or subtract from a date

This service enables you to add or subtract days, months and years to a date to calculate a past or future date.

Design changes: What is new and why?

Start Date

Month:	Day:	Year:	Date:	Add/subtract:	Years:	Months:	Weeks:	Days:
9	24	2014		(+) Add				2550

Today

Include a time ▸   Include only certain weekdays ▸

Calculate new date

From **Wednesday, September 24, 2014**
Added 2550 days

Result: Friday, September 17, 2021

The result is Friday, September 17, 2021. When I went to *Torah Calendar* and verified this date, I knew I had something that was going to change the world! The result was non other than the eve of Yom Kippur 2021 that falls on the eve of Shabbat (Saturday), nonetheless. Verify for yourself be viewing the 7th month of Tishri above. Within just a matter of 5 minutes time, the Creator had revealed to me his mow'ed or his *Appointed Feast* of good things to come, the eve of Yom Kippur and the eve of Tabernacles 2021! What an amazing Revelation and Double Confirmation!

This leads me to ask the question: What are the odds of these dates falling on the eve of the sixth Feast Day of Yom Kippur and the eve of the seventh Feast Day of Tabernacles 2021, especially when one factors in that these two separate dates of June 7th, 1967 and September 24th, 2014 spanning a difference of over 47 years as well as the significance of what they represent? There should be no doubt that the Creator has His hand at play in this considering that He is an Elohim with purpose, order and the highest degree of intelligence.

239

At that moment, I understood the significance of June 7th, 1967, but had no idea why the eve of Yom Teruah, September 24th, 2014 was giving me a confirmation to the eve of Yom Kippur 2,550 days in the future. It was at that time that I began to research online what might happen on September 24th, 2014. I was looking for potential military drills that may led to war, major geopolitical events around that time, an asteroid strolling by earth or even world leaders making announcements. After what had seemed liked a few hours time, I eventually came across a news article that stated that President Obama would be heading the "chairmanship" of the UNSC on September 24th, 2014. I knew in my spirit that this was "The Event" that would tie into the eve of Yom Teruah, because I was aware he had done so previously in 2009.

It would have been this defining moment that I knew I would need to abandon my book and to place all of this new revelation on a website as noted in prior chapters. Ultimately it were these two confirmations or "witnesses" that sealed this revelation for me and that would ultimately change the world!

From that day forward, I would make other remarkable connections and would place these connections and revelations in visual representations using Photoshop. One such graph would be the following graph labeled, *The Divine Confirmations*, where I have incorporated June 7th, 1967, the final two tetrads, the Creator's Jubilee, Daniel's 7th *week*, the final 70th *week*, the Shmitah cycles as well as the two confirmations resulting in the eve of Yom Kippur and Tabernacles of 2021. See the following graph.

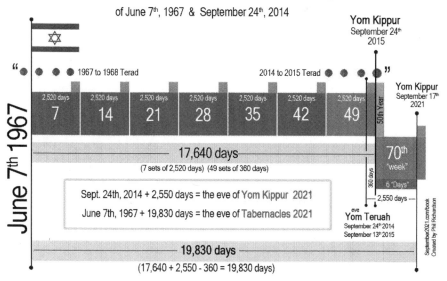

The Divine Confirmations
of June 7th, 1967 & September 24th, 2014

Yom Kippur
September 24th
2015

1967 to 1968 Terad   2014 to 2015 Terad

Yom Kippur
September 17th
2021

2,520 days	2,520 days	2,520 days	2,520 days	2,520 days	2,520 days	2,520 days
7	14	21	28	35	42	49

June 7th 1967

50th Year

17,640 days
(7 sets of 2,520 days) (49 sets of 360 days)

70th
"week"

360 days

6 "Days"

Sept. 24th, 2014 + 2,550 days = the eve of Yom Kippur 2021

June 7th, 1967 + 19,830 days = the eve of Tabernacles 2021

2,550 days

eve
Yom Teruah
September 24th 2014
September 13th 2015

September2021zoombook
Created by Phil Richardson

19,830 days
(17,640 + 2,550 - 360 = 19,830 days)

Notice the use of the simple math associated with these two confirmations as indicated on the graph. In addition, the confirmation of September 2021 results in a difference of 360-days between the eve of Yom Teruah 2014 and the eve of Yom Teruah 2015 and is the reason for the subtraction of the 360 days that results in the 19,830 days. Back in August 2014, I assumed that the seven years of tribulation would begin on Yom Teruah 2014 because of the fact that the seven 360-day cycles +30 days (2,550 days) fit so well in between 2014 and 2021, and because of all of the confirmations and connections the Creator was revealing to me at that time.

As it turned out, there was no start of tribulation in 2014 as originally thought. Like so many Christians, the assumption of the seven years of tribulation is predominately pushed in churches, publications, books, tv programs and teachings with no alternative aside from a possible 3.5 year period of time, simply because Scripture indicates seven years for various reasons. What I began to realize back in November of last year was that there would be no 7 years of tribulation, but rather 6 years. As you will see in a moment, this theory makes the most sense.

Six Years of Tribulation

First and foremost, there is no question that September 24, 2014 was a pivotal point in time. Not only do we have a future confirmation date, but we have the beginning of the final 2,550 day countdown until all is complete as referenced in the 9th chapter of Daniel by the completion of the 70th *week* that will begin on Yom Kippur 2015 with the final year being cut short on the eve of Yom Kippur 2021.

As you may recall in the past chapter, Yom Teruah 2014 to Yom Kippur 2021 qualifies for the 2,550 day period of time that not only lines up with Torah Calendar, but also with the Metonic Lunar Moon cycle of 86 moons +10 days and the 1,335 days that finalizes on the eve of Shavuot 2018, as discussed. The only other time this would work would be from 2017 to 2024, but there are problems associated with these dates as previously discussed and thus would not qualify. As you may recall, the 1,335 days would not qualify starting in 2015 or 2016, but may qualify in 2017; however, starting the 1,335 days from Yom Teruah 2017 and counting out would place the ending of the 1,335 days on Shavuot 2022 that would go beyond the two confirmation dates. This means that the 1,335 days only qualifies beginning on Yom Teruah 2014 and thus, would confirm September 24th, 2014 as being a key date in fulfilling Bible prophecy.

What you will notice from the graph, *The Divine Confirmation* is this 360-day window of time that we are in the midst of as I write this book identified on the graph between Yom Teruah 2014 to Yom Teruah 2015. I like to identify this period of time as the eye of the storm where all seems calm and surreal at the moment. This period of time is also the *49th 360-day cycle Shmitah* of the Creator's Jubilee as indicated by the small blue square.

Once this 49th Shmitah ends, as it will on the eve of Yom Teruah, we will have entered the 6,000th year on Tishri 1, 2015. I believe this *Appointed Feast* will set off a chain of events that will usher in the *6 Years of Tribulation* according to this graph and what is written in this book.

Keep in mind that the Creator has an *Appointed Time* for everything especially as it relates to His final 7 year plan. If the Shmitah Release Days of 2001, 2008 and 2015 represents judgment as a "Release" of wealth, then these final two jubilees, the Creator's 50th Year of Jubilee beginning Yom Kippur 2015 and the more common solar jubilee beginning Yom Kippur 2017 will represent mega-judgments in the form of wiping out wealth, capitol and more.

As you may recall, the Shmitah Release Day is that last day of the 2,520 day Shmitah cycle (seven sets of 360-days) that will finalize on Elul 29, 2015 on the civil calendar, destined for the "Release of Debt" as a blessing and liberation of his people. The Jubilee had an even greater blessing attached as this blessing would be for an entire year with a return of the land to its original owners and a re-uniting of clans, tribes and families.

Because the world is under judgment, these final two 50th Year of jubilees will represent a wiping away of wealth versus a wiping away of debt, thus the term *mega judgment*. This leads me to discuss the final graph of this book that I have titled as the *"The Richardson Theory."*

The Richardson Theory

Because most of these events described in this book are future events, I must state them in theory and thus the identification of this next to final graph titled, *"The Richardson Theory."* As I was stating, the final two jubilees identified as the 50th Creator's and the 50th Solar represent mega judgments. Please see the graph titled, *The Richardson Theory that* identify the two jubilees. In addition, notice how everything ties together much like a puzzle coming together. Represented on this graph is the *3 Pillar Foundation* that highlights the major Fall Feasts of September 2015, the final *Super Blood Moon* of the Tetrad, the *2017 Mid-Tribulation Sign* that places the first few verses of the 12th chapter of the Book of Revelation on Yom Teruah 2017 that would usher in the *Solar 50th Year of Jubilee,* along with *the two confirmations dates* falling on the eve of Yom Kippur and Tabernacles of 2021. Keep in mind that all of these graphs presented within this book may be viewed in high definition and downloaded from my site, *September2021.com.*

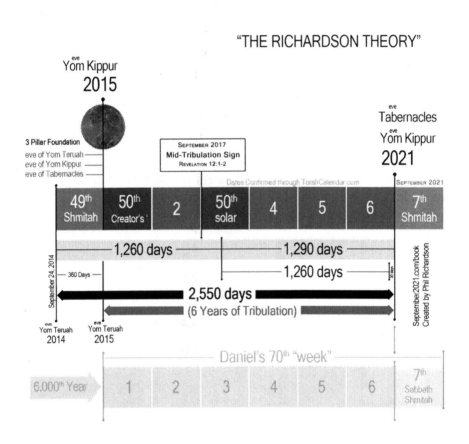

In addition, notice that the *49th Shmitah* accounts for year number one of the seven year countdown (2,550 days) until Yom Kippur 2021 with the

50th Year of the Creator's Jubilee accounting for year number one of the six year countdown until Yom Kippur 2021. Notice how all of these dates fit perfectly and how they associate with the two jubilees and with His *Appointed Feasts*.

Notice how the two jubilees fall in year one and year three of the *6 Years of Tribulation* as well as *Daniel's 70th week*. While the jubilees are appointed for judgment to the world, they should represent Liberation to those who have the seal of YHVH or to those who place their trust in the Creator and to His Son, Yahshua. It will be during this period of time that might offer liberation with regard to the land of Israel and the Jewish people yet during a time of great distress. Part of the Creator's plan is to use this great distress in order to reveal to the Jewish People their true Messiah and to bring many to righteousness.

The End of the 2,550 Days and the Connection to September 2021

Up to this point, I have not really covered the significance of September 2021 and what it might represent. Part of *"The Richardson Theory"* is to discuss my theory as it relates to September 2021. As discussed extensively, the ending of the 2,550 days will fall on a future Yom Kippur and in this case, will finalize on Yom Kippur 2021. My belief and part of my theory is that this will be the day that Yahshua places His feet back on the Mount of Olives and proceeds by force taking the dominion away from the enemy and entering Jerusalem for his Millennial reign as *King of Kings and Lords of Lords*.

This may be the same day that He defeats his enemies as a conquering King since Yom Kippur is the day designated for Judgment by the Almighty. Prior to this, and according to my theory, He will rescue his saints during the *Appointed Feast* of Yom Teruah, the feast *"where no man knows the day or hour,"* an idiom that identifies a groom coming for his bride. Keep in mind that this event, known as the *Rapture of the Church*, may happen more than once during these final 6 years with Liberation identified as the 50th Year of Jubilee being the likely period of time for this event to take place. More specifically, this event could take place between the eve of Yom Teruah to Yom Kippur with the blowing of the shofar covering a period of four years when these jubilees fall from 2015 to 2018. Although this event of the Groom coming for his Bride will take place during Yom Teruah or its eve, there is a slight chance it could take place on the eve or the Day of Yom Kippur as it is a day of the blowing of the shofar as well and there are many passages that allude to the righteous being saved on the day of wrath.

In addition, *"The Richardson Theory"* states that the final 7th year of Daniel's 70th *week* will take place back on Earth, meaning that the final year of the *Great Wedding Feast* will take place from Tabernacles 2021 to Tabernacles 2022. Of course, much Bible prophecy must take place in order for this to become a reality and as such is simply a theory at this point in time.

The 7 Witnesses and the Divine Order of Seven

If you have read this far, then undoubtedly you have picked up on the divine order of what has been presented. What I am about to reveal will absolutely confirm this even further. As stated, my theory identifies September 2021 as being the month that will usher in the return of the Messiah for all people, but especially for the Jewish people who will again be heard saying, *"Hoshia-na to the Son of Dawid! Blessed is He who is coming in the Name of יהוה! Hoshia-na in the highest!"* (John 12:13) as Yahshua Himself declared that He would not return until He would hear those words again, "And truly I say to you, you shall by no means see Me until the time comes when you say, 'Blessed is He who is coming in the Name of יהוה!'" *(Matthew 23:37-39).*

This leads me to discuss the divine order of His return. Please view *"The Richardson Theory"* graph once more and take notice of the Shmitah pattern located at the bottom of the graph. This Shmitah pattern of 6 days/weeks/months/years/millennia and then the beginning of the 7th has been heavily identified throughout this book and there is no exception as to the return of the Messiah. As a matter of fact, the Scripture states that He (Yahshua) is the Master of the Sabbath, "For the Son of Adam is Master of the Sabbath" (Matthew 12:8).

Based upon my theory, His return will follow the Shmitah pattern and will end the 6th and will usher in the BEGINNING of the :

- 7TH MILLENNIUM
- 7TH MILLENNIAL YEAR
- 7TH YEAR OF TRIBULATION
- 7TH MONTH OF TISHRI
- 7TH DAY AS IN DAYS OF DANIEL'S WEEK
- 7TH FEAST DAY OF TABERNACLES
- 7TH YEAR FROM THE "SUPER BLOOD MOON"
- 7TH YEAR OF DANIEL'S 70TH WEEK
- 7TH SHMITAH

...and the completion of the 2,550 days (7 years or 7 sets of 360-day cycles +30 days) that will identify the true Messiah on Yom Kippur 2021! The 30 days following the 2,520 days will fall on the 6th month of Elul and will signify Teshuvah or the final 40 days of Repentance of the Nations until all is complete. Please see the graph for verification.

All of this represents order to the highest degree possible! As a matter of fact, I cannot think of anything that it's lacking. This follows the Shmitah cycle precisely much in the same way that Friday, the 6th day, would come

247

to an end at sunset and at that moment would usher in the 7th day of Shabbat or Saturday. This is the same pattern we repeatedly see over and over again.

One last point I would like to make has to do with the Shmitah Year. Remarkably, Torah Calendar places the beginning of the 7th day Shmitah on Yom Teruah 2021 as can be seen on their calendar system. It is remarkable how everything lines up so well!

It's Too Perfect!

At this point I would like to Submit my theory to the scientific community of believers of these final 6 years until the return of the *Lion of Judah* back to Earth realizing that our Creator does not operate by chance, but rather with order and esteem, not lacking in anything as He is omnipotent, omnipresent and who sits outside the constraints of time. There is no doubt that this will challenge you in your own preconceived notions and belief systems regarding Bible eschatology and the reality of where we are on the prophetic timeline as well as the understanding of how Christianity has steered off course and needs to be corrected in certain false belief systems that have been adopted by just about every denomination.

This book was written in Boldness and goes against the flow of the acceptable thought patterns within Christianity of "date setting" as the message is LOUD and CLEAR! As the Creator is known as the *Eleventh Hour God,* this book and the revelation associated with it is a message in this eleventh hour as I am finalizing my final thoughts in early August 2015, just moments before September 2015. One thing is for sure, September 2015 will offer clarity to what is written here!

What we can Expect

"Son of man, speak to the children of your people, and you shall say to them, 'When I bring the sword upon a land, and the people of the land shall take a man from their borders and shall make him their watchman, and he sees the sword coming upon the land, and shall blow the ram's horn and shall warn the people, then whoever shall hear the sound of the ram's horn and shall not take warning, if the sword comes and takes him away, his blood is on his own head. 'He heard the sound of the ram's horn, but he did not take warning, his blood is on himself. But he who takes warning shall deliver his being. *'But if the watchman sees the sword coming and shall not blow the ram's horn, and the people shall not be warned, and the sword comes and takes any being from among them, he is taken away in his crookedness, and his blood I require at the watchman's hand.'* "And you, son of man, I have made you a watchman for the house of Yisra'ěl. And you shall hear a word from My mouth and you shall warn them for Me" (Ezekiel 33:2-7).

I consider myself as an Ezekiel 33 Watchman and as such, it is my desire to sound the ram's horn of Alarm (Teruah) in order to warn people and to win souls for the kingdom. This is really the reason behind this book, to sound the alarm and to point people towards Yahshua in my attempt to *"Wake Up Humanity"* out of their Laodicean Slumber and to bring a message of hope and unity through the only one that can offer Yeshua (Salvation).

If the world is headed towards the fulfillment of the 70th *week* of Daniel's prophecy, as is written and identified in this book, then I fully expect major world events to begin happening at a quickening speed unlike anything we have experienced in the past. Here is a list of events that I have compiled that I believe will be at the forefront starting this Yom Teruah and into the 50th Year of Jubilee.

Revival and the Great Harvest of Souls

I wanted to start out on a positive note especially considering what is about to take place in the world. Often times the Creator uses judgment and tribulation for the purpose of revival with the intended goal of winning souls for the kingdom who otherwise might be destined for hell. The two weeks following 9-11 was such a time of revival whereby the citizens of this nation as a collective whole took up the call of repentance. I remembered during that time of mourning that the churches of America were packed as the yearning of our spirits were to seek the unshakable grounds of the Almighty. 9-11 happened one week prior to the *Shmitah Release Day* of 2001 and as such the call to repentance began 7 days prior to the 10 days count down to Yom Kippur. How appropriate considering that the Almighty has brought restoration for two additional Shmitah patterns of 14 years.

As we approach the 14th (two witnesses as in two Shmitah cycles) year anniversary of 9-11 that will take place three days prior to the *Shmitah Release Day* of 2015, will we truly seek repentance as a nation much like the case in 2001? More importantly, will the Creator pass-over his judgment on a nation and world that continue to rebel against Him or will He allow another "terrorist" attack possibly on the second Shmitah anniversary of 9-11?

It is my unshakable view that part of the Creator's plan is to use tribulation in order to bring restoration and the beginnings of the great revival and Harvest of Souls for the Kingdom to come. This means for those reading this, that you have been commissioned for **such a time as this** in playing a part in the Great Commission spoken of by Yahshua and it is for this reason we have been born in this generation that will see the return of the King!

The Almighty U.S. Dollar is headed for a serious collapse! The BIS (The Bank of International Settlements) know as the "World's Bank" of Banks that most people have never heard of, has introduced the *Third Basel Accord*, named after their headquarters located in Basel, Switzerland. This Accord is scheduled to be implemented in 2015 or later and came to fruition as a result of the financial crises back in 2007/2008, that being the last Shmitah year. According to Wikipedia, "Basel III focuses primarily on the risk of a run on the bank by requiring differing levels of reserves for different forms of bank deposits and other borrowings." [1] To put it another way, the BIS, that sets policy for the Federal Reserve and all other central banks inclusive of the largest banks in the world, is anticipating a *"Run on The Banks"* and they are setting policy to deal with this event! Thus far, there are over 200 countries that have agreed to this Accord inclusive of the United States.

Additionally, both Russia and China have been calling for a new "Bretton Woods" agreement in hopes of dethroning the US Dollar as the reserve currency of the world replacing it with the Chinese' Yuan. When one realizes that both China and Russia have been stockpiling gold for the past 10 years, moving it from the West and to the East, then it becomes clear that these two countries are anticipating becoming the major power players of the world's economy, militarily and political influence along with the BRICS nations. They are simply waiting for the right moment to make their power play onto the world scene.

It should be clear that fiat based currencies inclusive of credit will become a thing of the past as they are not backed up by anything with the exception of the "good faith of the government." The idea behind the *Basel III Accords*, is to restructure these fiat currencies of the world based upon the assets or debts of that particular countries currency. This means that after this "Reset," currency will either rise or drop in value depending on the amount of debt or assets a country has. It is expected that the U.S. Dollar will lose value based upon the debt and obligations of the United States and the fact that our gold (assets) have been flowing to the East, "Fiat currency is becoming a thing of the past due to ongoing pervasive fraud and devaluation of paper currency – now it will have to be backed by assets (precious metals, oil, etc.)." [2]

The Distress of Nations

Yahshua spoke of a time of great distress among the nations, "For nation shall rise against nation, and reign against reign. And there shall be scarcities of food, and deadly diseases, and earthquakes in places" (Matthew 24:7). The catalysis for this prophecy is undoubtedly a collapse of the world's financial systems that would result in the eventual collapse of the U.S. Dollar as well as other fiat currencies that are pegged to the dollar. This will not happen overnight, yet once it happens, there will be a rapid deceleration of wealth especially through this "Economic Reset" that will more than likely take place within the Creator's 50th Year of Jubilee.

This, along with war, will cause this distress on the nations as the rising super powers of the world, Russia and China, will emerge from the financial ashes, no longer submitting to the demands and wishes of Washington.

6 Years of Tribulation and War

"And I looked and saw a white horse, and he who sat on it holding a bow. And a crown was given to him, and he went out overcoming and to overcome. And when He opened the second seal, I heard the second living creature saying, 'Come and see.' And another horse, fiery red, went out. And it was given to the one who sat on it to take peace from the earth, and that they should slay one another. And a great sword was given to him. And when He opened the third seal, I heard the third living creature say, 'Come and see.' And I looked and saw a black horse, and he who sat on it holding a pair of scales in his hand... And I heard a voice in the midst of the four living creatures saying, 'A quart of wheat for a day's wage, and three quarts of barley for a day's wage. And do not harm the oil and the wine.' And when He opened the fourth seal, I heard the voice of the fourth living creature saying, 'Come and see.' And I looked and saw a pale horse. And he who sat on it had the name Death, and the grave followed with him. And authority was given to them over a fourth of the earth, to kill with sword, and with hunger, and with death, and by the beasts of the earth" (Revelation 6:2-8).

The above passage from the sixth chapter of the Book of Revelation concerns the first in a series of "seals" being loosened in heaven, *"And one of the elders said to me, 'Do not weep. See, the Lion of the tribe of Yehudah, the Root of Dawid, overcame to open the scroll and to loosen its seven seals' "* (Revelation 5:5). The only one who has authority to loosen the seals is none other than Yahshua.

It is my understanding that the "seals" identify the riders as being "kings," with the horses representing the nation or kingdom of that king. We see that the Antichrist rides the white horse with white representing that nation as being a peaceful and righteous nation whereby he is able to conquer and overcome in a time of "peace." The second horse identified by the second seal is a nation identified with the color red that take peace away from the earth through war. Following this red "nation" is the black horse that brings scarcity that would follow a worldwide financial collapse and a worldwide war. If the horses represent nations, then this black nation seems to be identifying the rogue nation state of ISIS with their black flag of death. Likewise, red seems to indicate those nations that have red on their flag that are able to bring war such as China and Russia, while the Pale [3] (Green) horse seems to identify the Islamic State and Islamic nations with their green flags that represent these nations. As a matter of observation, the Muslim Brotherhood, Iranian, Iraqi, Jordanian, Pakistan, Libyan, Syrian, Saudi Arabian, Lebanese, Sudanese, Ethiopian, Kuwait and Palestinian flags all contain the exact same green in their flags.

As the breakdown of the rule of law continues to grow within the Middle East, we are seeing the rise of a Caliphate of Muslim nations uniting in their common battle cry of death to the West and to Israel. Nothing has changed with the exception of the West giving them more power and influence (notice that these nations are given power and are not the source of power). It will be this rising Caliphate that will more than likely fulfill the requirements as the pale horse.

From my perspective, the Islamic countries along with the rogue State of ISIS will be given power to kill up to 25% of humanity through terrorist acts and by the sword. Although the most powerful nations have declared war on ISIS through UN resolutions #2178 and the like, I guarantee you that we haven't seen the last of ISIS!

This leads me to briefly discuss an additional theory as relates to the 7 seals of Revelation chapter 6. It struck me the other day, that the loosening of the seals may correspond to the 360-Day cycles and the divine connection associated with them especially as it relates to the beginning of the Fall Feast days. To make my point, we need to identify the rider of the white horse. We know that Yahshua will come back on a white horse, with the white horse representing a righteous government or kingdom with the rider representing Yahshua as King. We know that the Antichrist is a false messiah and attempts to mimic the true King by being the rider on a white horse as well.

If the "President" of the UN is that rider and the US is that nation, then the loosening of the first seal began last year exactly on the eve of Yom Teruah 2014. This would mean that it is possible that the loosening of the second seal would occur one 360-Day cycle later that just happens to fall on the eve of Yom Teruah 2015 or possibly in 2016 as a pattern has not been established. From my perspective, in order for this to become a reality, there would need to be a resolution or announcement with regard to America, Russia and/or China as it relates to war. If this happens on Yom Teruah or its eve, then we will indeed have a pattern to go off of. It is to early to tell at this point, but something worth observing nonetheless.

Lights, Camera, Action!

"The coming of the lawless one is according to the working of Satan, with all power and signs and wonders of falsehood, and with all deceit of unrighteousness in those perishing, because they did not receive the love of the truth, in order for them to be saved. And for this reason Elohim sends them a working of delusion, for them to believe the falsehood, in order that all should be judged *who did not believe the truth, but have delighted in the unrighteousness.*" (II Thessalonians 2: 9-12)

This passage from II Thessalonians concerns great deception and falsehoods that will arise in the latter days and is very likely in reference to this whole phenomena with extraterrestrials as I believe these "entities" will be used to deceive mankind. I have seen this push by the media through documentaries, tv shows, magazines, video games and movies as we are being programmed to believe that mankind was seeded on this planet by ancient aliens.

The idea is prevalent even among some of the top scientific minds. As an example, top evolutionist and scientist, Richard Dawkins was asked in the documentary, *Expelled* as narrated by Ben Stein, on how life might have evolved and he stated, "Well, it could come about in the following way. It could be that at some earlier time, somewhere in the universe, a civilization evolved, probably by some kind of Darwinian means, probably to a very high level of technology, and designed a form of life that they seeded onto perhaps this planet. Now that is a possibility, and an intriguing possibility. And I suppose it's possible that you might find evidence for that if you look at the details of biochemistry, molecular biology, you might find a signature of some sort of designer." Moments before in the interview he emphatically denied any type of Creator or God, yet had no problem implying that aliens might be our "designers." Keep in mind that Mr. Dawkins is one of the brightest evolutionary scientist out there. How could he possibly believe in any type of "designer" when the entire Theory of Evolution is void of any type of designer inclusive of aliens?

We even see this idea pushed by the Discovery Channel in their series known as "Ancient Aliens," leaving us with the impression that Adam and Eve were seeded in order to populate the earth, as well as movies such as Prometheus directed by Ridley Scott, whereby the opening scene shows intelligent "beings" seeding planet earth, known in evolutionary studies as panspermia. The hypothesis of panspermia proposes the belief that microscopic life forms arrived on earth and eventually evolved into humans. Even Stephen Hawking believes this idea as he has stated, "Life could spread from planet to planet or from stellar system to stellar system, carried on meteors."[4] And this guy is the brightest of the brightest?

If that were not enough, we see this push by not only science, but also by the Vatican who recognize these alien species. It was Tom Horn and Chris Putnam, authors of *Petrus Rómanus: The Final Pope is Here* and *Exo-Vaticana* who both paid a visit to the Vatican's most advanced telescope known as L.U.C.I.F.E.R., an acronym standing for *Large Binocular Tele-scope Near-infrared Utility with Camera and Integral Field Unit for Ex-tragalactic Research,* located on Mount Graham in the mountains near Safford, Arizona.[5] Yes, Lucifer is another name for the devil and this should tell you something about the Vatican and their whole deceptive be-lief system.

What these two researchers and authors discovered was a connection be-tween the Vatican and their work on "extraterrestrial intelligence." As a matter of fact it was leading Vatican astronomer and top Jesuit Priest, Guy Consolmagno who admitted how contemporary societies will soon "look to The Aliens to be the Saviors of humankind." [6] This idea of alien life be-coming the saviors of mankind will eventually manifest and become that great delusion foisted upon mankind thanks to secretive governmental projects such as *Project Blue-Beam.* [7] The reality is that these aliens are de-monic entities, all being orchestrated by Satan. Will you believe the lie?

The Beginning of the 7th Millennium

First off, the beginning of the 7th millennium is a much anticipated and highly significant event with regard to the Jewish people as it is known as Olam Haba or "The World to Come." It is also significant because many well meaning Rabbis [8] believe that the Messiah must appear before "The World to Come" can begin. As quoted from the article, "When asked about the timing of the Messiah's arrival, Rabbi Kanievsky answered, 'At the end of the Sabbatical year.' Several people have asked the Rabbi to ver-ify this and he has given the same answer each time. *This year is the Sab-*

batical year and it will be ending on the 29th day of Elul, which, by the Gregorian calendar falls on Saturday, September 12, 2015."

Because of the great significance with regard to the 7th Millennium, I would like to discuss when the beginning of the 7th Millennium will take place through what has been presented thus far and with the aid of a few external sources.

The beginning of the 3rd millennium did not begin on the year 2,000 but rather it began January 1st, 2001. [9] This can be confusing because it would seem that the third millennium would have begun in the year 2,000 as some believe. To gain a clear understanding of this, we need to see what *Torah Calendar* has to say regarding the beginning of the 7th Millennium.

According to *Torah Calendar*,[10] we are approaching a critical time that seems to be between the year 6,000 and the year 6,001. As I have stated, I believe that *Torah Calendar* is off one year because they have not accounted for the 50th Year of the Creator's Jubilee that will have its beginning on Yom Kippur 2015. Instead, they have accounted for it beginning this past Yom Kippur 2014 as confirmed on their website, which seems to be incorrect for reasons that I will explain. The image taken from their website, [11] *Age of the Messiah to the Age of Life* will be used to explain this. View the following image.

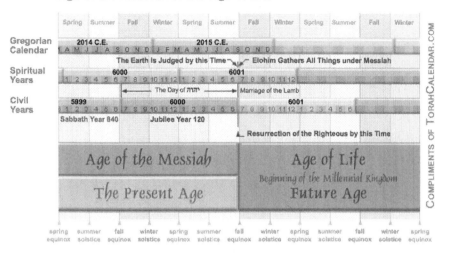

Age of the Messiah to the Age of Life

Notice on this image that they have *identified* "The Day of YHVH" as a one year period of time with a *corresponding* "Jubilee Year 120" (the 50th Year of the 120th Jubilee) that, according to Torah Calendar, took place between Yom Kippur 2014 and Yom Kippur 2015. The context of this phrase, "*The Day of YHVH,*" comes from the 58th & 61st chapters of Isaiah. "…Do you call this a fast, and an acceptable day to יהוה?" (Isaiah 58:5). This identifies the "Great Day" of Yom Kippur while, "to proclaim the acceptable year of יהוה, and the day of vengeance of our Elohim" (Isaiah 61:2) describes the Day being Yom Kippur and the Year being *the 50th Year of Jubilee.*

To recap, the "*Day of YHVH*" is a period of time reserved for the Creator's judgment that would fall on the *Appointed Feast* of Yom Kippur. Clearly the world has not experienced mayhem that would have begun Yom Kippur last year and as such, this calendar system is off by one 360-Day cycle as stated by myself in prior chapters. Keep in mind that Torah Calendar states a one year period of judgment within the *Day of YHVH* happening on the now corrected dates from Yom Teruah 2015 to Yom Kippur 2016.

259

My goal in identifying these discrepancies is not to downplay *Torah Calendar* or what they have written but rather to reinforce their amazing website and their ideas one year in advance beginning this September 2015 and finalizing in September 2016. Thus, year 6,000 would begin September 14th/15th of 2015 and the year 6,001 would begin Yom Teruah 2016 with Yom Kippur representing — *"The Earth is Judged by this Time."*

To clarify, the viewpoints being expressed by *Torah Calendar* do not necessarily reflect my viewpoint with regard to judgment. As such, I do not necessarily believe that the *Day of YHVH* must take place on Yom Kippur 2016; however, with that said, that may change based upon what takes place this coming year.

In addition, *Torah Calendar* makes mention of the *"Marriage of the Lamb"* indicating that they believe that the Groom will come for His Bride on the now corrected date of Yom Teruah 2016. According to Torah Calendar, "The end of the Present Age and the Age of the Messiah initiates the Age of Life or the Millennial Kingdom on Day 1 / Month 7 / Year 6001. The righteous dead are to be awakened by the sound of the last trump (1 Corinthians 15:52)." [12] Notice that their Year 6001 is correct however it is reserved for Yom Teruah 2016 and not Yom Teruah 2015.

Thus, the *"Age of Life,"* according to their spiritual understanding would begin in September 2016 that would end the *"Age of Messiah"* otherwise known as the *Church Age of Grace* as well as the 120th jubilee. According to my understanding of the information presented, the beginning of the *7th Millennium* would thus begin Yom Teruah 2016 as the *"Age of Messiah"* would end and the *"Age of Life"* would begin. It is my belief that Christianity will be required to get rid of their paganism and to begin to start calling upon the Creator's true name —Yahweh, as the period of grace ends and more will be required at the turn of the 7th Millennium!

As you can see, the period of time from September 2015 to September 2016 will be a critical period of time of teshuvah (repentance) and getting your spiritual house in order. *If Torah Calendar is correct, then Yom Teruah 2016 may be the time destined for the Groom coming for his Bride!*

The "Destroyer of the Eye!"

As stated in the Introduction, there are specific meanings behind Hebraic names. The Creator's name spelled in Hebrew as יהוה (YHVH) is made up of the Hebrew letters Yod Hey Vav Hey with each of these Hebrew letter having a meaning:

- THE LETTER VAV IS THE SYMBOL OF A NAIL.
- THE LETTER HEY IS THE SYMBOL OF REVELATION AS IN "BEHOLD, I BRING YOU REVELATION."
- THE SYMBOL ATTACHED TO THE LETTER YOD HAS A MEANING OF "HAND OR HAND ATTACHED TO AN ARM."

Putting it all together, we find that YHVH's name literally means:

- BEHOLD! THE NAIL IN THE HAND THAT BRINGS REVELATION!

But what about the Son's name? What deep meaning is associated with His name aside from "YHVH is Salvation?"

We find that Yahshua's (יהושע) name is made up of the Hebrew letters Yod, Hey, Vav, Shin and Ayin. Much like the meaning behind the Father's name, the meaning behind the Son's name is astounding especially as it relates to our day and age.

- THE HEBREW LETTER VAV IS THE SYMBOL OF A NAIL.

261

- THE LETTER HEY IS THE SYMBOL OF REVELATION AS IN "BEHOLD, I BRING YOU REVELATION."
- THE SYMBOL ATTACHED TO THE LETTER YOD HAS A MEANING OF "HAND OR HAND ATTACHED TO AN ARM."
- THE SYMBOL BEHIND THE LETTER SHIN IS THE PICTOGRAPH OF TEETH OFTEN ASSOCIATED WITH CONSUMING OR DESTROYING AS IN THE CONSUMING FORCES OF FIRE.
- THE SYMBOL ASSOCIATED WITH THE LETTER AYIN IS AN EYE.

Putting it all together the name of Yahshua literally means:

- **BEHOLD! THE NAIL IN THE HAND THAT DESTROYS THE EYE!**

When you realize that *the New World Order* is identified as being the all seeing eye on top of the pyramid, then you realize just how powerful his name is. For a visual representation of this, just view the backside of the U.S. One Dollar Bill and notice *the All Seeing Eye* on top of the Pyramid with the inscription underneath that reads in latin, *NOVUS ORDO SECLORUM* translates as *a new order of the ages* or a *New World Order.* [13] This phrase has been expressed by many world leaders including just recently by Pope Francis, "Francis issued an impassioned call for a new world order where the goods of the Earth are shared by everyone, not just exploited by the rich." [14]

This is part of the reason why I make reference to the United States as possibly being *Mystery Babylon.* Aside from my country being a wealthy country, it has influenced all the "kings of the earth"; housing the entity establishing "World Government" (the United Nations); home to the all powerful U.S. Dollar and is protected by the Pacific and Atlantic Oceans, *"O you who dwell by many waters, Abundant in treasures, Your end has come..."* (Jeremiah 51:13). It is interesting to see that the monetary system that was established by the Bretton Woods Conference of 1944, bears the image of *the All Seeing Eye* that will be destroyed by the one who is destined to do so.

Tearing Down the Veil Between Jew and Gentile

Part of the reason for this book is to help the reader identify the veil of lies and misperception that have separated Jews and Gentiles. Keep in mind that the Jewish People originated from the tribe of Judah and are Israelis, yet Israel has been identified as the northern kingdom of Israel that has been identified by the ten tribes of Israel that were dispersed throughout the world. When I use the phrase "Jew and Gentile," I am using it in a way that most people understand it, in other words, the Jewish people and everyone else. For simplicity sakes, I use Gentile to identify Christians as is the common perception within the churches.

Both sides of the veil, Jews and Christians, have hidden knowledge and revelation that the opposite group needs in order to complete the puzzle. For the Jew, the hidden knowledge and revelation concerns their true Messiah— Yahshua who is embraced by the Gentiles. It will be He who will save both Jew and Gentile at their greatest hour of need. For the Gentile believer in Yahshua, the hidden knowledge and revelation concerns the 7th day Sabbath, the significance of the Feast Days, the Torah, and a need to separate from paganism.

If it were not for my insatiable desire to dispense with false belief systems within Christianity and to embrace the truths that the Jews hold dear, then the revelation behind this book would have never come about. Knowing this, it is my goal to bring unity through the Messiah as He is the only one that can do so as prophesied concerning him.

I have made mention of false belief systems throughout this book; however, I have left a few until now. It should be evident that the Shmitah principle of 6 years and then the seventh as a rest is highly important to

263

the Creator. This same Shmitah pattern is identified in the weekly Sabbath that begins Friday at sunset and ends Saturday at sunset. It is my belief that those who have the seal of YHVH during these final 6 years will be those who honor and obey his commandments especially concerning the 7th weekly Sabbath or rest. This Sabbath day principle is part of the *Marriage Covenant* that we should be honoring as it shows the Bridegroom that we truly love him if we obey his commandments, *"He who possesses My commands and guards them, it is he who loves Me. And he who loves Me shall be loved by My Father, and I shall love him and manifest Myself to him"* (John 14:21). There are numerous Scriptures that speak of keeping and guarding His commandments. Here are a few:

"Here is the endurance of the set-apart ones, here are those guarding the commands of Elohim and the belief of יהושע." (Revelation 14:12)

"Blessed are they that do his commandments, that they may have right to the tree of life, and may enter in through the gates into the city." (Revelation 22:14)

"And He said to them, "The Son of Adam is Master of the Sabbath." (Luke 6:5)

"By this we know that we love the children of Elohim, when we love Elohim and guard His commands. For this is the love for Elohim, that we guard His commands, and His commands are not heavy," (1 john 5:2-3)

"And by this we know that we know Him, if we guard His commands. The one who says, "I know Him," and does not guard His commands, is a liar, and the truth is not in him." (1 John 2:3-6)

"Not everyone who says to Me, 'Master, Master,' shall enter into the reign of the heavens, but he who is doing the desire of My Father in the heavens. "Many shall say to Me in that day, 'Master, Master, have we not prophesied in Your Name, and cast out demons in Your Name, and done many mighty works in Your Name?' "And then I shall declare to them, *'I never knew you, depart from Me, you who work lawlessness!'* " (Matthew 7:21-23, "lawlessness *being Torahlessness*,")

Shout, O Daughter of Jerusalem!

Many Jewish People believe that they will be saved in a future Yom Kippur as briefly touched on in the first chapter. As I have laid out, part of *"The Richardson Theory"* identifies Yahshua as being the one who will save the Jewish People on that special *Day* of Yom Kippur 2021.

At this point, I would like to highlight some Scriptures within the Tanakh that have been fulfilled by Yahshua/Jesus and some Scriptures that still speak of his return.

"Rejoice greatly, O daughter of Tsiyon! Shout, O daughter of Yerushalayim! See, your Sovereign is coming to you, He is righteous and endowed with deliverance, humble and riding on a donkey, a colt, the foal of a donkey. "And I shall cut off the chariot from Ephrayim and the horse from Yerushalayim. And the battle bow shall be cut off. And He shall speak peace to the nations, and His rule is from sea to sea, and from the River to the ends of the earth." (Zechariah 9:9-10) Much like Isaiah 61, there is a separation of almost 2,000 years from "the foal of a donkey" to "And I shall cut off the chariot from Ephrayim..." This verse speaks of Yahshua.

"And I shall pour on the house of Dawiḏ and on the inhabitants of Yerushalayim a spirit of favour and prayers. And they shall look on Me whom they pierced, and they shall mourn for Him as one mourns for his only son. And they shall be in bitterness over Him as a bitterness over the first-born." (Zechariah 12:8-10)

" 'See, the days are coming,' declares יהוה, 'when I shall raise for Dawid a Branch of righteousness, and a Sovereign shall reign and act wisely, and shall do right-ruling and righteousness in the earth. 'In His days Yehudah shall be saved, and Yisra'ĕl dwell safely. And this is His Name whereby He shall be called: 'יהוה our Righteousness.' " (Jeremiah 23:5-6)

"Elohim, therefore, has highly exalted Him and given Him the Name which is above every name, that at the Name of יהושע every knee should bow, of those in heaven, and of those on earth, and of those under the earth." (Phillippians 2:10)

"But He was wounded for our transgressions; He was crushed for our iniquities; upon him was the chastisement that brought us Shalom, and with his stripes we are healed." (Isaiah 53:5)

"But you, Bĕyth Lehem Ephrathah, you who are little among the clans of Yehudah, out of you shall come forth to Me the One to become Ruler in Yisra'ĕl. And His comings forth are of old, from everlasting." (Micah 5:2)

"For a Child shall be born unto us, a Son shall be given unto us, and the rule is on His shoulder. And His Name is called Wonder, Counsellor, Strong Ĕl, Father of Continuity, Prince of Peace. Of the increase of His rule and peace there is no end, upon the throne of Dawiḏ and over His reign, to establish it and sustain it with right-ruling and with righteousness from now on, even forever. The ar-dour of יהוה of hosts does this." (Isaiah 9:6-7)

"And one of the elders said to me, "Do not weep. See, the Lion of the tribe of Yehuḏah, the Root of Dawiḏ, overcame to open the scroll and to loosen its seven seals." (Revelation 5:5)

I would like to make one more point with connecting Yahshua to Yom Kippur and that has to do with the Ten Commandments. The first time the Ten Commandments were presented to Israel, they were broken on the 50th day of Shavuot by Moses as he observed Israel defiling themselves with the golden calf. I believe that the breaking of the first set of Ten Commandments was no accident as YHVH has a hand in everything that happens. The shattering of the Ten Commandments symbolizes not only a broken marriage covenant between Israel and YHVH, but also represents the southern kingdom (the Jewish People) rejecting their true Messiah who came as a Bridegroom to Israel as *the Humble Messiah* spoken of by the Prophets. Much like the Ten Commandments, the *Word of YHVH* was broken and *cut short* through His sacrificial death that likewise was prophe-sied to take place.

According to *Chabad.org*, "On 7 Sivan, Moses went up onto the moun-tain . . . On 17 Tammuz, the tablets were broken. On the 18th, he burned the [Golden] Calf and judged the transgressors. On the 19th, he went up for forty days and pleaded for mercy. On 1 Elul, he went up to receive the second tablets, and was there for forty days. On 10 Tishrei, Gd restored His goodwill with the Jewish people gladly and wholeheartedly, saying to Moses, 'I have forgiven, as you ask,' and gave him the Second Tablets." [15]

267

It would have been on Tishri 10 of Yom Kippur *that the Restored set of Ten Commandments* was presented, the first time being broken in pieces, yet this time fully restored and accepted by Israel. The spiritual connection is that Yahshua will be presented a second time and this time will be fully accepted by Israel and those who make up his Bride as it is Yahshua who has restored the marriage covenant as well.

Interestingly enough, the time period between Shavuot to Yom Kippur is 120 days. My point is that the 120 days is represented by the three ages of man being 40 as in 40 jubilees times three equaling 120 jubilees or 6,000 years and it will be after 6,000 years when the true Messiah is presented in much the same way that Yehoshua entered the promise land in that year of Jubilee when Moses was 120 years old (120 jubilees).

"And Mosheh called Yehoshua and said to him before the eyes of all Yisra'ĕl, "Be strong and courageous, for you are going with this people to the land which יהוה has sworn to their fathers to give them, and you are to let them inherit it. "And it is יהוה who is going before you, He Himself is with you. He does not fail you nor forsake you. Do not fear nor be discouraged." And Mosheh wrote this Torah and gave it to the priests, the sons of Lĕwi, who bore the ark of the covenant of יהוה, and to all the elders of Yisra'ĕl. And Mosheh commanded them, saying, "At the end of seven years, at the appointed time, the year of release, at the Festival of Booths," (Deuteronomy 31:7-10).

Some Additional Facts and Observations:

Almost two millennia have passed since Yahshua was on this earth, yet the revelation concerning Him have been re-ignited in these latter days as new knowledge and revelation concerning Him have been and are being revealed. This revelation is not only coming forth through the written word of the Bible, but also through archeological discoveries. One such discovery was of the actual crucifixion site of Yahshua as discovered by Ron Wyatt and his two sons back in 1981.[16] The evidence uncovered suggests that this location was the actual site and not those sites traditionally accepted and monopolized by big religious institutions.

Other discoveries made by Mr. Wyatt are some of the most profound in the history of mankind, yet most people have no idea because the mainstream media never has made mention of his discoveries, nor ever will for that matter. Once you understand that true knowledge and power are hidden, then you can see why this revelation will never be made public partly because it would conflict with the agenda pushed by the media and the pop culture.

Other archeological discoveries made by Mr. Wyatt have been of the true Mount Sinai,[17] the Red Sea crossing located in the Gulf of Aqaba[18] and of Noah's Ark located in the Mountains of Ararat.[19] All of these discoveries have been scientifically documented and can be further researched by going to http://wyattmuseum.com

One of the most profound discoveries made by Mr. Wyatt and his two boys was that of the Ark of the Covenant located below the crucifixion site as documented by Mr. Wyatt as being discovered on January 6th, 1982. You can research this further by visiting his site and the testimonial video[20] documenting this discovery as well as the testimonial video of the Messiah's blood on the Mercy Seat that poured through the crack to the cave below after the great earthquake recorded in Scripture. [21]

The revelation concerning the Messiah's blood as discovered on the Mercy Seat points to Yahshua as not only as being the Ultimate Atoning Sacri-

fice, but also of the Order of Melchizedek who were both King and Priest.
22

Blessed are Those Who Shall be Found Watching!

Contrary to what is being preached from the pulpits, we are to be discern-
ing the signs and times by watching and trying to determine His return so
as to avoid being caught by surprise as a *thief in the night.*

Will you be found watching or will you be caught by complete surprise?
We are not to be ignorant of the times in which we live. If this book has
had any impact on you, I pray that it would be your desire to understand
the times so that you can be a light unto the nations because the harvest of
souls will be great.

"Let your loins be girded and your lamps burning, and be like men
waiting for their master, when he shall return from the wedding, that
when he comes and knocks they open to him immediately. *"Blessed
are those servants whom the master, when he comes, shall find
watching. Truly, I say to you that he shall gird himself and make
them sit down to eat, and shall come and serve them.* "And if he
comes in the second watch, or in the third watch, and find them so,
blessed are those servants." (Luke 12:35-38, emphasis added in bold)

I would like to end this book by encouraging you to seek truth because the
deception is so deep and many fall into its trap. Yahshua Himself made
the following proclamation, "יהושע said to him, "I am the Way, and the
Truth, and the Life. No one comes to the Father except through Me"
(John 14:6). What an amazing and truly astonishing statement! Not only
is He proclaiming to be the Truth, but the Life and ultimately the Way to
the Father as there is no other means to do so. My prayer is that you will

follow Him, as He is the Good Shepherd and the only method by which, eternal life can be achieved!

Index

Scripture that supports calling upon the true name of the Creator Yáhweh:

Genesis.4:26, 12:8, 13:4, 16:13, 26:25, Exodus 3:15, 5:23, 9:16, 15:3, 20:7, 33:19, 34:5-6, Leviticus 18:21, 19:12, 20:3, 22:2,32, 24:11-16, Numbers 6:27, Deuteronomy 5:11, 6:13, 10:8,20, 14:22, 18:5,7, 18:19-22, 28:10,58, 32:3, Psalms 5:11, 7:17, 8:1,9, 9:2,10, 18:49, 20:5,7, 22:22, 23:3, 25:11, 29:2, 31:3, 33:21, 34:3, 44:5,8,20, 45:17, 48:10, 52:9, 54:1,6, 63:4, 66:2,4, 69:29,36, 72:19,10,18 21, 75:1, 76:1, 79:6,9, 80:18, 83:16,18, 86:9,11-12, 89:24, 91:14, 92:1, 96:2,8, 97:12, 99:3, 100:4, 102:21, 103:1, 105:1-12, 106:8,47, 111:9, 113:3, 115:1, 116:4,17, 118:10-12,26, 119:55,132, 124:8, 129:8, 135:1,3,13, 138:2, 142:7, 143:11, 145:1-2,21, 148:5,13, 149:3, Proverbs 18:10, 30:4,9, Isaiah 4:1, 12:4, 18:7, 25:1, 26:13, 29:23, 41:25, 42:8, 43:7, 47:4, 48:1-12, 50:10,51:15, 52:5-6, 56:6, 59:19, 63:12,14,16,19, 64:2,7, 65:1, Jeremiah 3:17, 10:6,16,25, 11:21, 12:16, 14:7,9,14-15,21, 15:16, 16:21, 23:25,27, 25:29, 26:9, 29:21, 32:18,34, 33:2, 34:15,16,).

Mystery Babylon:

I realize that this subject might be offensive to some people and as such I suppose your position would be to at least consider the possibilities of what

272

is written here. What I have come to realize is that often time's ancient Scriptures are attributed to double prophetic fulfillments as the case with Daniel's 7th *week* prophecy as mentioned within this book. Some of the Scriptures that have applied to actual Babylon in Iraq may apply to the Latter Day *Mystery Babylon* that in reality is a deep network made up of the world's power players such as the United States; the U.N.; the Vatican; the Basel and London based banking systems inclusive of the IMF, World Bank, BIS, and the Federal Reserve; Bilderberg and the global elite; the mega corporations; and Luciferian Freemasonry that seems to tie it all together. With that said, therein lies a particular *"Nation"* that houses a *"Great City"* whereby all of the nations of the world have been corrupted. We can zero in on this *Great City* by identifying the Scripture associated with it.

Listed are additional passages that describe this latter day *Great City* known as Babel.

"And you said, 'I am mistress forever,' so that you did not take these matters to heart, and did not remember the latter end of them. "And now, hear this, you who are given to pleasures, who dwells complacently, who says in your heart, 'I am, and there is none but me. I do not sit as a widow, nor do I know the loss of children.' " (Isaiah 47:7-8)

"The sea has risen over Babel, she has been covered with the roaring of its waves." (Jeremiah 51:42)

"Lift up a banner on the walls of Babel, strengthen the watch, station the watchmen, prepare the ambush. For יהוה has both planned and done what He spoke concerning the inhabitants of Babel. *You who*

273

dwell upon many waters, great in treasures, your end has come, the measure of your greedy gain." (Jeremiah 51:12-13)

"And they threw dust on their heads and cried out, weeping and mourning, and saying, 'Woe! Woe, the great city, in which all *who had ships on the sea became rich by her wealth!* For in one hour she was laid waste.' " (Revelation 18:19)

As you have read these verses, what Nations or *Great Cities* come to mind? Do these Scriptures speak of Russia, the European Union, Rome, Mecca, England or the United States? In the 18th chapter of the Book of Revelation, John describes a nation who will reign in these latter days who, according to the prophets, will be abundantly wealthy, militarily powerful and who will dwell by many waters that surround her. The verse that describes the great city, "in which all who had ships on the sea became rich by her wealth," would automatically eliminate Mecca, Moscow and the Vatican as being a possibility since these cities have no ports and especially deep sea ports that would be required for large ships of the merchants of the world.

Although the United States makes up only 5% of the population of the world, it makes up 50% of all of the wealth of the planet with a military force that is still the standard of the world and the envy of every nation. Indeed, we are a wealthy and powerful country by every standard available.

The northern tribes of Israel more than likely make up a majority of her people and is the reason why there is such a strong connection to the Jewish people. The prophecies speak of the sea coming up over her and being covered by a multiple of waves. This prophecy has not happened, but clarifies that this nation is directly bordered by the oceans and would not speak of a literal Babylon in Iraq since their geographical location would not support these Scriptures. Babylon will also cause the slain of Israel to fall. This seems to identify the land of Israel, as this *Mystery Babylon* will eventually turn her back on Israel, as will all nations in the latter days according to the prophets.

My final point is to discuss the following verses as it relates to Babel burning with fire in one hour.

"Because of this her plagues shall come in one day: death and mourning and scarcity of food. And she shall be burned up with fire, because יהוה Elohim who judges her is mighty. 'And the sovereigns of the earth who committed whoring and lived riotously with her shall weep and mourn over her, when they see the smoke of her burning, standing at a distance for fear of her torture, saying, '**Woe! Woe, the great city Babel, the mighty city, because your judgment has come in one hour!' And the merchants of the earth weep and mourn over her, because no one buys their merchandise any more**" – (Revelation 18:8-11)

Keep in mind, that it is New York City that houses the United Nations and their strong-arm, the UNSC, that forms World Government! It is also the reason why the Shmitah patterns point to this city with the fall of the U.S. Stock markets on Elul 29, 2001/2008 on the *Shmitah Release Days* and is the city that makes the connection to the nine *Harbingers* of judgment.

It has taken me a while to form my opinions with regard to America, but it didn't fully click until I researched and discovered the connection to the plagues of fire mentioned in Revelation 18:8-11. It wasn't until I read and watched videos regarding the open vision that Dumitru Dudman [1] had on April 22,1996 and Henry Grover [2] had in 1986. It would be wise to discern whom this *Great City* might refer too because the time is late!

A Summary of the Nine Harbingers

" THE HARBINGERS" [3]

Based on Isaiah 9:10, - *"The bricks have fallen, but we will build with hewn stones: the sycamores are cut down, but we will plant cedars in their place,"* the northern 10 Tribes of Israel refused to repent after they were struck by the Assyrians - which was a warning from the Lord. Instead of listening to the alarm, of turning back, and humbling themselves in repentance, they boasted of their resolve, that they would rebuild stronger and better than before. They ignored the warning and rejected the call to return. They defied it. Sadly, their defiance led to the nation's total destruction years later. The ancient prophecy forms the key to the nine harbingers of judgment, which are given to a nation in danger of judgment – each of which have reappeared on American soil – marking America as the nation in danger of judgment.

The First Harbinger: The Breach. In 732 B.C., the hedge of protection was removed and Israel's enemies invade the land and wreak havoc. The calamity traumatizes the nation but it takes place on a limited scale, as with 9/11. The warning is the removal of the hedge. On September 11, 2001, America's hedge of protection was removed – the breach of America's security, and was a sign that God has lifted His protective hand.

The Second Harbinger: The Terrorist. It was the dark shadow of Assyrian terror that loomed over the kingdom of Israel. The danger against which the prophets had warned. And when, years later, Israel's final judgment came, the Assyrians would again be the means through which it would happen. So, too, the attack on America is carried out by terrorists. The

Assyrians were a Semitic people, children of the Middle East. So too were the terrorists of 9/11.

<u>The Third Harbinger:</u> The Fallen Bricks. The most visible signs of the attack on ancient Israel were that of the fallen buildings and the ruin heaps of fallen bricks. The third harbinger is the sign of the fallen bricks of the fallen buildings. On Sept 11, 2001, Americans were confronted with the same sign, fallen bricks of the fallen buildings of the wreckage of Ground Zero. America was not turning back to God. It was a short-lived spiritual revival that never came.

<u>The Fourth Harbinger:</u> The Tower. Israel defiantly began rebuilding on the devastated ground, vowing to rebuild higher and stronger. So, too, in the wake of 9/11, American leaders vowed to rebuild at Ground Zero higher and stronger – the Tower begins to rise at Ground Zero. Those involved act unwittingly.

<u>The Fifth Harbinger:</u> The Gazit Stone. We will rebuild with quarried stone - The Israelites carve out quarried stone from mountain rock and bring it back to the ground of destruction where clay bricks once stood. Three years after 9/11, a stone is quarried out of the mountain rock of New York. This massive stone was brought back to Ground Zero. In ancient Israel this stone became a misplaced embodiment of the nation's confidence in its own power. So too the massive stone at Ground Zero became the symbolic cornerstone of the rebuilding. Public ceremonies accompanied the stone placement. Plans to rebuild Ground Zero would be frustrated for years. Eventually they would remove the stone from GZ altogether.

<u>The Sixth Harbinger:</u> The Sycamore. The Sycamores have been cut down - The attack on ancient Israel resulted in the striking down of the sycamore tree, a biblical sign of national judgment. The fallen sycamore is a sign of uprooting, a warning and, in ignoring the warning, it becomes a prophecy of judgment. On 9/11, as the North Tower fell it sent debris and wreckage which struck and uprooted an object – a sycamore tree growing at Ground Zero. The tree was made into a symbol and named The Sycamore of Ground Zero. When it fell in ancient Israel it prophesied the nation's downfall and the end of its kingdom. What happens to America depends on if the warning is heeded.

<u>The Seventh Harbinger:</u> The Erez Tree. But we will plant cedars in their place - In their defiance of God, the Israelites replace the fallen sycamore with a Cedar tree. The cedar, being stronger than the sycamore becomes a symbol of the nation's arrogant hope that it will emerge from the crisis stronger than before. The English name for this tree is "Cedar," but the Hebrew word is "Erez." Erez stands not only for cedar but for a conifer tree of the panacea family. In November of 2003, a tree was lowered at the corner of Ground Zero into the soil where the fallen sycamore once stood. The tree was a conifer, a panacea tree, the biblical Erez. A ceremony was held around the tree and it, too, became a symbol – entitled The Tree of Hope. There is always hope. A nation's true hope is found only in returning to God.

<u>The Eight Harbinger:</u> The Utterance. The Eighth Harbinger was the public speaking of the ancient vow of defiance. For this harbinger to manifest, the vow would have to be spoken in the nation's capital by a national leader, as it had been in ancient Israel. On Sept 11, 2004, every object mentioned in the prophecy of Isa 9:10 had manifested. The public utterance of the prophecy had to take place publicly, which happened on Sept

11, 2004 when VP candidate John Edwards, giving a speech in the capital city, quoted this exact Scripture word for word in Wash., DC. Without realizing it, he was joining the two nations together and, without realizing it, pronouncing judgment on America. The ancient and the modern were bound together.

<u>The Ninth Harbinger:</u> The Prophecy. The Ninth Harbinger is the proclaiming of the ancient vow as prophecy, as a matter of public record, and spoken before the words come true. On Sept 12, 2001, the day after 9/11, America issues its official response to the attack. The one in charge of issuing the response was Tom Daschle, Senate Majority Leader. As he closes his speech he makes a declaration – he proclaims the ancient vow of defiance, word for word, to the world. By doing so he prophesies the nation's future course, all of which comes to pass. "

NOTES

¹ William F. Dankenbring, "Time Prophecies of Daniel," http://www.triumphpro.com/isaac-newton-and-end-time-prophecies-of-daniel.pdf (accessed March 15, 2015).

² "Dead Sea Scrolls," *Wikipedia*, https://en.wikipedia.org/wiki/Dead_Sea_Scrolls (accessed March 20, 2015).

³ Blue Letter Bible, "Strong's # H3068 for The Lord," http://www.blueletterbible.org/lang/lexicon/lexicon.cfm?strongs=H3068&t=KJV (accessed July 15, 2015).

⁴ BlueLetterBible, "Strong's # H3050 for Yeh or Yah," http://www.blueletterbible.org/lang/lexicon/lexicon.cfm?strongs=H3050&t=KJV (accessed July 27, 2015).

⁵ Dan Baxley, "Yahshua, or Yahushua, or Yahoshua, or Yeshua, or Y'shua – His Name?"*Removing the Fog of Religion,* http://www.yahshuaservant.com/yahushua--or-yahshua--not--yeshua.htm (accessed January 14, 2015).

⁶ "Passover Day a High Sabbath," http://yahuyahweh.org/eaoy/pdf/Passover_Day_A_High_Sabbath.pdf (accessed on August 1, 2015).

⁷ "Easter," *Remnantofgod.org,* http://www.remnantofgod.org/easter.htm (accessed March 16, 2015).

⁸ "Zeitgeist (film series)," *Wikipedia,* https://en.wikipedia.org/wiki/Zeitgeist_%28film_series%29 (accessed February 17, 2015).

⁹ "Is Christmas Christian?," *remnantofgod.org,* http://www.remnantofgod.org/xmas.htm#date (accessed March 17, 2015).

¹⁰ Institute for Scripture Research, "Home page of their website," http://isr-messianic.org/ (accessed August 7, 2015)

[11] The Scripture associated with this is Ezekial 37:16, "And you, son of man, take a stick for yourself and write on it, 'For Yehudah and for the children of Yisra'ĕl, his companions.' Then take another stick and write on it, 'For Yosĕph, the stick of Ephrayim, and for all the house of Yisra'ĕl, his companions.' " We all have access to the Creator through two methods, either the stick (Branch) of Judah or the stick (Branch) of Ephraim through Yahshua.

Chapter 1

The Latter Days are all About the Ancient Jewish Wedding

[1] As a means of clarification, when the word week is highlighted with Parenthesis such as "week," it is being used to identify 7 prophetic years of 360-Day cycles or exactly 2,520 days.

[2] "Rosh Hashanah: Names, Themes, and Idioms," http://bibleprophesy.org/trumpets.htm (accessed August 4, 2015)

[3] BlueLetterBible, "Strong's # H4150 for Mow'ed," http://www.blueletterbible.org/lang/lexicon/lexicon.cfm?Strongs=H4150&t=KJV (accessed August 7, 2015).

[4] Blue Letter Bible " Strong's # H226 for Signs," http://www.blueletterbible.org/lang/lexicon/lexicon.cfm?Strongs=H226&t=KJV (accessed August 9, 2015)

[5] Rev. Marjorie, "The Remez Series Part 5: A Thief in the Night as Jewish Idiom and Remez Statement," , http://www.sweetmanna.org/RemezAThiefInTheNight-JewishIdiomLesson5.html (accessed March 23, 2015).

[6] Judah Gabriel Himango, "Torah Tuesdays: Everything there is to know about the Red Heifer," http://judahgabriel.blogspot.com/ (accessed February 25, 2015).

[7] "Luke 1:5-17," YOUVERSION, https://www.bible.com/bible/316/luk.1.isr98 35 (accessed February 22, 2015).

[8] Glenn Kay, "Jewish Wedding Customs and the Bride of Messiah," *Congregation Netzar Torah Yeshua*, http://messianicfellowship.50webs.com/wedding.html (accessed January 28, 2015).

[9] "Ancient Jewish History: The Two Kingdoms," https://www.jewishvirtuallibrary.org/jsource/History/Kingdoms1.html (accessed on August 1, 2015).

[10] "The Kings of Israel and Judah," http://www.britam.org/kings.html (accessed on August 1, 2015).

[11] Tony Garland, "Ten Tribes Lost?" *Spiritandtruth.org*, http://www.spiritandtruth.org/teaching/Book_of_Revelation/commentary/htm/topics/ten_tribes.html (accessed February 2, 2015).

[12] The Scripture associated with this is Matthew 15:24, "And He answering, said, 'I was not sent except to the lost sheep of the house of Yisra'ël.' "

[13] BlueLetterBible, "Strong's # H259 for echad," http://www.blueletterbible.org/lang/lexicon/lexicon.cfm?Strongs=H259&t=KJV (accessed August 7, 2015)

Chapter 2

Daniel! Seal The Book Until The Time of The End!

[1] "Agriculture in Israel," *Wikipedia*, accessed February 29, 2015, https://en.wikipedia.org/wiki/Agriculture_in_Israel

[2] Baruch S. Davidson, "When is the next Jubilee year?" *Chabad.org*, http://www.chabad.org/library/article_cdo/aid/513212/jewish/When-is-the-next-Jubilee-year.htm (accessed February 1, 2015).

[3] "Holocaust," *About.com*, http://history1900s.about.com/cs/holocaust/p/balfourdeclare.htm%29 (accessed February 3, 2015).

[4] "Timeline of Jerusalem," *Wikipedia,*
https://en.wikipedia.org/wiki/Timeline_of_Jerusalem (accessed February 4, 2015).

[5] Torah Calendar, "Using the Creation Calendar,"
http://torahcalendar.com/USINGCAL.asp (accessed August 1, 2015).

[6] Denise Hassanzade Ajiri, Yahoo News, accessed on July 30, 2015,
http://news.yahoo.com/iran-calls-israels-nuclear-disarmament-182055986.html

Chapter 3

6,000 Years of Man's Rule

[1] Terry Hurlbut, "The earth originally had a 360-day calendar," *examiner.com,*
Accessed February 4, 2015, http://www.examiner.com/article/the-earth-originally-had-a-360-day-calendar

[2] "Hebrew Calendar," *Wikipedia,*
http://en.wikipedia.org/wiki/Hebrew_calendar (accessed February 5, 2015).

[3] "Hillel II," *Wikipedia,*
http://en.wikipedia.org/wiki/Hillel_II (accessed February 5, 2015).

[4] "The Creation Calendar Made Simple,"
http://torahcalendar.com/PDF/CalendarSimple.pdf (accessed February 14, 2015).

[5] "Studying the Hebraic Roots of Christianity," *Hebraic Heritage Ministries International,* accessed February 5, 2015, http://www.hebroots.com/lul7_8.html

[6] Leo Hohmann, "Mahdi to Return by 2016, Followed by Jesus?" *WND Faith,* accessed April 4, 2015,
http://www.wnd.com/2015/03/mahdi-to-return-by-2016-followed-by-jesus/?cat_orig=faith

[7] "Maitreya," *Wikipedia,* https://en.wikipedia.org/wiki/Maitreya (accessed April 10, 2015).

[8] Torah Calendar, "The 7,000 Year Plan of Elohim," http://torahcalendar.com/PLAN.asp (accessed July 20, 2015).

Chapter 4

September 2015 and the Feast of Yom Teruah

[1] Blue Letter Bible, " Strong's # H8643 for Teruah," http://www.blueletterbible.org/lang/lexicon/lexicon.cfm?strongs=H8643&t=KJV (accessed August 9, 2015).

[2] Rabbi Dr. Hillel Ben David (Greg Killian), "The Significance of Yom Teruah (Rosh Hashanah),"

[3] Jonathan Cahn, The Mystery of the Shemitah (published by FrontLine Charisma Media/Charisma Book House Group 2014), 13

[4] Jonathan Cahn, The Mystery of the Shemitah (published by FrontLine Charisma Media/Charisma Book House Group 2014), 7

[5] Ibid., 15

[6] Ibid., 129-130

[7] Ibid., 164

[8] Ibid., 197

[9] "Mt. Sinai, Red Sea Crossing, and Sodom and Gomorrah," http://www.arkdiscovery.com/red_sea_crossing.htm (accessed February 16, 2015).

[10] Jonathan Cahn, The Mystery of the Shemitah (published by FrontLine Charisma Media/Charisma Book House Group 2014), 38

[11] Ibid., 41-42

[12] Ibid., 15

[13] "Bretton Woods Conference," Wikipedia, http://en.wikipedia.org/wiki/Bretton_Woods_Conference (accessed February 20, 2015).

[14] "Oslo Accords," *Wikipedia,*
http://en.wikipedia.org/wiki/Oslo_Accords (accessed March 1, 2015).

[15] Wikipedia, "Taba Summit," https://en.wikipedia.org/wiki/Taba_Summit (accessed August 1, 2015).

[16] "Annapolis Conference," *Wikipedia,*
http://en.wikipedia.org/wiki/Annapolis_Conference (accessed March 23, 2015).

[17] Kevin Liptak, "Now that he has a deal with Iran, Obama must face Congess," http://www.cnn.com/2015/07/14/politics/iran-nuclear-deal-congress-obama-block/ (accessed July 22, 2015).

[18] "Netanyahu warns Iranians of 'very bad' nuclear deal," *BBC News*, March 5, 2015,
http://www.bbc.com/news/world-middle-east-31749088 (March 22, 2015).

[19] Matthew Ayton, "Can new life be injected into the Israel-Palestine Peace Process?" *The National*, May 25, 2015, June 1, 2015,
http://www.thenational.ae/opinion/comment/can-new-life-be-injected-into-the-israel-palestine-peace-process (accessed July 22, 2015).

[20] "'Jade Helm' military exercise causing political firestorm in Texas, western states," *Fox News*, May 6, 2015,
http://www.foxnews.com/politics/2015/05/06/jade-helm-military-exercise-causing-political-firestorm-in-texas-western-states/ (June 2, 2015).

[21] Ibid.

Chapter 5

September 2015 and the Feast of Yom Kippur

[1] "Sir Isaac Newton," *Blue Letter Bible,*

https://www.blueletterbible.org/commentaries/newton_isaac/ (accessed May 12, 2015).

[2] Sir Robert Anderson, "The Coming Prince," *What Saith the Scripture,* http://www.whatsaiththeScripture.com/Voice/The.Coming.Prince.3.html (accessed May 15, 2015).

[3] Doctor Peterson, "How do you work the BC & AD math problems" http://mathforum.org/library/drmath/view/64396.html, (accessed July 27, 2015).

[4] Jake Sherman, "Pope will address Congress in September," *Politico,* February 5, 2015, http://www.politico.com/story/2015/02/pope-address-us-congress-114939.html (accessed May 2, 2015).

[5] Susan Davis, "Pope Francis to Address Congress," *USA Today*, February 5, 2015, http://www.usatoday.com/story/news/politics/2015/02/05/pope-francis-congress-boehner/22923081/ (accessed March 4, 2015).

[6] "Leaders gather at Vatican for historic meeting on climate change and sustainable development," *United Nations,* http://theeconomiccollapseblog.com/archives/in-september-the-un-launches-a-major-sustainable-development-agenda-for-the-entire-planet (accessed May 25, 2015).

[7] Michael Snyder, "In September, The UN Launches a Major Sustainable Development Agenda for the Entire Planet," *The Economic Collapse,* May 11, 2015, http://theeconomiccollapseblog.com/archives/in-september-the-un-launches-a-major-sustainable-development-agenda-for-the-entire-planet (accessed May 24, 2015).

Chapter 6
September 2015 and the Feast of Tabernacles

[1] Jonathan Cahn, The Mystery of the Shemitah (published by FrontLine Charisma Media/Charisma Book House Group 2014) pg. 65

[2] Rev. Marjorie, "Rosh Hashanah The Wedding of the Messiah, Part 12," *Sweet Manna from Heaven,* http://www.sweetmanna.org/FallFeastsWedding-MarriageofTheBridePart12.html (accessed May 4, 2015).

[3] "A New Look at the Deep Meaning of the Feast of Tabernacles," http://www.hope-of-israel.org/tabernac.htm (accessed on August 1, 2015).

[4] "Modern Jewish History: The Spanish Expulsion," *Jewish Virtual Library,* https://www.jewishvirtuallibrary.org/jsource/Judaism/expulsion.html (accessed April 15, 2015).

[5] "The Creation Calendar," *Torahcalendar.com,* http://torahcalendar.com/Linkpage.asp?D=23&P=5152&M=0&S=0&R=0&H=0&U=0&F=0 (accessed April 25, 2015).

[6] "Vayelech," *Wikipedia,* https://en.wikipedia.org/wiki/Vayelech (accessed April 28, 2015).

Chapter 7
September 2017 and the Mid-Tribulation Sign

[1] Rogers, J. H. (February 1998). "Origins of the ancient constellations: I. The Mesopotamian traditions". *Journal of the British Astronomical Association, no.1* 108: 9–28.

[2] N.M. Swerdlow, "The Babylonian Theory of the Planets" p.17 (Princeton University Press, 2/9/1998)

[3] "12th Century Rabbi Predicted Israel's Future," http://www.wnd.com/2012/11/12th-century-rabbi-predicted-israels-future/ (accessed August 1, 2015).

[4] Phil Richardson, "The 7 Kings of Revelation & the 8th King, Petrus Romanus...The Final Pope!!", *September 2015.com*, http://september2015.com/the-7-kings-of-revelation-the-8th-king-petrus-romanus-the-final-pope/ (accessed May 25, 2015).

Chapter 8
September 2014 and the Final 2,550 Days

[1] Phil Richardson, 'The 6 Years of Tribulation Starts September 2015 on Yom Teruah," *September2015.com*, September2015.com (accessed April 24, 2015).

[2] Phil Richardson, "Latest Videos and Graphs," *September2015.com*, september2015.com/latest-videos (accessed April 24, 2015).

[3] "It is noteworthy that the prophecy was given at Babylon, and the Babylonian year consisted of twelve months of thirty days. That the prophetic year is not the ordinary year is no new discovery. It was noticed sixteen centuries ago by Julius Africanus in his Chronography, wherein he explains the seventy weeks to be weeks of Jewish (lunar) years, beginning with the twentieth of Artaxerxes, the fourth year of the 83rd Olympiad, and ending in the second year of the 202nd Olympiad; 475 Julian years being equal to 490 lunar years."

[4] "Discipleship Study Questions," *TorahCalendar.com*, http://torahcalendar.com/GRADEQUIZ2.asp?Q=25 (accessed June 24, 2015).

[5] Ibid.

[6] "Metonic Cycles and the 70th Week of Daniel," http://endtimepilgrim.org/metonic.htm (accessed May 24, 2015).

[7] Judaism 101: "Jewish Calendar," http://www.jewfaq.org/calendar.htm (accessed August 7, 2015).

[8] "The Security Council," *United Nations Security Council*,

http://www.un.org/en/sc/ (accessed May 23, 2015).

[9] Ibid.

[10] "What is the Security Council?." *United Nations Security Council,* http://www.un.org/en/sc/about/ (accessed April 23, 2015).

[11] "President of the United Nations Security Council," *Wikipedia,* http://en.wikipedia.org/wiki/President_of_the_United_Nations_Security_Council#2015. E2.80.9319 (accessed April 27, 2015).

[12] Infowars.com, "In Violation of the Constitution: Obama Takes on Chairmanship of the UN Security Council," http://www.infowars.com/in-violation-of-the-constitution-obama-takes-on-chairmanship-of-un-security-council/ (accessed August 5, 2015).

[13] "In Violation of the Constitution: Obama takes on chairmanship of UN Security Council," September 14, 2009, http://www.infowars.com/in-violation-of-the-constitution-obama-takes-on-chairmanship-of-un-security-council/ (accessed March 4, 2015).

[14] Bradley A. Blakeman, "Obama's Policies Weaken U.S. in Middle East," *Newsmax,* December 3, 2012, http://www.newsmax.com/BradleyBlakeman/Obama-Middle-East-policy/2012/12/03/id/466287/#ixzz3cCrBw6q0 (accessed April 5, 2015).

[15] Patrick Goodenough, "Sen. Coats Says Obama is 'Desperate for a Deal' with Iran: Recalls Clinton's North Korea 'Mistake', April 28, 2015, http://www.cnsnews.com/news/article/patrick-goodenough/sen-coats-says-obama-desperate-deal-iran-recalls-clinton-s-north (accessed May 4, 2015).

[16] "President of the United Nations Security Council," *Wikipedia,* http://en.wikipedia.org/wiki/President_of_the_United_Nations_Security_Council#2015. E2.80.9319 (accessed April 27, 2015).

[17] Wikipedia, "Presidents of the United Nations Security Council," https://en.wikipedia.org/wiki/President_of_the_United_Nations_Security_Council (accessed August 2, 2015).

[18] Rravda.Ru, "Palestinian state expected to materialize in Spetember 2015," http://english.pravda.ru/news/world/04-06-2015/130883-palestinian_state-0/ (accessed July 26, 2015)

[19] Michael Snyder, "Something Else Coming In Setember: A UN Resolution Establishing A Palestinian State," May 31, 2015, http://endoftheamericandream.com/archives/something-else-coming-in-september-a-un-resolution-establishing-a-palestinian-state (accessed August 1, 2015)

Chapter 9

Putting It All Together: The Connection to September 2021

[1] "Basel III," *Wikipedia*, https://en.wikipedia.org/wiki/Basel_III (accessed April 27, 2015).

[2] "Global Currency Reset in Process: The Fed Can't Exit Easy Monetary Policy as USD Comes Under Attack, China and Russia Suggesting a New Bretton Woods, One Quadrillon Dollars of Derivatives Time Bomb is Set to Explode," *Investment Watch*, August 9, 2013, http://investmentwatchblog.com/global-currency-reset-in-process-the-fed-cant-exit-easy-monetary-policy-as-usd-comes-under-attack-china-and-russia-suggesting-a-new-bretton-woods-one-quadrillion-dollars-of-derivatives-time-bomb/#mRozVgGOLIMrRp8g.99 (accessed March 23, 2015).

[3] Blue LeterBile.com, "Strongs # G5515 chloros," http://www.blueletterbible.org/lang/lexicon/lexicon.cfm?Strongs=G5515&t=KJV (accessed August 5, 2015).

[4] "Panspermia," *Wikipedia*, https://en.wikipedia.org/wiki/Panspermia (accessed April 23, 2015).

[5] Thomas R. Horn, "Exo-Vaticana," *Thomas Horn*, http://www.newswithviews.com/Horn/thomas185.htm (accessed April 13, 2015).

[6] Ibid.

[7] "Project Blue Beam," *Watcher Files,* http://www.thewatcherfiles.com/bluebeam.htm (accessed May 13, 2015).

[8] Breaking Israel News, "Leading Israeli Rabbi Says The Arrival of the Messiah is Imminent," http://www.breakingisraelnews.com/44534/leading-israeli-rabbi-messiah-imminent-jewish-world/#MwsFOQGocykZqDyb.97 (accessed August 7, 2015).

[9] "Wikipedia," https://en.wikipedia.org/wiki/3rd_millennium (accessed July 30, 2015).

[10] "The 7,000 Year Plan of Elohim," http://torahcalendar.com/PLAN.asp (accessed July 30, 2015).

[11] Ibid

[12] Ibid.

[13] "The NWO, Freemasonry & Symbols on the Dollar Bill," http://freedom-school.com/dollarbill.html (accessed June 12, 2015).

[14] Simon Tomlinson, "The Pope's new world order: Francis calls for the 'goods of the Earth' to be shared by everyone – not exploited by the rich at the expense of the poor," *MailOnline.* July 8, 2015. http://www.dailymail.co.uk/news/article-3153552/The-Pope-s-new-world-order-Francis-calls-goods-Earth-shared-not-exploited-rich-expense-poor.html#ixzz3fWRC5mUx (accessed July 10, 2015).

[15] "The 120 Day Version of the Human Story," http://www.chabad.org/parshah/article_cdo/aid/2508/jewish/The-120-Day-Version.htm, (accessed August 1, 2015).

[16] "The Ark of Covenant Special Article," *Wyatt Archaelogical Research,* http://wyattmuseum.com/the-ark-of-the-covenant-special-article/2011-338 (accessed June 3, 2015).

[17] "Mt. Sinai,"*Wyatt Archaelogical Research,* http://wyattmuseum.com/discovering/mt-sinai (accessed July 5, 2015).

[18] "Red Sea Crossing," *Wyatt Archaelogical Research,* http://wyattmuseum.com/discovering/red-sea-crossing (accessed July 5, 2015).

[19] "Noah's Ark," *Wyatt Archaelogical Research,*

http://wyattmuseum.com/discovering/noahs-ark (accessed July 5, 2015).

[20] "The Ark of the Covenant Found in Israel," *YouTube.com*, https://www.youtube.com/watch?v=-87sjeFzrzs (accessed July 5, 2015).

[21] "Ron Wyatt Discovers the Blood of Jesus Christ and Ark of the Covenant! - Nsearch Radio," youtube.com, https://www.youtube.com/watch?v=3i0RBDRnwAo (accessed July 30, 2015).

[22] Gavin Finley, "The Order of Melchizedek, the Dual Offices of the Coming Messiah as Priest and King," http://endtimepilgrim.org/melchizedek.htm (accessed July 30, 2015).

INDEX

[1] "A Vision Received by Brother Dumitru Duduman April 22, 1996," http://www.handofhelp.com/vision_36.php (accessed July 30, 2015).

[2] "Henry Grover Russian Invasion of America," http://americaslastdays.blogspot.com/p/henry-gruver-russian-invasion-of-america.html (accessed July 30, 29015).

[3] "Jonathan Cahn: The Harbinger by the 700 Club," http://www.cbn.com/700club/guests/bios/jonathan_Cahn_010312.aspx (accessed July 30, 2015).

47722317R00168

Made in the USA
Middletown, DE
01 September 2017